ISLAMIC SURVEYS 8

BELL'S INTRODUCTION TO THE QUR'ĀN

completely revised
and enlarged by

W. MONTGOMERY WATT

EDINBURGH
at the University Press

EDINBURGH UNIVERSITY PRESS
22 George Square, Edinburgh
85224 171 2
North America
Aldine Publishing Company
529 South Wabash Avenue, Chicago
Library of Congress
Catalog Card Number 77-106474
Printed in Great Britain by
T. & A. Constable Ltd, Edinburgh

FOREWORD TO THE REVISED EDITION

When the suggestion of a revised edition of Richard Bell's *Introduction to the Qur'ān* was first made in discussions with the Secretary of Edinburgh University Press, I was attracted by the idea of doing something to maintain the influence of a great scholar, and was emboldened by the success of Theodor Nöldeke's pupils in revising and continuing his work. The task, however, as I soon realized, is not without its difficulties. Richard Bell was my greatly respected teacher under whom I did much of my study of Arabic and who guided me in the preparation of the thesis which eventually appeared as *Free Will and Predestination in Early Islam*. On one or two points, however, I am unable to accept his theories about the Qur'ān, as I indicated in the article 'The Dating of the Qur'ān: a review of Richard Bell's Theories' (*Journal of the Royal Asiatic Society*, 1957, 46-56). Consequently it seemed best that, following the example of Friedrich Schwally (see p. 175 below), I should speak in my own name throughout and refer to Bell in the third person, especially where I disagreed with him. The sincerest tribute to such a scholar is to take his views seriously and criticize them frankly. It is my hope that the present revision will enable a new generation of scholars to appreciate the importance of Bell's painstaking analysis of the Qur'ān.

Despite the fact that I speak in my own name and that there are few paragraphs without some slight changes, the core of the book is still essentially Bell's work. Though I have studied parts of the field in connection with the biography of Muḥammad, and have here and there looked at some of the issues raised by Bell, I have undertaken no special research in the preparation of this revision. The additions are mostly elementary matters that seemed appropriate to an 'introduction', such as a more extensive bibliography. I have also tried to arrange the material more logically. I believe Bell's original text to have been based on his lectures to students, which he brought together and lightly revised shortly before his death when literary activity was becoming difficult.

One major change in the form of expression has seemed desirable. Bell followed his European predecessors in speaking of the Qur'ān as Muḥammad's own, at least in his *Introduction*. Various remarks he made to me, however, lead me to think that he would have had a considerable measure of sympathy with the views I have expressed about Muḥammad's prophethood, most recently in *Islamic Revelation in the Modern World*. With the greatly increased contacts between Muslims and Christians during the last quarter of a century, it has become imperative for a Christian scholar not to offend Muslim readers gratuitously, but as far as possible to present his arguments in a form acceptable to them. Courtesy and an eirenic outlook certainly now demand that we should not speak of the Qur'ān as the product of Muḥammad's conscious mind; but I hold that the same demand is also made by sound scholarship. I have therefore altered or eliminated all expressions which implied that Muḥammad was the author of the Qur'ān, including those which spoke of his 'sources' or of the 'influences' on him. On the other hand, I believe we are justified in speaking of the 'influences' of the external world on the Arabian environment (cf. p. 185); and that we are likewise justified in noticing a 'development' in the outlook of the community of believers; and such a development presumably requires to be met by a change of emphasis in the revelation.

A novel feature is the Index to the Qur'ān. In my own work I have found of great value the index included in H. U. Weitbrecht Stanton's *Teaching of the Qur'ān* (London, 1919), and I have attempted to produce something similar, but more in accordance with the outlook and interests of today.

The transliteration of Arabic words is essentially that of the second edition of *The Encyclopaedia of Islam* (London, 1960, continuing) with three modifications. Two of these are normal with most British Arabists, namely, *q* for *ḳ*, and *j* for *dj*. The third is something of a novelty. It is the replacement of the ligature used to show when two consonants are to be sounded together by an apostrophe to show when they are to be sounded separately. This means that *dh*, *gh*, *kh*, *sh*, *th* are to be sounded together; where there is an apostrophe, as in *ad'ham*, they are to be sounded separately. The apostrophe in this usage represents no sound, but, since it only occurs between two consonants (of which the second is *h*), it cannot be confused with the apostrophe representing the glottal stop (*hamza*), which never occurs between two consonants.

In the Qur'ānic references, where the verse-number in Flügel's edition differs from that in the standard Egyptian edition, that of Flügel is given after a stroke. Identical digits are not repeated except in the case of numbers from 10 to 19 (where one must distinguish 12/8 from 12/18).

I am indebted to Mr Alford T. Welch for revising the Table of Suras and for many valuable general comments; and to Miss Helen Pratt for typing with great accuracy a large part of the text and not least the Index to the Qur'ān.

It has seemed appropriate to include this *Introduction* in the Islamic Surveys Series since their aims are very similar.

W. Montgomery Watt

THE CONTENTS

INTRODUCTION

Few books have exercised a wider or deeper influence upon the spirit of man than the Qur'ān. By Muslims it is regarded as a revelation from God. It is used in their public and private devotions, and is recited at festivals and family occasions. It is the basis of their religious beliefs, their ritual, and their law; the guide of their conduct, both public and private. It moulds their thought, and its phrases enter into literature and daily speech. A book thus held in reverence by over four hundred millions of our fellow-men is worthy of attention. It also demands serious study; for it is by no means an easy book to understand. It is neither a treatise on theology, nor a code of laws, nor a collection of sermons, but rather a medley of all three, with other things thrown in. Its 'revelation' was spread over a period of some twenty years, in the course of which Muḥammad rose from the position of an obscure religious reformer in his native Mecca to that of virtual ruler of Medina and most of Arabia. As it reflects the changing circumstances, needs and purposes of the Muslims during these years, it naturally varies much in style and content, and even in teaching. Its arrangement is unsystematic, and though the Arabic in which it is written is, on the whole, intelligible, there are difficult passages whose meaning, as the Arabs say, is known to God alone.

One of the features of the second half of the twentieth century is the great increase in contacts between adherents of different religions. A consequence of this is that it is no longer possible for the occidental scholar to pontificate about the religions of Asia as he did in the nineteenth century. The adherents of these religions now belong to the same intellectual world as the occidental scholar, and will criticize him if he fails to understand and appreciate their religion as a religion. The term 'dialogue' is often applied to this new relationship between adherents of different religions. Though the term is vague, it implies, with reference to the Qur'ān in particular, a reverent attitude towards it as a holy book and respect for Muslim beliefs about it, even if these are not shared.

ONE

THE HISTORICAL CONTEXT

1. The international situation

The Qur'ān was 'revealed' in the early part of the seventh century AD in the towns of Mecca and Medina in west-central Arabia. About the same time the missioners of Columba were bringing the Christian faith to Scotland and northern England, while those of Augustine of Canterbury were spreading northwards and westwards from Kent. In France the Merovingian kings exercised a largely nominal rule. The Roman empire of the West had succumbed to the barbarians, but the Eastern Roman or Byzantine empire, with its capital at Constantinople, had escaped their ravages. Under Justinian (528–65) the latter had attained a position of settled power and civilization, but in the half-century following his death it had fallen into confusion, partly owing to attacks from without by other barbarians, and partly because of internal troubles and incompetent rulers.[1]

In the east Byzantium had a serious rival in the Persian empire of the Sassanids, which stretched from Iraq and Mesopotamia in the west to the eastern frontiers of modern Iran and Afghanistan. Its capital was at Ctesiphon (al-Madā'in), some twenty miles south-east of the site of the later city of Baghdad. The history of the Middle East in the later sixth and early seventh centuries is dominated by the struggle between these two giants. Towards the end of the reign of Justinian a fifty years' peace had been agreed on, but this had not been kept, and the long final war to the death began in 602. Taking advantage of the weakness of the Byzantines, Khosrau II of Persia commenced hostilities alleging as his pretext revenge for the murder of the emperor Maurice, from whom he had, at the beginning of his reign, received aid. Phocas (602–10), who had displaced Maurice, was beset by apathy and active revolt at home and was in no position to ward off the Persian attack. Asia Minor was overrun. At the lowest ebb of the fortunes of Byzantium in 610, Heraclius, son of the governor of North Africa, appeared with a fleet before Constantinople. Phocas was deposed and Heraclius crowned emperor. The tide might be said to have turned.

Nevertheless there were still troubles ahead for the Byzantines. Their European provinces had been overrun by barbarians from the north, and years passed before Heraclius could make headway against the Persians. These meanwhile turned southwards, and conquered Syria and Egypt in 614. The sack of Jerusalem after a revolt against the Persian garrison, the slaughter of the inhabitants, and the carrying off of what was believed to be the true Cross, stirred the emotions of Christians throughout the Byzantine empire, and enabled Heraclius to reorganize his forces. After dealing with the Avars, who threatened Constantinople from the north, he turned in 622 against the Persians. In a series of campaigns in Asia Minor he met with some success, but in 626 the Persians were besieging Constantinople though briefly and unsuccessfully. A bold invasion of Iraq by Heraclius in 627 was crowned by the defeat of a Persian army. Though Heraclius withdrew soon afterwards, the strains produced in the Persian empire by the long series of wars now made themselves felt. In February 628 Khosrau II was murdered, and the son who succeeded him had many opponents and wanted peace. The great struggle was virtually ended, and the Byzantines had had the best of it. The negotiations for the evacuation of the Byzantine provinces dragged on until June 629, and it was September before Heraclius entered Constantinople in triumph. The Holy Rood was restored to Jerusalem in March 630.

The struggle of the two great powers had more relevance to Arabian politics than is immediately obvious. The struggle was indeed comparable to that between the Soviet bloc and the Atlantic powers in the decades after the Second World War. As each side in the latter tried to gain the support of relatively small neutral states, so in the sixth and seventh centuries each side sought to extend its own sphere of influence in Arabia and to reduce that of the other side. Not much could be done with the nomads of the desert except contain them, and this was done by paying semi-nomadic groups on the borders of the desert to stop nomadic raids into the settled country – the Ghassanids on the Byzantine border at Petra and other places, and Lakhmids on the Persian border with their centre at Hira. On the periphery of Arabia, however, there were many possibilities of gaining influence. About 521 the Christian empire of Abyssinia or Ethiopia occupied the fertile highlands of the Yemen in south-west Arabia; and this was done despite theological differences, with the full support and perhaps encouragement of the Byzantine empire. The Yemen remained under the Abyssinians until about 575, when they were expelled by a sea-borne expedition from Persia. Persia also gained control of a number of small towns on the eastern and southern coasts of Arabia. This was normally done by supporting a pro-Persian faction. The incident about 590 associated with the name of ʿUthmān ibn-al-Ḥuwayrith is to be regarded as an attempt by the Byzantines to gain control of Mecca by helping this man to become a puppet ruler there. Meccan interest in the struggle of the two empires is reflected in a passage of the Qur'ān [30.2/1-5/4], usually taken to be a prophecy of the final victory of the Rūm or Byzantines[2]; and there may be one or two other references to the war. Some of the later successes of Muḥammad in Arabia may be due to the fact that, with the decline of Persia about 628, most of the pro-Persian factions turned to Muḥammad for support and became Muslims.

2. Life in Arabia

The religion of Islam is popularly associated with life in the desert, and, though there is an element of truth in this idea, it is misleading unless properly qualified. Islam has nearly always been first and foremost a religion of townsmen paying little attention to the special needs of agriculturists or pastoral nomads. The first home of Islam was Mecca, then an extremely prosperous commercial centre; and its second home was Medina, a rich oasis with some commerce also. Yet both Mecca and Medina stood in close relationship to the surrounding nomads.

By the end of the sixth century the great merchants of

Mecca had gained a monopolistic control of the trade passing up and down the western coastal fringe of Arabia to the Mediterranean. The winter and summer caravans are referred to in 106.2 and traditionally went southwards and northwards respectively. The route southwards went to the Yemen, but there was an extension to Abyssinia, and goods were probably also transported to and from India by sea. This route had probably become important because the alternative route from the Persian Gulf to Aleppo had been made dangerous by the war between the Byzantines and the Persians. In order to be able to use these long caravan routes safely the Meccans had to be on good terms with nomadic tribes capable of protecting the caravans over the various sections of the route. The guarantors were of course paid for their trouble; but the prestige and military power of the Meccans, together with their diplomatic skill, seem to have ensured the smooth working of the system.

The fact that the Qur'ān was first addressed to people engaged in commerce is reflected in its language and ideas. A reference to Mecca's commercial prosperity and its caravans has just been mentioned. An American scholar, C.C. Torrey, made a special study of *The Commercial-Theological Terms in the Koran*,[3] and came to the conclusion that they were used to express fundamental points of doctrine and not simply as illustrative metaphors. Among the Qur'ānic assertions of this kind are the following: the deeds of men are recorded in a book; the Last Judgement is a reckoning; each person receives his account; the balance is set up (as for the exchange of money or goods) and a man's deeds are weighed; each soul is held in pledge for the deeds committed; if a man's actions are approved he receives his reward, or his hire; to support the Prophet's cause is to lend a loan to God.[4]

While the Meccans were in constant business relations with the nomads, they also had a deeper connection with the desert. It was only a generation or two since they had given up nomadic life to settle in Mecca. In many ways the people of Mecca still retained the outlook of the nomads. The malaise and discontent in Mecca may be largely traced to the tension and even conflict between nomadic mores and the new way of life which commercial activity fostered. It is this nomadic way of life above all which is presupposed in the Qur'ān. Nomadism is one of the great achievements of the human spirit. Arnold Toynbee has spoken of it as a *tour de force*; it presupposes the domestication of animals, especially the camel, and this must have taken place when men were living in oases and partly dependent on agriculture; thus, presumably when conditions in the oases grew more difficult, the owner of camels leaves this for the even more difficult life of the desert or steppe.[5] Only a high degree of excellence in the art of living in community will enable men to make a success of life in the desert. One of the claims to greatness of Islam as a religion is that it took the human virtues or excellences, tempered in the fire of desert life, and made them accessible to other men.

The basis of life in the desert is the pasturing and breeding of camels. The staple food of the nomad is the milk of the camels. It is only occasionally that their flesh is eaten. By selling surplus camels or by receiving fees for guaranteeing the safety of caravans the nomads may become able to purchase dates from the oases, and even luxuries like wine. Sheep and goats were also kept, but these had to remain on the edge of the desert where there were wells. The camel-nomad, on the other hand, could at certain seasons of the year go into the sandy desert (*nafūd*) where there were no wells. In the rainy season or spring (*rabīʿ*) there were many valleys and hollows with plentiful but short-lived vegetation. From this the camels could gain sufficient food and liquid to keep themselves and their owners well fed and free from thirst. Arabian rainfall is erratic, however, and the nomad has to vary his movements according to its incidence in any particular season. Once the spring vegetation has disappeared, the nomad has to go to other tracts of land where there are wells and perennial shrubs. Since the camel is thus so basic to life in Arabia, references in the Qur'ān to 'cattle' (*anʿām*) should primarily be understood of camels.

Because of the constant pressure of population on food-supplies, the struggle to maintain existence against rivals was unending. For mutual defence against enemies and for mutual help against nature, men banded themselves together in groups, usually based on kinship. Raids by one group upon another were almost a national sport among the Arabs. A favourite practice was to appear unexpectedly with overwhelming force at some point where the other party was weak; the men in charge of the camels would flee – without losing face, since the enemy had overwhelming force – and the raiders would make off with the camels. The size of the effective groups was relatively small; but for certain purposes small groups would act together with other groups on the basis of a real or feigned kinship through descent from a common ancestor. Groups of different sizes are roughly indicated in English by such terms as 'family', 'clan', 'tribe', 'federation of tribes'. A tribe or clan, besides those who were full members by birth, usually had attached to it various other persons who looked to it for protection. This attachment took several forms, such as 'confederate' (*ḥalīf*), 'protected neighbour' (*jār*) and 'client' (*mawlā*). The confederate had made an alliance with an individual or group on terms of at least nominal equality, whereas the other attached persons were in some sense inferior.

Protection by the group was an essential feature of life not only in the deserts of Arabia but also in a town like Mecca and an oasis settlement like Medina. It was linked with the idea of retaliation or 'an eye for an eye' – the *lex talionis* of the Old Testament [*Exodus*, 21.24f., etc.]. The principle of retaliation, coupled with corporate responsibility, was a relatively effective way of keeping peace in the desert and preventing wanton crime. According to primitive ideas there was no need or obligation to respect human life as such; but a man would avoid injuring or killing another if the latter was of the same tribe, or an allied tribe, or if he belonged to a group that was powerful and certain to exact vengeance. An understanding of this system and its ramifications is necessary for a proper appreciation of many incidents in Muḥammad's career. He was able to continue in Mecca despite opposition because his own clan of Hāshim, though many members of it disapproved of his new religion, was in honour bound to avenge any injury to him. At the same time the system prevented punishment, as now understood, by the executive body of the municipality of Mecca or Medina. If the head of the council in Mecca, even with the consent of the whole council, had tried to punish an offender, the latter's clan would have felt justified in taking vengeance. In such a case only the head of the offender's own clan could punish him. At various points in the Qur'ān concepts from this sphere are applied metaphorically to God. He does not fear the consequences (*sc.* retaliation) of his punishing the tribe of Thamūd [91.15]; he gives 'neighbourly protection' (*yujīr*) to all, but 'neighbourly protection' against him is never given (*sc.* because no one is strong enough' [23.88/90].

The extent of the sense of unity among the Arabs before Islam is a point about which there has been some dispute. There cannot have been anything comparable to Arab nationalism as now understood, since the Arab's basic attachment was to the tribe or clan. There were, however, widely accepted common customs, such as those connected with retaliation. Above all, however, there seems to have been some feeling of having a common language, Arabic; there are several references to the revelations to Muḥammad as 'an Arabic Qur'ān' [12.2; etc.] or as being 'in an Arabic tongue' [46.12/11]. Difficulties implicit in these statements will be considered in a later chapter. It would seem that there were various mutually intelligible dialects, and that the people who spoke them regarded themselves as 'clear-speakers' in contrast to a foreigner who was a 'confused speaker' (*'ajamī*). There were also theories of a common descent, or rather of two groups, sometimes distinguished as northern and southern Arabs, each descended from a common ancestor, though the two were not related.[6] Whatever the truth behind these accounts, it seems clear that some of the 'southern' tribes had taken to nomadic life after being settled in the Yemen. There had been in South Arabia for a thousand years a great civilization based partly on trade and partly on elaborate irrigation. The breakdown of the irrigation system, often called the bursting of the dam of Ma'rib (and referred to in 34.16/15), is now known from inscriptions to have been rather a series of events, extending at least from 451 to 542, and may have been the result rather than the cause of economic decline.[7] South Arabian influences on Mecca in Muḥammad's time may have been important, but there is little agreement on this point.

Apart from the Yemen there were a number of oases in western Arabia where agriculture was practised. The chief of these was Medina (literally 'the town'), previously known as Yathrib. The main crop was dates, but cereals were also grown. In agricultural development at Medina and elsewhere a leading part had been played by Jews – an unusual rôle in the light of medieval European conceptions of the Jew as a trader and financier. Certain Arabs had settled in the oasis of Medina at some time after the Jewish settlement, and these Arabs had become politically dominant. In other oases – Taymā', Fadak, Wādi l-Qurā, Khaybar – the settlers were predominantly Jewish. The ultimate ethnic origin of these Jewish tribes and clans is not clear. They had adopted the social forms and customs of the Arabs, and differed only in religion; some may have been Arab groups who had adopted Judaism, and in any case there had been much intermarriage.[8]

The religious situation in Arabia about AD 600 was complex. The presence of these settlements of Jews in oases and of a considerable number of Jews in the Yemen led to a gradual spread of some Jewish ideas. There was also much Christian influence, though it was more diffuse. Trade had brought the Meccans into contact with the Byzantine and Abyssinian empires, which were Christian. Christianity had spread in the Yemen, especially when the country was under Abyssinian control. Sections of some of the nomadic tribes had become Christian. Apart from this we hear of only isolated individuals like Waraqa ibn-Nawfal at Mecca, the cousin of Muḥammad's first wife Khadīja. This was sufficient, however, to ensure that there was some penetration of Christian ideas into intellectual circles in Arabia. On the other hand, the reason why more Arabs did not become Christian is doubtless in part the fact that Christianity had political implications; the Byzantine and Abyssinian empires were officially Christian (Orthodox or Monophysite), and Nestorian Christianity was strong in the Persian empire.[9]

Apart from Judaism and Christianity, there are traces in the Qur'ān and elsewhere of forms of the old Semitic religion. Names of particular deities are mentioned [53.19f.; 71.23/2]. These were not comparable to the Greek gods, but were rather local forms taken by the general Semitic worship of male and female powers.[10] In so far as these deities had primarily belonged to an agricultural phase in the life of the

Arabs, they were hardly relevant to nomadic society; and stories of the period suggest that the nomads had no profound respect for them. The chief driving power in nomadic life came from what may be called 'tribal humanism',[11] that is, a belief in the virtues or human excellence of a tribe or clan (and its members) and in the transmission of these qualities by the tribal stock. For men whose effective belief was this, the motive behind most actions was the desire to maintain the honour of the tribe. The question of honour is omnipresent in the numerous examples of pre-Islamic poetry that have been preserved.

Apart from tribal humanism and the old paganism, there appears to have been present among some Arabs a form of belief in which a supreme deity or 'high god' was acknowledged in addition to the lesser deities. This may be inferred from a number of passages where polytheists are depicted as admitting that God is creator and provider and as praying to him in a moment of crisis.[12] It is probable that such a belief was widespread, and also that a few people were moving on from this to belief in one God only. In later Muslim works it is assumed that there were a number of such persons – some names are given – and that they used the name of *ḥanīf* (singular). In the Qur'ān this word is applied primarily to those who professed what is called 'the pure religion of Abraham' – a pure monotheism which was later allegedly corrupted by Jews and Christians. The matter is complex,[13] but the point to be emphasized here is that any 'pure monotheist' prior to Muḥammad – and there may well have been some – did not call himself a *ḥanīf*. In the Qur'ān the word belongs to the teaching about the relation of Islam to Judaism and Christianity and not to affairs about AD 600. Nevertheless the Qur'ān also gives hints of much religious ferment at that period.

3. Muḥammad's career[14]

The career of Muḥammad is a subject of study in itself and will only be briefly sketched here so as to indicate its main phases in so far as some knowledge of them is necessary for the understanding of the Qur'ān. Not surprisingly there are virtually no references to the period of Muḥammad's life prior to his call to be a prophet. The chief exception is the passage in 93.6-8, which speaks of his orphanhood and poverty. This is explained more fully by the Traditions. When Muḥammad was born in Mecca about AD 570 his father was already dead, and his mother died when he was about six. He was then under the care of his grandfather 'Abd-al-Muṭṭalib, and, when he in turn died, of his uncle Abū-Ṭālib, who lived until a year or two before Muḥammad's Hijra or emigration to Medina in 622. His poverty may be ascribed to the fact that by Arab customary law a minor could not inherit, so that nothing came to Muḥammad from either his father or his grandfather. The fortunes of the clan as a whole may have been in decline, since Abū-Ṭālib, for long head of the clan, was apparently not a wealthy man. He did, however, undertake trading journeys to Syria, and Muḥammad is said to have been to Syria with him. Later he was commissioned by a woman of moderate means, called Khadīja, to take charge of her goods on a trading journey of this type, and he was so successful that she married him, she then being about forty and he twenty-five. He presumably continued to trade with their joint capital for the next fifteen years or longer.

The next phase of Muḥammad's career began when he was about forty. His years of poverty must have made him fully aware of the spiritual malaise affecting Mecca as a result of its material prosperity. He is said to have been in the habit of meditating on such matters. About 610 in the course of his meditations he had some strange experiences, and came to the conclusion that he was receiving messages from God to communicate to the people of Mecca. At first the messages were simply remembered by Muḥammad and his friends, though later some may have been written down by Muḥammad's secretaries. After his death all that was extant, written or remembered, was collected and written down to constitute the Qur'ān as we know it. This simple statement covers many disputed points which will be dealt with later. For a few years after receiving the first revelation Muḥammad made no public proclamations, but communicated the messages privately to friends sympathetic to the outlook and attitude prescribed in them. The main emphasis was on a call to worship God in gratitude for his goodness to the Meccans as a whole and to each individual. Many of the revealed passages spoke of various natural events as signs of God's goodness.

In due course, however, Muḥammad had to pass over to a public proclamation of the Qur'ānic message, and this led sooner or later – the chronology of the Meccan period is uncertain – to opposition from the richest merchants in Mecca. Probably even during the phase of private communication the messages had contained a warning that those who disregarded the divine messages would inevitably be punished either in this life or in the life to come. After opposition appeared these warnings became more frequent. Stories of previous messengers or prophets were recounted or alluded to in the messages in order to convince the audience of the certainty of punishment. Presumably because the opposition to Muḥammad was associated with a recrudescence of the old religion with its idol-worship, the Qur'ānic messages now include a vigorous attack on idols and an insistence on monotheism. The stories of previous messengers also gave encouragement to Muḥammad and the band of followers that had gathered round him. It is difficult to assess the extent of persecution, but it was bitterly resented by the Muslims, as those eventually came to be known who accepted the Qur'ānic messages. By a process of inference it appears that on the death of Abū-Ṭālib the new chief of Muḥammad's clan, Abū-Lahab (another uncle), withdrew the protection of the clan from Muḥammad, alleging that he had forfeited the right to it by asserting that the ancestors of the clan were in Hell. This is doubtless the reason for the fierce attack on Abū-Lahab in sura 111.

Persecution and withdrawal of protection made it impossible for Muḥammad to continue his mission in Mecca. An opportunity presented itself of migrating to the oasis of Medina some two hundred miles to the north, and Muḥammad and seventy of his followers decided to go there. This event was the Hijra (latinized as 'Hegira') or Emigration; and the Islamic era begins with the beginning of the Arabian year in which it took place, viz. 16 July 622.[15] Most of the Arabs of Medina made an agreement with Muḥammad, accepting his claim to be a prophet and recognizing him as chief of the 'clan' of Emigrants. For the first few years at Medina Muḥammad was far from being ruler of the oasis, since there were eight other clan chiefs of roughly equal status. In time, however, through the military success of the expeditions or razzias undertaken by the Emigrants assisted by the men of Medina, Muḥammad's power greatly increased.

The first eighteen months or so after the Hijra were occupied not merely with a general adjustment to the new situation by all concerned but more especially by attempts on Muḥammad's part to gain the support of the Jewish clans and small groups in Medina. Time and again he is instructed in the Qur'ān to appeal to them in various forms. Then, when it appears that few of them are going to respond to his appeals, he is told to criticize them, and shown that the religion he is proclaiming is the pure religion of Abraham which the Jews and Christians have corrupted. What is found in the Qur'ān is mainly evidence for the intellectual aspects of the dispute between Muḥammad and the Jews, but there are also a few references to the expulsion of Jewish clans. There are also places where both Jews and Christians are attacked. There was no active hostility against Christians until the last two or three years of Muḥammad's life, and so it would seem that the criticisms of the Jews were sometimes continued into this period. What is known as 'the break with the Jews' occurred about March 624, shortly before the battle of Badr. The chief outward mark of this realignment of forces in Medina was that the Qibla or direction faced in prayer was changed from being towards Jerusalem, like the Jews, to being towards Mecca. This was an indication that the new religion was to be specifically Arab, and that Muḥammad was going to rely more on the 'arabizing' party among his followers than upon the 'judaizing' party.

The same month of March 624 also saw the throwing down of the gauntlet by the Muslims to the power of Mecca. Already in January 624 a handful of Muslims had captured a small Meccan caravan from under the noses of the Meccans, as it were. In March, however, a band of just over three hundred Muslims led by Muḥammad himself won a surprise victory at Badr over a much larger force from Mecca and killed about half the leading men of Mecca. This was a challenge to the Meccan commercial empire which the great merchants could not ignore. About a year later they invaded the Medinan oasis and had the better of the fighting near mount Uḥud, but failed to inflict very heavy losses on Muḥammad, far less to dislodge him. The Qur'ān reflects both the exhilaration of the Muslims after the victory of Badr, which seemed to them God's vindication of their cause, and their dismay after Uḥud when they feared that he had abandoned them. There are rather fewer references in the Qur'ān to the later incidents in Muḥammad's struggle with the Meccans. In 627 they besieged Medina for a fortnight along with nomadic allies, but had no success. In March 628 Muḥammad attempted to perform the pilgrimage to Mecca with 1,600 men; though he was stopped by the Meccans and had to postpone his pilgrimage to the next year, he signed a treaty with them at al-Ḥudaybiya which put an end to hostilities. An incident between nomads allied to the two sides was construed by Muḥammad as a breach of the treaty, and he marched on Mecca with 10,000 men in January 630 and entered the city as conqueror with virtually no fighting. He showed great leniency to his former enemies, the Meccans, and most of them became his associates in the final phase of his career and acknowledged him as the Messenger of God.

This final phase was constituted by the expansion of Muḥammad's authority into most regions of Arabia, and his 'reconnaissance in force' of one of the routes used in the subsequent Arab expansion beyond Arabia. Even before 630 a few nomadic tribes had become Muḥammad's allies and had recognized his political as well as his religious authority. Two or three weeks after his victorious entry into Mecca Muḥammad took his 10,000 Muslims and also 2,000 Meccans to a place towards the east called Ḥunayn, and there met a concentration of nomads hostile both to himself and to the Meccans. For some time the issue of the battle hung in the balance, but it ended in the absolute rout of Muḥammad's opponents. After this there was no possible concentration of nomads in Arabia (apart from the north) which could take the field against the Muslims. Soon most of the tribes of Arabia began sending deputations to Medina to seek alliance with Muḥammad. By the time of his death on 8 June 632 he was effective ruler of most of Arabia, though in the case of several tribes there was also a strong faction hostile to him, who were biding their time to throw off the yoke of Medina. It would seem, however, that for some years before his death Muḥammad had realized that the extension of his rule and of what may be called the *pax islamica* over the nomadic tribes of Arabia must go hand in hand with an outlet for their energies into regions beyond Arabia. In this connection it is to be noted that the greatest of all Muḥammad's expeditions, that to Tabūk in the north, seems to have had as its strategic aim the opening of the route for expansion into Syria. This expedition, which is mentioned at several points in sura 9, lasted from October to December 630 and comprised 30,000 men. On the whole, however, the Qur'ān has few references to this last phase.

ANNEX A

Chronology of Muḥammad's career

c. 570 *birth at Mecca*
c. 595 *marriage to Khadīja*
c. 610 *first revelation*
c. 613 *beginning of public preaching*
c. 619 *deaths of Khadīja and Abū-Ṭālib*
16 July 622 *beginning of era of Hijra*
September 622 *arrival in Medina*
c. February 624 *change of* qibla
March 624 *battle of Badr*
March 625 *battle of Uḥud*
April 627 *siege of Medina*
March 628 *treaty of al-Ḥudaybiya*
January 630 *conquest of Mecca; battle of Ḥunayn*
October-December 630 *expedition to Tabūk*
March 632 *pilgrimage of farewell*
8 June 632 *death*

ANNEX B

Ḥanīf

The word *ḥanīf* occurs twelve times in the Qur'ān, two of these instances being of the plural *ḥunafā'*. The basic usage is doubtless that in 3.67/0, where it is said that Abraham was neither a Jew nor a Christian but a *ḥanīf*, a *muslim*, not one of the 'idolaters'. There are similar historical statements about Abraham worshipping God as a *ḥanīf* in 6.79 and 16.120/1, but the word *muslim* is not used there. Next there are a number of explicit or implicit commands to Muḥammad and the Muslims to follow the creed or religion of Abraham as a *ḥanīf* [2.135/29; 3.95/89; 4.125/4; 6.161/2; 16.123/4]. In the remaining passages [10.105; 22.31/2; 30.30/29; 98.5/4] there is no mention of Abraham, but the command is given to Muḥammad (or the Muslims or the people of the Book) to serve God 'as a *ḥanīf*, not one of the idolaters'. Thus the word is connected solely with Abraham himself or with 'the religion of Abraham' as that is conceived in the Qur'ān and, as applying to Islam, contrasted with Judaism and Christianity as well as with paganism.

Later Muslim scholars always take the word in this sense, sometimes also using *ḥanīf* as equivalent of 'Muslim', and the *ḥanīfiyya* as equivalent of 'Islam'. The latter word was found instead of Islam in Ibn-Mas'ūd's copy of the Qur'ān at 3.19/17. Muslim scholars also tried to show that there were men just before Muḥammad who were seeking the *ḥanīfiyya* or pure monotheism. There certainly appear to have been men seeking a purer or more adequate religion, but they cannot have called themselves by the name of *ḥanīf*, since, had they done so, the name could not have been equated with 'Muslim'. It seems that pre-Islamic Arab poets used *ḥanīf* for 'pagan' or 'idolater', and this was certainly the Christian usage, derived from Syriac by taking the plural *ḥunafā'* to represent the Syriac plural *ḥanpé*. Christians used this point in mocking criticism of Muslims, and the latter seem eventually to have abandoned calling themselves *ḥunafā'*. A much fuller discussion will be found in *EI*², art. '*ḥanīf*'.

TWO

MUḤAMMAD'S PROPHETIC EXPERIENCE

1. Criticisms of the claim to prophethood

Muḥammad's claim to be a prophet and messenger and to receive messages from God to be conveyed to his fellow Arabs has been criticized and attacked almost from the day it was first put forward. From the Qur'ān itself we learn that the pagan Meccans called the messages 'old-world tales' (*asāṭīr al-awwalīn*),[1] while the Jews of Medina mocked Muḥammad's claims. These criticisms were taken up by Christian scholars. In medieval Europe there was elaborated the conception of Muḥammad as a false prophet, who merely pretended to receive messages from God[2]; and this and other falsifications of medieval war-propaganda are only slowly being expunged from the mind of Europe and of Christendom.

The first step towards a more balanced view was taken by Thomas Carlyle when he laughed out of court the idea of an impostor being the founder of one of the world's great religions.[3] Various later scholars followed this with attempts to save Muḥammad's sincerity, but sometimes at the expense of his sanity. Gustav Weil sought to prove that he suffered from epilepsy.[4] Aloys Sprenger went further and suggested that in addition Muḥammad suffered from hysteria.[5] Sir William Muir retained something of the false-prophet idea; he pictured Muḥammad as an earnest and high-souled messenger and preacher while at Mecca, who, when he went to Medina, succumbed to the wiles of Satan for the sake of worldly success.[6] D. S. Margoliouth had no qualms about accusing him of having deliberately mystified the people, and pointed to the history of spiritualism as showing how easily human beings with unusual powers fall into dishonesty.[7] Theodor Nöldeke, while insisting on the reality of

Muḥammad's prophetic inspiration, and rejecting the idea that he suffered from epilepsy, thought that he was subject to overpowering fits of emotion which led him to believe that he was under divine influences.[8] Recent writers have on the whole been more favourable and have taken the view that Muḥammad was absolutely sincere and acted in complete good faith. Frants Buhl emphasized the far-reaching historical significance of the religious movement he inaugurated[9]; while Richard Bell spoke of the eminently practical character of his activity even as a prophet.[10] Tor Andrae examined Muḥammad's experience from a psychological standpoint and found it genuine, and also held that he had a prophetic message for his age and generation.[11]

In the adverse opinions more attention was paid to certain Traditions than to the evidence of the Qur'ān itself. Too little allowance also was made for the fact that the Muḥammad whom we know best was to all appearance healthy both in body and in mind. It is incredible that a person subject to epilepsy, or hysteria, or even ungovernable fits of emotion, could have been the active leader of military expeditions, or the cool far-seeing guide of a city-state and a growing religious community; but all this we know Muḥammad to have been. In such questions the principle of the historian should be to depend mainly on the Qur'ān and to accept Tradition only in so far as it is in harmony with the results of Qur'ānic study. The Qur'ān, however, though it apparently chronicles without reserve the gibes and reproaches of his opponents, mentions nothing that would support the belief in some diseased condition in Muḥammad. The opponents indeed said he was *majnūn*, but that meant either simply that they thought his conduct crazy, or that they regarded his utterances as inspired by jinn, as those of soothsayers were supposed to be. Had they been able to point to any evident signs of disease in him we should almost certainly have heard of this. Medieval conceptions must therefore be set aside, and Muḥammad regarded as a man who sincerely and in good faith proclaimed messages which he believed came to him from God.

2. Qur'ānic descriptions of revelation and prophethood

One of the latest and clearest descriptions of revelation in the

Qur'ān is in 2.97/1, where Gabriel is said to have brought it (the message) down upon the Prophet's heart by God's permission. That this was the account accepted by Muḥammad and the Muslims in the Medinan period is certain. Tradition is unanimous on the point that Gabriel was the agent of revelation. When Tradition carries this back to the beginning, however, and associates Gabriel with the original call to prophethood, the scholar's suspicions are aroused since Gabriel is only twice mentioned in the Qur'ān, both times in Medinan passages. The association of Gabriel with the call appears to be a later interpretation of something which Muḥammad had at first understood otherwise.

It is to be noted that in 2.97/1 there is no assertion that Gabriel appeared in visible form; and it may be taken as certain that the revelations were not normally mediated or accompanied by a vision. The Qur'ān indeed mentions two occasions on which Muḥammad saw a vision [53.1-12, 13-18]. Strictly read, these verses imply that the visions were of God, since the word *'abd*, 'slave' or 'servant', describes a man's relation to God and not to an angel; this interpretation is allowed by some Muslim commentators. In 81.15-25, however, the vision is re-interpreted as that of an angel. This indicates a growing and changing understanding of spiritual things in the minds of Muḥammad and the Muslims. At first they assumed that he had seen God himself, but later they realized that that was impossible, and therefore concluded that the vision was of a messenger of God, that is, an angel. Similarly the experience of receiving messages or revelations may have been interpreted differently at the beginning of his mission and at the close of the Medinan period. Yet, however the visions are interpreted or explained, to Muḥammad they were undoubtedly real. At the same time they were unique; there is no mention of any other visions, if we except that before the expedition to al-Ḥudaybiya [48.27]. There is just a little in the Qur'ān to support the hypothesis adopted by Tor Andrae[12] that Muḥammad actually heard voices; but the fact that the revelations took the form of words might be held to show that Muḥammad was closer to the auditory than to the visual type of inspiration. Both the visible appearance of God and the hearing of his voice are excluded by 42.51/0: 'it is not fitting for any human being that God should speak to him except by "revelation" or from behind a veil, or by sending a messenger to "reveal" by his permission what he will'.

What then is meant by 'reveal' and 'revelation', or, as they are rendered in the Bell translation, 'suggest' and 'suggestion'? The Arabic verb and noun, *awḥā* and *waḥy*, have become the technical terms of Islamic theology for the communication of the messages or revelations to Muḥammad. In accordance with 2.97/1 they have come to imply the recitation of the words of the Qur'ān to him by the angel Gabriel. In the Qur'ān itself the words are commonly used of this special form of communication, but they are not confined to it. There are several examples of their use in a more general sense. Thus the word *awḥā* is used in 19.11/12 of Zechariah (Zacharias), after he had become dumb, 'making a sign' or 'indicating' to the people that they should glorify God. Satans (or demons) of jinn and men 'suggest' specious ideas to one another [6.112]. The recipient of *waḥy*, even from God, is not always a prophet, or even a human being. God 'suggests' to the bee to take houses for herself in the hills and trees and the arbours which men erect [16.68/70]. At the Last Day the earth will give up its burdens because its Lord has 'suggested' to it to do this [99.2-5]. God 'suggested' to each of the seven heavens its special function [41.12/11].

Even when the recipient is a prophet what is communicated is usually not the words of a revelation but a practical line of conduct, something to do, not to say. Thus it is 'suggested' to Noah to build the ark, and he is to build it under God's eyes and at his 'suggestion' [11.36/8f.; 23.27]. To Moses it is 'suggested' to set out with his people by night [20.77/9; 26.52], to strike the sea with his staff [26.63], to strike the rock with his staff [7.160]. To Muḥammad himself it is 'suggested' that he should follow the religion of Abraham [16.123/4]. These practical 'suggestions' are often formulated in direct speech, as if a form of words had been put into a person's mind [cf. 17.39/41 and previous verses].

There are cases too in which the formula has reference to doctrine rather than to conduct; for example, 'your God is One God' [18.100; 21.108; 41.6/5]. Usually the formula is short, the sort of phrase which after consideration of a matter might flash into a person's mind as the final summing up and solution of it. There are indeed a few passages in which the verb seems to mean the communication of somewhat lengthy pieces to the Prophet; for example in 12.102/3, 'stories of what is unseen (or absent)' may refer to the whole story of Joseph.[13] Even in such passages, however, the actual verbal communication of the stories is not certainly implied. The fundamental sense of the word as used in the Qur'ān seems to be *the communication of an idea by some quick suggestion or prompting*, or, as we might say, by a flash of inspiration. This agrees with examples given in the dictionaries (such as *Lisān al-'Arab*, s.v.) where it is implied that haste or quickness is part of the connotation of the root.

An explanation of the frequent use of this term in connection with the Prophet's inspiration might be that there was something short and sudden about it. If Muḥammad was one of those brooding spirits to whom, after a longer or shorter period of intense absorption in a problem, the solution comes in a flash, as if by suggestion from without, then the Qur'ānic use of the word becomes intelligible. Nor is this merely a supposition. There is evidence to show that the Prophet, accessible enough in the ordinary intercourse of men, had something withdrawn and separate about him. In the ultimate issue he took counsel with himself and followed his own decisions. If decisions did come to him in this way, it was perhaps natural that he should attribute them to outside suggestion. The experience was mysterious to him. He had before him the example of the soothsayer (*kāhin*) who probably claimed that he spoke by outside prompting. Once or twice, probably near the beginning of his mission, when his hesitations had caused him more than usually intense and long-continued mental exertion, the decision had come to him accompanied by a vision. He has assumed that it was God who had appeared to him and 'suggested' that he should speak to the people in public. It is to be noted that in the passage where these visions are described, nothing is said about the Qur'ān. A 'suggestion' came to him, but this was simply that he should speak – at least such is the natural interpretation – and it is his 'speaking' which is explained and defended [53.4, 10].

These considerations to some extent justify the hypothesis favoured by Richard Bell that originally the *waḥy* was a prompting or command to speak. The general content of the utterance was perhaps 'revealed' from without, but it was left to Muḥammad himself to find the precise words in which to speak. Sura 73.1-8 was interpreted by Bell of the Prophet taking trouble over the work of composing the Qur'ān, choosing the night-hours as being 'strongest in impression and most just in speech', that is, the time when ideas are clearest and when fitting words are most readily found.[14] A similar experience when after effort and meditation the words in the end came easily as if by inspiration, may well have led him to extend to the actual words of his deliverances this idea of suggestion from without. A curious isolated passage [75.16-19] seems to encourage him to cultivate this deliberately: 'Move not thy tongue that thou mayest do it quickly; ours it is to collect it and recite it; when we recite it follow thou the recitation; then ours it is to explain it'. This has always been taken as referring to the reception of the Qur'ān, and if we try to get behind the usual mechanical interpretation we can picture Muḥammad in the throes of composition. He has been seeking words which will flow and rhyme and express his meaning, repeating phrases audibly to himself, trying to force the continuation before the whole has become clear. He is here admonished that this is not the way; he must not 'press', but wait for the inspiration which will give the words without this impatient effort to find them. When his mind has calmed, and the whole has taken shape, the words will come; and when they do come, he must take them as they are given him. If they are somewhat cryptic – as they may well happen to be – they can be explained later. If that be the proper interpretation of the passage, it throws light on a characteristic of the Qur'ān which has often been remarked on, namely, its disjointedness. For passages composed in such fashion must almost of necessity be comparatively short.

In some such way, then, Muḥammad's claim to inspiration might be understood. It has analogies to the experience which poets refer to as the coming of the muse, or more closely to what religious people describe as the coming of guidance after meditation and waiting upon God. 'Guidance' is in fact one of the Qur'ān's favourite words for the message. Muḥammad's experience was interpreted in various ways. At first he assumed that it was God who spoke to him, just as he had assumed that it was God who had appeared to him in his visions. Then, according to 42.51/0 ff., this idea was rejected in favour of the idea of a spirit implanted within him. Later, when through increasing familiarity with Jewish and Christian ideas he had learned of angels as messengers of God, he assumed that it was angels who brought the message. Finally, he adopted Gabriel as the special angel who prompted him on God's behalf. There are passages in the Qur'ān illustrating all these various ideas. Yet always the essence of the experience is the same: he was prompted, 'suggestions' were made to him, the message was brought down upon his heart. That these promptings, however mediated, came ultimately from a divine source, he was convinced. He may, indeed, have had occasional doubts. He realized, perhaps as a result of the false step which he made in recognizing the pagan deities as intercessors, and of other mistakes which he may have made, that Satan sometimes took a hand in the prompting.[15] From the assurances that he was not mad, nor prompted by jinn, it may perhaps be inferred that he sometimes wondered if this was the case. In general, however, he was convinced that the 'suggestions' were from God.

That this experience of 'suggestion' or 'guidance' is a real one, no one who has ever become deeply absorbed in a difficult problem will deny. But the habit of expecting such experiences, and the attempt to induce them, are not without their dangers. We cannot force the answer which we wish, or indeed any answer, at the time we wish it. Muḥammad seems to have experienced this also, 18.24/23. It is when the mind is more or less passive that such 'suggestions' come, but it makes a great difference whether this passive attitude is the result of a heavy strain upon the mental and spiritual powers, or is cultivated as a state of more or less mental vacancy. Between these two poles there is the danger that meditation becomes a brooding over passing troubles, or that it allows too easy a response to external stimuli. Of some of these dangers Muḥammad seems at times to have been conscious, as is shown by 5.101; 22.52/1. In later life when events pressed upon him and decisions were imperative, and when questions arose which he could not avoid answering, he no doubt tried to force the revelation, though there is no proof that this in fact happened. After a revelation about special marriage privileges for himself, his young wife 'Ā'isha is said to have remarked sarcastically, 'Your Lord hastens to do your pleasure'.[16] If this story is true, it shows that there was a conscious rectitude in Muḥammad not to be perturbed by such an insinuation. Actually, even in his later days, there were revelations which were contrary to his own natural desires. He was exhorted to steadfastness when his inclination was to compromise, he was urged to policies which he felt to be difficult, and he was taken to task for things he had done or had omitted to do. In all this Muḥammad must have been, as he claimed, a passive recipient.

About the details of Bell's theory there is an element of conjecture, and one may be justified in maintaining an attitude of reserve towards them. One difficulty which he does not meet is that *awḥā* is not the only verb in the Qur'ān commonly used for 'reveal'. There are also *nazzala* and *anzala*; and these two words in their various forms occur about three times as often as the derivatives of *awḥā* (about 250 instances as against 78). *Nazzala* and *anzala*, however, both mean 'to send down'; and it may be that Muḥammad and the Muslims were content with a naïve view of the process of revelation. The central point, however, which is not meant to be contradicted by Bell's theory, is that the ultimate source of the Qur'ānic messages is God. Of this Muḥammad was utterly convinced and on this conviction he built up his claims to authority. At the same time he was also modest about himself. He was only a human being to whom 'suggestions' came, a channel through whom divine messages were communicated to the Arabs [18.110; 41.6/5]. The guidance by *waḥy*, however, was all that the long line of previous prophets had experienced; the one exception was Moses, to whom God had spoken directly [7.144/1; 19.52/3].

Finally, it should be added that neither a psychological account of the precise nature of Muḥammad's prophetic experience nor an insistence on his sincerity, answers the final question, 'Is the Qur'ān true? Is it really a message from

God?' This point will be touched on again at the end of the concluding chapter. Muḥammad surrounded his experiences with some degree of awe and mystery. This does not detract from the sincerity of his own belief in them. They were mysterious to himself, and, if they were what he believed them to be, they were worthy of awe. He regarded them always as something separate and distinct; and, as just noted, they often conflicted with his own desires and inclinations. The claim that they were from beyond himself could not have been altogether a pose.

Of the essential sincerity of Muḥammad, then, there can be no question. We need not, however, go to the other extreme and picture him as a modern saint. The age was a rude one to our ideas, even in the most enlightened parts of the world, and Arabia was not one of these.

3. The conception of the prophetic function

Closely connected with this question of the precise form of Muḥammad's experience of revelation is the further question of how the prophetic function is to be conceived. The changing circumstances of his life – the transition from the preacher of Mecca to the statesman of Medina and then to the ruler of much of Arabia – necessarily affected the use of his time. The changes are reflected in the Qur'ān; and indeed it must in large part have been the Qur'ān which made Muḥammad consciously aware of the new aspects of his function, and even directed the development of the function.

Although in English and other European languages it is usual to speak of Muḥammad as 'prophet' or its equivalent, the word commonly applied to him in the Qur'ān is *rasūl* or 'messenger' (also translated 'apostle'). This is likewise the word used in the Shahāda, or confession of faith: 'there is no deity but God, Muḥammad is the messenger of God'. The word *rasūl* can be applied to anyone who is sent with a message. In 81.19 it is used of an angel bearing a message to Muḥammad (which is specially appropriate, since angel comes from the Greek word for 'messenger'). It is insisted that there had been a long line of messengers before Muḥammad, and that therefore there was nothing novel in his position [46.9/8]. The obvious fact was admitted, of course, that for some time before Muḥammad there had been no messengers of this kind; this was described by saying that he came after a 'break' or 'gap' (*fatra*) in the series [5.19/22]. After his initial experiences of 'suggestion' or 'revelation', Muḥammad may well have been puzzled to know what to make of them. There is a story in the Traditions (though not referred to in the Qur'ān) that in this situation he was encouraged by Waraqa ibn-Nawfal to regard his experiences as similar to those of prophets in the past; Waraqa was a cousin of Muḥammad's wife Khadīja and was also a Christian. On such a point the Traditions may not be wholly reliable, but it is certain from the Qur'ān that from an early date the Muslims assumed an identity in essentials between Muḥammad's experiences and those of previous prophets and messengers. The stories of such persons in the Qur'ān show that Muḥammad had a distinguished spiritual ancestry.

Those 'sent as messengers' (*mursalīn*, roughly equivalent to the plural *rusul*) are also described in 6.48 as 'announcers' and 'warners' (*mubashshirīn*, *mundhirīn*); and likewise in 33.45/4, 48.8 and 35.24/2 Muḥammad himself is spoken of as an 'announcer' and 'warner' (*bashīr*, *nadhīr*). The idea that the function of the messenger is to warn his own people is frequent in the earlier passages of the Qur'ān. Sometimes the word 'warn' is used absolutely without an object, though one may gather from other passages the kind of object implied; in 92.14 it is the fire, that is, Hell, and in 78.40 it is punishment in the life to come. There are also passages in which a messenger has to warn his people that they will be punished by a temporal calamity (as Ḥūd warned 'Ād in 46.21/0). It has sometimes been held, especially by European scholars, that the earliest message of the Qur'ān was a warning of either eschatological or temporal punishment.[17] This theory would be supported by the view held by a few Muslim scholars but not the majority, that the first passage of the Qur'ān to be revealed was the beginning of sura 74, for this contains the words 'rise and warn' [74.2]. On the other hand, it would seem that the more positive message of sura 106 – to be grateful to God and worship him – also belongs to a very early period. It would thus be mistaken to restrict the earliest message to 'warning'.

The word *bashīr*, also used of Muḥammad, has been rendered 'announcer'. When it is coupled with 'warner', some contrast may be intended; the warner tells men of possible punishment, while the announcer informs them of the rewards of the upright. It is sometimes thought that the corresponding verb *bashshara* means 'to announce good news'; and in Christian Arabic the noun *bishāra* is used for 'good news' or 'gospel'. In a number of places, however, the Qur'ān uses *bashshara* of punishment.[18] While this might be understood as 'giving good tidings' in an ironical sense, it seems better to take it simply as 'announce'. The dictionaries suggest that the basic meaning of the word is to announce something which produces a change in a man's *bashra* or complexion; mostly this is done by good news, such as the birth of a child, but it might also be done by very bad news. The word *bashīr*, however, seems to indicate that Muḥammad's function is not confined to 'warning'.

Another word used of Muḥammad is *mudhakkir*, which is normally 'one who reminds, admonishes, exhorts', and correspondingly the message is referred to as a *tadhkira*, 'reminder, admonition'. The root, however, has a rich semantic development in Arabic which makes it impossible in English to indicate all its connotations. Although the first stem of the verb, *dhakara*, is usually translated 'remember' or 'mention', there is often no special emphasis on calling to mind something that was previously known and has been forgotten. The thought seems to be rather that of keeping something before the mind, and also adopting an appropriate attitude. Thus the second stem *dhakkara* (of which *mudhakkir* is the participle) would mean 'to put something before a person's mind in such a way that he adopts an appropriate attitude', and this may be approximately rendered by 'admonish' or 'exhort'. In the Qur'ān the meaning is in fact very close to 'warn', as in 50.45 where Muḥammad is instructed to 'admonish by the *qur'ān* (revealed messages) whoever will fear God's threat'. Even the simple word *dhikr*, often 'remembrance' or 'mention', takes on a suggestion of 'warning' in 7.63/1 and 69/7 where groups are told that 'a *dhikr* from their Lord' comes upon their messengers so that they may warn (*andhara*) them.

The primary function of a 'warner' is to convey a message to his people; but, since the warning is aimed at a redirection of the activity of the whole community, it may be said to have a political aspect. It would certainly appear that some of Muḥammad's opponents were afraid of a growth of his political influence, for it is insisted in 88.21f. that he is 'only a warner (*mudhakkir*), not an overseer (*musayṭir*)'. In this connection it is interesting to note that in 7.188 Muḥammad is told to make it clear to his opponents that his function is only to convey specific messages which are given to him; he has no general knowledge of the 'unseen' (including the future) of which he could make use to his own advantage. As already noted it is insisted that Muḥammad is truly human, like all the previous messengers sent to different peoples; and like them also he has a wife and children.[19] Such statements are designed to correct a misapprehension which must have been current among some of the people, namely, that a messenger from God must be an angelic or semi-divine being. On the contrary, the warner is an ordinary human being without special powers, but one who has been selected by God to perform this function of warning [40.15; etc.].

The Arabic word properly translated 'prophet' is *nabī*, which is derived from Aramaic or Hebrew.[20] It occurs more frequently than the words just considered, but much less frequently than *rasūl*. According to Nöldeke's chronology it first occurs in the second Meccan period, but by Bell's dating all the instances are Medinan with the possible exception of 17.55/7. This might indicate that the Muslims became familiar with the word through their contacts with the Jews of Medina. It is further to be noted that *nabī* is not applied to any of the messengers in the Arabian tradition, such as Hūd and Ṣāliḥ, but only to personages mentioned in the Old or New Testaments (assuming that Idrīs may be identified with Ezra or Enoch).[21] By way of exception, however, Muḥammad himself is regarded as a prophet in the Qur'ān and often addressed as such [e.g. 33.1, 6, 7; 66.1, 8f.]. In 33.40 he is spoken of as 'the seal of the prophets' (*khātam an-nabiyyīn*), a phrase which perhaps originally meant 'the one confirming previous prophets', though it has also been given other interpretations. Later Muslim scholars debated at length whether the rank of *nabī* or *rasūl* was higher, and whether every prophet had to be a messenger or *vice versa*; but these questions have little relevance to the study of the Qur'ān itself.[22] In the Qur'ān the chief difference between the two words is that *nabī* is only applied to men connected with the Judaeo-Christian tradition, for Muḥammad was regarded as continuing and reforming that tradition.

The new functions which devolved upon Muḥammad as messenger and prophet after he went to Medina are reflected in a number of Qur'ānic passages. The responsibilities which fell to him as chief of the 'clan' of Emigrants could have been interpreted in a purely secular way. The clearest statement is perhaps that in 4.105/6 (dated by Bell shortly after Uḥud): 'We have sent down to you the Book with the truth in order that you may judge between the people on the basis of what God has shown you'. Similarly in 5.42/6 (perhaps a little earlier) Muḥammad is told that, if Jews come to him to settle a dispute, and if he agrees to do so, 'he is to judge between them fairly'; the following verse with a reference to the Jews' rejection of the Torah might be taken to imply that judgement was on a basis of scripture. In the light of these verses two other passages [6.89; 3.79/3] which speak of men receiving the Book, the *ḥukm* and prophethood, are probably to be interpreted in the same way; *ḥukm* is from the same root as the word translated 'judge' in 5.42/6, and may be rendered 'judgement' or 'jurisdiction'. With this may be compared 2.151/46 in which the Muslims of Medina are told: 'we have sent a messenger among you, one of yourselves, to recite to you our verses (or signs), to cleanse you (from the impurity of paganism), and to teach you the Book and *ḥikma* . . .'; the last word normally means 'wisdom' and is regarded as of foreign origin,[23] but one wonders if here it has been influenced by the Arabic root.

Another interesting passage is 4.59/62-64/7 where the believers are told to obey God and the Messenger and to bring matters of dispute to God and the Messenger for decision.[24] Decision by God and the Messenger is probably meant to describe decision by Muḥammad on the basis of a revealed text. It also seems probable that obedience to God and the Messenger does not mean direct obedience to the Messenger, but only obedience to him in so far as he is proclaiming the divine message; so this would be primarily obedience to the message. If people disobey and then repent, however, the Messenger may ask pardon for them [4.64/7]. This last point is probably to be understood eschatologically, since the picture normally given by the Qur'ān is that, when men are judged on the Last Day, the Messenger to their community will be present to bear witness against them (presumably to testify that they have duly had the message communicated to them).[25]

In a sense, then, there has been development in the Qur'ān but it is not really change. The new aspects are present from the beginning in the conception of the warner. It was the change in the circumstances of Muḥammad and the Muslims that made it necessary for these aspects to become explicit. The process of development, therefore, is not to be taken as exposing an inconsistency in the Qur'ān but as showing the adaptation of its essential teaching to the changing ideas and changing needs of the Muslims.

4. The writing down of the Qur'ān

It seems probable that for a time, perhaps for years, it was only in their memories that Muḥammad and the Muslims retained the passages revealed to him. This was the normal practice in a predominantly oral culture; the pre-Islamic Arabic poems were treated in the same way. It is also probable, however, that much of the Qur'ān was written down in some form during Muḥammad's lifetime. The problems involved in this matter, however, are of much greater complexity than might be expected. This is because later apologetes for Islam, challenged by Christians and others to point to a miracle of Muḥammad's which would authenticate his claim to prophethood, asserted that the Qur'ān itself was his miracle. The assertion has some basis in the Qur'ān itself where the unbelievers are challenged to produce a similar sura or suras or book [10.38/9; 11.13/16; 28.49]; but the apologetes went beyond this and interpreted various verses in such a way as to enhance the miraculous character of the Qur'ān. One of the chief points they made was that Muḥammad could neither read nor write.

The same tendency may underly the taking of 96.4 to

mean '(God) taught the use of the pen', which is the normal interpretation of Muslim scholars. Partly on the basis of this interpretation European scholars for a time assumed that in Muḥammad's day writing was a recent introduction into Arabia, was known to only a few and was still regarded as a marvel. While many simple people still regarded it as something magical or supernatural, it is now known that it was by no means a recent introduction. The verse, too, with the following one, runs literally: 'who taught by the pen, taught man what he did not know'; and this may be interpreted: 'who taught man by the pen (that is, by books) what he did not (otherwise) know', and referred in the first place to previous revelations. Even with this interpretation, however, writing is still regarded as something novel and wonderful.

However ordinary people in Mecca *felt* about writing, archaeological evidence shows that some forms of writing had been known in Arabia for many centuries.[26] There are inscriptions in the South Arabian language going back far beyond the Christian era. Inscriptions found in north-west Arabia in the Nabataean, Liḥyānic and Thamūdic alphabets belong to the centuries preceding the appearance of Muḥammad. For Classical Arabic and the Arabic script the earliest instance is three graffiti on the wall of a temple in Syria, which are dated about AD 300, while four Christian inscriptions have been found belonging to the sixth century. Though this evidence is meagre, one is justified in assuming that, where inscriptions on stone or metal occur, writing on some more convenient material was also well known. When these various scripts are compared with one another, it is clear that the development is one of written forms, which tend to grow more cursive and so less suitable for inscriptional use.

No indisputably early inscriptions have yet been found in the neighbourhood of Mecca and Medina. Mecca, however, was a mercantile town, dependent on its trade for its very existence, and in regular communication with regions where writing was commonly used. The Meccan merchants must have kept some record of their transactions, and it may be assumed that writing was well enough known there. The indirect evidence of the Qur'ān confirms this. Its imagery is steeped in a mercantile atmosphere,[27] and implies the keeping of accounts in writing. The Judgement-day is the day of reckoning, when the books will be opened, and when everyone will be shown his account, or will be given his account to read. The angels write the deeds of men, and everything is recorded in a book. Even if some of these images were previously used by Christians, they would not have been adopted had they not been understood in Mecca. The Qur'ānic regulation that debts should be recorded in writing [2.282f.] shows that even in Medina (where this was revealed) persons able to write were not difficult to find. It is reported in Tradition that some of the Meccans captured at Badr earned their ransom by teaching Medinans to write.[28]

The report, widely accepted and found in many sources, that the first 'collection' of the Qur'ān was made by Zayd ibn-Thābit in the caliphate of Abū-Bakr (632–4), says that it was collected not only from 'the hearts of men' but also from pieces of parchment or papyrus, flat stones, palm-leaves, shoulder-blades and ribs of animals, pieces of leather and wooden boards.[29] This report is probably not authentic. Apart from the general difficulty about the date (to be considered in the next chapter), it is likely that the report was spread by people who wanted to contrast the relative poverty of Muḥammad and his Companions with the material luxury of Umayyad and early 'Abbāsid times. No doubt the things mentioned were occasionally used for writing in Mecca and Medina – as indeed most of them are known to have been used until recently by Muslims in East Africa – but there is no reason why papyrus should not have been in normal use at Mecca. For purposes of book-production papyrus had by this time given place in the Graeco-Roman world to pergament or parchment, which was prepared from the skins of animals, was more enduring and afforded a better surface. The word *raqq* in 52.3 probably refers to parchment, and in particular to the Jewish Law given at Sinai.[30] Perhaps the Torah was written on parchment at this period. Papyrus, however, continued to be produced, and was largely used for business purposes and private correspondence. It was made in rectangular sheets of moderate size. In former times rolls for the writing of books had been produced by pasting a number of such sheets together. Long rolls had gone out of fashion, but to a limited extent the sheets might still be pasted together or folded to form a book. Probably it is this material which is denoted by the word *qirṭās* in the Qur'ān [6.7, 91], for that is derived from the Greek *chartēs*, meaning a leaf or sheet of papyrus. Since this is an early borrowing, and was probably not taken directly from Greek, it is conceivable that it may have undergone a change of meaning; but this is unlikely, since the word appears to have still had the significance of papyrus in the days of the caliphs.[31] The verse 6.91 may then imply that the Jews used papyrus for writing out separate portions of the Torah, while 6.7 would indicate the possibility of a book being made of papyrus; this may be the kind of book intended when the Qur'ān speaks of a book being sent down to Muḥammad [e.g. 6.92].

What material was denoted by *ṣuḥuf* we have no means of knowing. The word occurs several times in the Qur'ān, usually in connection with the revelation generally [20.133; 80.13; 98.2], or with the revelation to Abraham and Moses [53.36/7f.; 87.18f.]; in 81.10, however, and probably also in 74.52, it refers to the record of man's deeds. The word is from ancient South Arabian, but occurs in Arabic poetry before Muḥammad's time.[32] The singular *ṣaḥīfa* probably denotes a sheet of writing material, and so would not specify what it consists of. The plural *ṣuḥuf* one would naturally take to mean separate (unbound) sheets, but it is possible that the *ṣuḥuf* of Moses and Abraham mentioned in the Qur'ān implied something in the nature of a book. What the words conveyed to the first hearers would depend on what they were familiar with in Muḥammad's practice or otherwise.

In the light of this familiarity with writing and writing materials at Mecca and elsewhere, we may turn to the question whether Muḥammad himself could read and write. For Muslims it has become almost a dogma that he could do neither. It enhances the miracle of the Qur'ān that it should have been delivered by one entirely unlettered. Early Muslim opinion was not so fixed, but on the whole it tended to the same conclusion. One of the chief arguments was from the application of the adjective *ummī* to Muḥammad in 7.157/6, 158. The word was alleged to mean 'unlettered', and one could point to 2.78/3, 'of them are *ummiyyūn* who do not know the book . . .', and argue that they did not know the book because they could not read and write. If the verse is carefully read, however, without a preconceived idea of its meaning, the most natural way to take it is of people without written scriptures. This meaning fits the other instances of the plural found in the Qur'ān [3.20/19, (?) 75/69; 62.2]; in the first two the *ummiyyūn* are associated with the Jews but distinct from them, while in the last Muḥammad is spoken of as a messenger raised up 'among the *ummiyyūn*, one of themselves'. All these facts make it virtually certain that *ummī* means 'non-Jewish' or 'Gentile', and that it is derived from the Hebrew phrase *ummōt ha-'ōlām*, 'the peoples of the world'. The use of the word by Arabs could also be influenced by the possibility of taking it as meaning 'belonging to the *umma* or community'; and in this case *ummī* could be rendered as 'native', that is, belonging to the Arab community. This gives a perfectly good sense for 'the *ummī* prophet' of 2.157/6 and 158; he is the Gentile or native prophet sent to the Arabs and sprung from among themselves. Thus there is no argument here for Muḥammad being completely unlettered, but at most for his being ignorant of the Jewish and Christian scriptures.[33]

A similar conclusion may be reached from examining another verse sometimes interpreted to mean that he could not write, namely, 29.48/7. Sale, following the Muslim commentators, rendered it; 'thou couldest not read any book before this, neither couldest write it with thy right hand'; but a more accurate translation would be: 'you were not reciting previously any book, not inscribing it with your right hand'. The verb *talā* used here – like *qara'a* from which *qur'ān* is derived – means both 'read' and 'recite', and from what we know of the circumstances of Muḥammad's time, the rendering 'recite' was more appropriate then. The verse simply means that he had not been a reader or writer of previous scriptures (that is, as a priest or scribe). This is confirmed by the following words: 'in that case those who invalidate (your claims) would have doubted'; that is, would justly have suspected that you were merely repeating what you had learned from these scriptures. Here again there is nothing which absolutely implies that Muḥammad had no knowledge of reading and writing.

The evidence from Tradition is equally inconclusive. In the story of his Call to be a messenger, he is said to have replied, when the angel said to him 'recite' (*iqra'*), *mā aqra'u* which may mean either 'I do not (cannot) recite' or 'what shall I recite?' This is presumably the earliest version of the Tradition.[34] Those scholars who wanted to emphasize the miraculous quality of the Qur'ān naturally chose the first interpretation, and there are also later forms of the Tradition where the words *mā anā bi-qārin* are substituted, and these can only mean 'I am not a reciter or reader'. On the other hand there are also versions of the Tradition where Muḥammad's reply has the form *mādhā aqra'u*, which can only mean 'what shall I recite?'. The probability is that the latter was the original meaning, so that there is certainly no conclusive evidence here that Muḥammad was unable to read and write.

Even if Tradition is accepted as generally reliable, it fails to prove that Muḥammad could write. Frequently when it is said that Muḥammad wrote, this only means that he gave instructions for a written message to be sent, since it is well known that, at least in his later years, he employed secretaries. In some forms of the story of the conclusion of the treaty of al-Ḥudaybiya in 628 he is stated to have written with his own hand. The emissary of the Meccans objected to the designation 'Messenger of God' in the heading of the treaty, and Muḥammad told 'Alī, who was acting as secretary, to substitute 'son of 'Abd-Allāh'. When 'Alī refused, Muḥammad took the document and himself deleted the title, and some versions add that he wrote the altered designation with his own hand. The whole incident of 'Alī's refusal may be an invention of his partisans to make a political point. The objection to the title and the dropping of it are perhaps indirectly confirmed by the insistence that 'Muḥammad is the messenger of God' in 48.29; but some forms of the story imply that the objection was raised before the title was written, and mention no change in the document.[35] Thus the evidence here for Muḥammad having written anything is weak.

A stronger, though indirect, argument may be drawn from the story of the expedition to Nakhla about two months before the battle of Badr. Previous expeditions had been unsuccessful because some people in Medina seemed to be passing on information to Muḥammad's enemies. To guard against such leakage, therefore, the leader of the expedition to Nakhla was given sealed orders – a written letter of instructions – which he was not to open until he was two days' march from Medina.[36] It is not certain that at this early stage of his career in Medina Muḥammad employed secretaries, and in any case the need for secrecy was such that the writing of the letter could only have been entrusted to someone of the greatest loyalty and discretion. It is therefore not impossible that Muḥammad wrote the letter with his own hand.

While there is thus no convincing proof that Muḥammad was able to write, it is not improbable that he could. He may well have learned the art in Mecca itself. Since he conducted business for Khadīja in his youth, and probably also on his own behalf, he must surely have been able to keep accounts. The Meccan gibe about 'old-world tales, which he has written for himself! they are recited to him morning and evening', even if 'has written' means 'has had written', at least shows that the critics thought that he was working with written material of some sort [25.5/6]. The retort in the following verse does not directly deny that this was so. Again the retort in 18.109 to a presumed gibe about the verbosity of the revelation – 'were the sea ink for the words of my Lord, the sea would fail before the words of my Lord would fail, though we brought as much again' – and the similar verse which speaks of all the trees of the world as pens, must imply that ink and pen was being used for the revelation [31.27/6].

An answer may now be given to the question whether Muḥammad could read and write. On the whole it seems likely that he could read and write as much as the average merchant of Mecca. On the other hand, from a general consideration of the form of the Biblical stories in the Qur'ān, and because *ummī* means one who does not know the previous scriptures, it may be taken as certain that Muḥammad had never read the Bible or even had it read to him [cf. 2.78/3]. These conclusions do not seem to be contrary to the doctrine of the miraculous character of the Qur'ān. A further point might be added. Some educationists would hold that a person may be illiterate and cultured and another person literate and uncultured; the first may have a rich store of traditional cultural lore, and the second may have lost all this in the process of learning to read cheap trash. It seems clear that, whether literate or not, Muḥammad was a cultured person by the standards of Mecca in his time, and this point would have to be noticed in any contemporary apologetic for the miraculous character of the Qur'ān. The point is also relevant to a consideration of the question of sources (chapter 11, section 2 below).

It remains to consider the state of the Qur'ān at the time of Muḥammad's death. Originally the revealed passages were preserved in the memories of Muḥammad and his Companions, and after his death 'the hearts of men' continued to be a place where the Qur'ān or parts of it were found; since the Qur'ān had not been 'collected', no one could have memorized the Qur'ān as a single whole, though a few might have memorized most of the parts. It is also known that parts of the Qur'ān had been written down. In the story of the conversion of ʿUmar ibn-al-Khaṭṭāb, this is said to have come about when he found his sister and her husband, who were Muslims, having sura Ṭā' hā' [20] read to them by a friend from a *ṣaḥīfa* (presumably a sheet of parchment or papyrus); ʿUmar asked to see it, and is said to have been able to read it for himself.[37] If this story is to be trusted (which is not at all certain), it shows that some revelations had been written down by the middle of the Meccan period.

After Muḥammad went to Medina his employment of secretaries is well attested. Among those used for the writing down of the revelations were ʿUthmān, Muʿāwiya, Ubayy ibn-Kaʿb, Zayd ibn-Thābit and ʿAbd-Allah ibn-Abī-Sarḥ.[38] A curious story is told about the last-named. While Muḥammad was dictating to him the passage beginning 23.12, he was carried away by wonder at this description of the creation of man; and, when Muḥammad paused after the words 'another creature', exclaimed 'blessed be God, the best of creators'. Muḥammad accepted this as the continuation of the revelation, and told him to write it down. This aroused doubt, however, in Ibn-Abī-Sarḥ, and later he gave up Islam and returned to Mecca; at the conquest of Mecca he was one of those proscribed, but was pardoned on the intercession of ʿUthmān.[39] This is the sort of story that could hardly have been invented. Other Traditions speak of Muḥammad telling his secretary to place a newly revealed passage after such and such an older passage. In the case of the legislative revelations at Medina it would be desirable to have them written down at once.

Even if it is allowed that many revealed passages had been written down in this way, it still remains to consider to what extent the revelations had attained something like the form of the Qur'ān as we know it. The solution of the problem seems to be largely a matter of degree. On the one hand, Muḥammad himself cannot have produced a complete recension of the Qur'ān. Had he done so, there would have been no need later for a 'collection' of the Qur'ān. In the story of the 'collection' under Abū-Bakr the latter is said to have hesitated when the suggestion was first made on the ground that this was something Muḥammad had never done; but this is a story on which in general little reliance can be placed. On the other hand, if different Companions had memorized different selections of passages, and had perhaps put short pieces together differently, one would have expected greater divergences in the various texts than in fact we find. There is therefore a presumption that Muḥammad himself had brought together many revealed passages and given them a definite order, and that this order was known and adhered to by his Companions. There is further support for this presumption in the Qur'ānic conception of 'the Book' (to be discussed in chapter 8, section 4).

It may further be suggested as a likely hypothesis that the units in which the revelations were arranged were suras. This is almost implied by the Qur'ānic challenges to opponents to produce similar suras [10.38/9; 11.13/16]. The suras in Muḥammad's time would not be identical with the present suras, but might contain the main part of each of the present suras. They may have had no fixed order. The work of the 'collectors' would therefore be to add to the embryonic suras at appropriate points all the verses and short isolated passages not already included somewhere but preserved in the hearts of men or on some of the miscellaneous writing materials on the list. While this view is no more than a hypothesis, it accords with most of the data about which we are reasonably certain.

What remains obscure is the relative amount of the material in Muḥammad's suras and that which had to be added to them. One would think that at most the material to be added might be as much again, and at the least perhaps one-fifth of the bulk of the suras.

THREE

THE HISTORY OF THE TEXT

1. The 'collection' of the Qur'ān

(a) *The 'collection' under Abū-Bakr.* There is a widespread report, found in many slightly differing forms, telling of a 'collection' of the Qur'ān in the caliphate of Abū-Bakr (632–4). According to this report[1] 'Umar ibn-al-Khaṭṭāb (who succeeded as caliph in 634) was perturbed by the fact that in the battle of Yamāma during the 'wars of the apostasy (*ridda*)' many of the 'readers' of the Qur'ān were killed. Since these were the men who had parts of the Qur'ān by heart, 'Umar feared that, if more of them died, some of the Qur'ān would be irretrievably lost. He therefore counselled Abū-Bakr to make a 'collection' of the Qur'ān. At first Abū-Bakr hesitated to undertake a task for which he had received no authority from Muḥammad, but in the end he gave his approval and commissioned Zayd-ibn-Thābit. The latter, who had been one of Muḥammad's secretaries, had no illusions about the difficulty of the task, but at length agreed. As mentioned above (p. 32), he then proceeded to 'collect' the Qur'ān 'from pieces of papyrus, flat stones, palm-leaves, shoulder-blades and ribs of animals, pieces of leather and wooden boards, as well as from the hearts of men'. The last passage to be found was 9.128/9f. – the two closing verses of sura 9. Zayd wrote what he 'collected' on sheets (*ṣuḥuf*) of equal size and gave them to Abū-Bakr. On the latter's death they passed to 'Umar, and on 'Umar's death to his daughter Ḥafṣa, a widow of the prophet.

This tradition is open to criticism on a number of grounds. For one thing it seems to assume that up to the time of Muḥammad's death there had been no authoritative record of the revelations and no attempt to bring some order into them;

but it has been already shown that this is unlikely. Then there are many discrepancies between this tradition and others and between the different versions of this tradition. Thus there is no unanimity about the originator of the idea of collecting the Qur'ān; generally it is said to have been ʿUmar, but sometimes Abū-Bakr is said to have commissioned the 'collection' on his own initiative. On the other hand, there is a tradition which says ʿUmar was the first to 'collect' the Qur'ān and completely excludes Abū-Bakr.[2] Again, the reason given for the step, namely the death of a large number of 'readers' in the battle of Yamāma has also been questioned. In the lists of those who fell in that campaign, very few are mentioned who were likely to have had much of the Qur'ān by heart.[3] Those killed were mostly recent converts. Besides, according to the tradition itself, much of the Qur'ān was already written in some form or other, so that the death of some of those who could recite it from memory need not have given rise to the fear that parts of the Qur'ān would be lost.

Perhaps the weightiest criticism of the tradition is that an official collection of this kind might have been expected to have had wide authority attributed to it, but of this we find no evidence. Other 'collections' of the Qur'ān seem to have been regarded as authoritative in different provinces. The disputes which led to the recension of the Qur'ān under ʿUthmān could hardly have arisen if there had been an official codex in the caliph's possession to which reference could have been made. Again the way in which ʿUmar himself is represented elsewhere as insisting that the verse of stoning[4] was in the Qur'ān, is hardly consistent with his having in his possession an official collection. Lastly, and most significant of all, the *ṣuḥuf* on which Zayd wrote the Qur'ān were, at the time when the revision came to be made, in the keeping of Ḥafṣa. Now Ḥafṣa was ʿUmar's daughter, and we are apparently to assume that since ʿUmar had become caliph by the time Zayd finished his work, the *ṣuḥuf* were handed to him, and from him passed to his daughter. If Zayd's collection was an official one, however, it is hardly probable that it would pass out of official keeping, even into the hands of the caliph's daughter. That Ḥafṣa had a copy of the Qur'ān on *ṣuḥuf* seems certain; but it is unlikely that it was an official copy made in the official way that tradition asserts.

It seems practically certain, then, that no complete 'collection' of the Qur'ān was officially made during the caliphate of Abū-Bakr. The traditional account so far considered was doubtless gradually elaborated to avoid the awkward fact that the first 'collection' of the Qur'ān was made by 'Uthmān, who was greatly disliked. On the other hand, there is no good ground for doubting that Ḥafṣa possessed a Qur'ān written on *ṣuḥuf*, whether this was written by herself, by Zayd, or by someone else.

(b) *The 'collection' under 'Uthmān.* The traditional account of what led to the next step in the fixing of the form of the Qur'ān implies that serious differences of reading existed in the copies of the Qur'ān current in the various districts. During expeditions against Armenia and Azerbaijan, we are told, disputes concerning the reading of the Qur'ān arose amongst the troops, who were drawn partly from Syria and partly from Iraq. The disputes were serious enough to lead the general, Ḥudhayfa, to lay the matter before the caliph, 'Uthmān (644–56), and to urge him to take steps to put an end to these differences. The caliph took counsel with senior Companions of the Prophet, and finally commissioned Zayd ibn-Thābit to 'collect' the Qur'ān. With Zayd were associated three members of noble Meccan families, 'Abd-Allāh ibn-az-Zubayr, Sa'īd ibn-al-'Āṣ and 'Abd-ar-Raḥmān ibn-al-Ḥārith. One of the principles they were to follow was that, in case of difficulty as to the reading, the dialect of Quraysh, the tribe to which the Prophet belonged, was to be given the preference. The whole Qur'ān was carefully revised and compared with the *ṣuḥuf*, which had been in Ḥafṣa's keeping and which were returned to her when the work was finished. Thus an authoritative text of the Qur'ān was established. A number of copies were made and distributed to the main centres of Islam. As to the exact number of these standard codices, and the places to which they were sent, the account varies; but probably one copy was retained in Medina, and one was sent to each of the towns, Kufa, Basra and Damascus, and possibly also to Mecca. Previously existing copies are said to have been then destroyed, so that the text of all subsequent copies of the Qur'ān should be based upon those standard codices.

This traditional account of the 'collection' of the Qur'ān under 'Uthmān is also open to criticisms, though they are not so serious as in the case of Abū-Bakr's 'collection'. The most serious difficulties are those connected with the *ṣuḥuf* of Ḥafṣa. Some versions of the story suggest that the work of the commissioners was simply to make a fair copy, in the dialect of Quraysh, of the material on these leaves. Some important material, however, has come to light since the publication of Friedrich Schwally's revised edition of the second volume of Nöldeke's *Geschichte des Qur'āns* in 1919. In particular there is a story of how the caliph Marwān when governor of Medina wanted to get hold of the 'leaves' of Ḥafṣa to destroy them, and eventually on her death persuaded her brother to hand them over.[5] Marwān was afraid lest the unusual readings in them might lead to further dissension in the community. On the whole it is unlikely that this story has been invented, for it implies that the 'leaves' of Ḥafṣa were unsuitable as a basis for the official text. The 'leaves' are not to be confused with a codex of the new official text said to have been given to Ḥafṣa. The most likely solution of the problem is to hold that, while Ḥafṣa may well have had 'leaves' on which she had written down many sūras, hers was in no respect an official 'collection'. It is perhaps specially mentioned to link up this account with that of the first 'collection' under Abū-Bakr. On the whole, then, it seems unlikely that the 'leaves' of Ḥafṣa were of primary importance. They cannot have contained more than what had been arranged in the 'book' by Muḥammad at the time of his death; and they can hardly have been the sole or main basis of the 'Uthmānic text.

Other criticisms are minor. There are various lists of the persons who helped Zayd. Schwally shows that the suggested names are all improbable.[6] He also questions the instruction to write the revelations in the dialect of the Quraysh (the tribe of Mecca) on the ground that the Qur'ān is in a partly artificial, literary language.[7] Perhaps the function of the commissioners was to help to 'collect' revelations from sources known to them. Schwally dismisses this possibility on the ground that the commission was mainly concerned to produce a fair copy of Ḥafṣa's 'leaves'; but since the new material shows that Ḥafṣa's 'leaves' were unsuitable as a basis for the new edition, Schwally's objection falls. Indeed, there is no reason now for rejecting two points in the traditional account: (1) the commissioners were to collect all the pieces of revelation they could find; (2) where men had remembered it with dialectal variations of the literary language, they were to make the Meccan forms standard.

This establishment of the text of the Qur'ān under 'Uthmān may be dated somewhere between 650 and his death in 656. It is the cardinal point in what may be called the formation of the canon of the Qur'ān. Whatever may have been the form of the Qur'ān previously, it is certain that the book still in our hands is essentially the 'Uthmānic Qur'ān. 'Uthmān's commission decided what was to be included and what excluded; it fixed the number and order of the suras, and the 'outline' of the consonantal text (that is, its shape when the dots distinguishing letters are omitted). If we remember that to preserve every smallest fragment of genuine revelation was an ineluctable requirement, the commission under Zayd must be adjudged to have achieved a wonderful piece of work.

2. The pre-'Uthmānic codices

While 'Uthmān's effort to obtain uniformity throughout the caliphate in the Qur'ānic text must on the whole have been successful in practice, the pre-'Uthmānic or non-canonical readings were by no means forgotten. Most of the larger commentaries on the Qur'ān such as those of aṭ-Ṭabarī and az-Zamakhsharī refer to such non-canonical readings from time to time. One or two Muslim scholars in the early tenth century made a special study of the early *maṣāḥif* (sing. *muṣ'ḥaf*). One such work, the *Kitāb al-maṣāḥif* of Ibn-Abī-Dāwūd (d. 928), survives and was published in 1937. It contains a note to the effect that he uses *muṣ'ḥaf* in the sense of 'reading' or 'set of readings', but the modern editor, Arthur Jeffery, thinks that this is an interpolation, and that when the author speaks of 'the *muṣ'ḥaf* of N' he means an actual written codex.[8] From the information given by Ibn-Abī-Dāwūd and from other sources Jeffery has drawn up a list of fifteen 'primary codices' and almost as many 'secondary codices', and from most of these he has collected at least a few non-canonical readings. The presumption is that at an early period certain Muslims began to write down as much as they could of the Qur'ān. At first these written collections would not necessarily be of interest to the Muslims in general, since men accustomed to the dominance of oral tradition tend to be suspicious of writing, and some Muslim scholars said the phrase 'to collect the Qur'ān' simply meant 'to remember the whole of the Qur'ān'. In the course of time, however, some of the written collections came to have special authority in various great centres of the Islamic world. In particular that of ʿAbd-Allāh ibn-Masʿūd was held in high regard in Kufa, and that of Ubayy ibn-Kaʿb in most parts of Syria.[9]

No copies exist of any of the early codices, but the list of variant readings from the two just mentioned is extensive, running to a thousand or more items in both cases. Ibn-Masʿūd (d. 653) was for a time a personal servant of Muḥammad's, but eventually settled in Kufa where he became an authority on religious matters on account of his interest in the subject and his close association with the Prophet. Ubayy ibn-Kaʿb was a Muslim from Medina who frequently acted as secretary for Muḥammad. The variant readings in the codices of both these men chiefly affect the vowels and punctuation, but occasionally there is a different consonantal text. For both, too, we have lists of the suras, and it is noteworthy that these differ from each other and also from the ʿUthmānic list in the order in which the suras are arranged. On the whole the longer suras come first as in the standard order. The names of the suras, too, are mostly the same as those normally used although in many cases alternatives exist (as will be explained in the next chapter); but it is conceivable that this uniformity in names is due to later transcribers of the lists who substituted the common names for unusual ones. There is, of course, no way of being certain that the contents represented by the names are identical; but on the other hand there is no indication that the contents were different except in respect of the variants noted.

Questions of the omission or addition of suras are also specially connected with these two early codices. The lists giving the order in which they placed the suras are not complete, but it would be rash to infer from this that suras absent from the list had been omitted from the codex. There are explicit statements, however, that Ibn-Mas'ūd omitted altogether the last two suras [113, 114], the Mu'awwidhatān or suras 'of taking refuge with God'; but these are a kind of charm or prayer of commendation, and may not originally have been regarded as part of the Qur'ān. It is also doubtful whether Ibn-Mas'ūd included the first sura or Fātiḥa. This also is a prayer, whose function is not unlike that of the Lord's Prayer in Christianity. Some scholars have argued that, if it were part of the Qur'ān it should have been preceded by the word *qul*, 'say', that is, a command to use it as a prayer. Ubayy seems to have included the three suras mentioned, and also to have had two other suras which are not in the standard text of the Qur'ān. The text of these suras has been preserved by some Muslim scholars. They are short prayers and, as in the case of the Fātiḥa, one might have expected them to be preceded by the word 'say'. Short as the text of them is, there are a number of points where the linguistic usage is not paralleled in the Qur'ān. Schwally, while noting this, thought they might nevertheless go back to Muḥammad,[10] but this is extremely doubtful. It is conceivable that they were used by Muslims in Muḥammad's time, but they cannot have been part of the Qur'ān. Of a different character are omissions of parts of the text for dogmatic reasons. Such is the declaration of the Khārijite sub-sect of the Maymūniyya that the sura of Joseph (12) was not part of the Qur'ān.[11] Their reason for this, however, seems to have been that it was not fitting that a love-story should be included in the Qur'ān. This declaration, then, hardly contributes to our knowledge of the history of the text.

Thus on the whole the information which has reached us about the pre-'Uthmānic codices suggests that there was no great variation in the actual contents of the Qur'ān in the period immediately after the Prophet's death. The order of the suras was apparently not fixed, and there were many slight variations in reading; but of other differences there is no evidence. The modern scholar, familiar with the way in which textual studies have elucidated the stages in the development of early European literary texts, would like to achieve something similar in the case of the Qur'ān, but for this the available information is insufficient, except in respect of the relation of the secondary codices to the primary codices.

3. The writing of the Qur'ān and early textual studies

While the promulgation of the 'Uthmānic text was a major advance towards uniformity, its importance may easily be exaggerated. For one thing, knowledge of the Qur'ān among the Muslims was based far more on memory than on writing. For another thing the script in which the Qur'ān was originally written was what is referred to as a *scriptio defectiva* in contrast to the *scriptio plena* in which it is now written. The nature of the early scripts is fairly well known from the study of early Qur'āns and fragments in some of the great libraries.[12] In the earliest examples only consonants are written, and even these are not adequately distinguished from one another, since the same written shape may sometimes indicate either of two consonants. One might say, then, that this *scriptio defectiva* was little more than an elaborate mnemonic device. It presupposed in the 'reader' some degree of familiarity with the text. A man with no knowledge of the Qur'ān but who understood the script would have had great difficulty in deciphering the writing, though not so much as a person unaware of the structure of Arabic words might suppose. Certainly, however, extensive memorization is presupposed, and this is the background of the improvement of the writing and the growth of textual studies. There was a special class of men, the *qurrā'* or Qur'ān-reciters (sometimes called 'readers'), who specialized in memorizing the sacred text. As the centuries passed their social character changed; eventually we find that this study of the text is chiefly associated with philology, and is a regular part of higher education.

By the time of the caliph 'Abd-al-Malik (685–705) the inadequacy of the existing script was clear to leading Muslims and improvements began to be made. The problem of the incorrect copying of the defective script had also to be dealt with. The traditional accounts of the passage to the *scriptio plena* do not tally with one another, nor with the findings of palaeography. It is virtually certain that the *scriptio plena* did not come into existence all at once, but only gradually by a series of experimental changes. One of the more probable traditional accounts ascribes the introduction of diacritical marks and vowel points to the initiative of al-Ḥajjāj, probably during his governorship of Iraq (694–714). The actual work is said to have been done by scribes such as Naṣr ibn-ʿĀṣim (d. 707) and Yaḥyā ibn-Yaʿmur (d. 746). It is hardly possible that the *scriptio plena* should have been introduced all at once by Abū-l-Aswad ad-Duʿalī (d. 688), as is sometimes suggested. Existing copies of the Qur'ān illustrate different methods of obviating deficiencies of the script; e.g. dots of different colours for the vowels instead of the signs now in current use. The chief matters to be dealt with were: (*a*) distinguishing between consonants with a similar shape; (*b*) the marking of long vowels, which eventually was mostly done by adding the consonants *alif*, *waw*, *yā'*; (*c*) the marking of short vowels; (*d*) certain other matters such as the doubling of consonants and the absence of a vowel after a consonant.

The process of improving the script was completed towards the end of the ninth century. It now became possible to enforce a greater measure of uniformity than was conceivable with the original script. It is not surprising, then, to find in the early tenth century a series of moves to ensure a measure of uniformity. These are chiefly associated with the name of Ibn-Mujāhid (859–935).[13] He was not, of course, the first to concern himself with securing uniformity in the text. Malik ibn-Anas (d. 795), the great scholar of Medina and founder of the Malikite legal rite, had explicitly stated that the performance of the worship behind someone who used the readings of Ibn-Masʿūd was invalid.[14] The more precise script, however, enabled Ibn-Mujāhid to make more exact regulations. As a result of his studies he wrote a book entitled 'The Seven Readings' (*Al-qirā'āt as-sabʿa*). He based himself on a Tradition to the effect that Muḥammad had been taught to recite the Qur'ān according to seven *aḥruf*, interpreted to mean 'seven sets of readings', though *aḥruf* is the plural of *ḥarf* which is properly 'letter'.[15] His conclusion was that the set of readings of each of seven scholars of the eighth century was equally valid, but that these seven sets alone were authentic.

The conclusions of the scholar were made effective by the

action of the courts. In 934 a scholar called Ibn-Miqsam[16] was forced to renounce the view that one was entitled to choose any reading of the consonantal outline that was in accordance with grammar and gave a reasonable sense. This decision was tantamount to an insistence that only the seven sets of readings were valid. In April 935 (about four months before the death of Ibn-Mujāhid) another scholar, Ibn-Shannabūdh, was similarly condemned and forced to retract his view that it was permissible to make use of the readings of Ibn-Masʿūd and Ubayy ibn-Kaʿb. Up to this time some scholars had apparently been in the habit of making some use of these readings in commenting on and elucidating the Qur'ān. The readings of ʿAlī ibn-Abī-Ṭālib were also rejected by Ibn-Mujāhid.

The seven sets of readings accepted by Ibn-Mujāhid represented the systems prevailing in different districts. There was one each from Medina, Mecca, Damascus and Basra, and three from Kufa. For each set of readings (*qirā'a*), there were two slightly different 'versions' (sing. *riwāya*). The whole may be set out in tabular form.[17]

District	*Reader*	*First Rāwī*	*Second Rāwī*
Medina	Nāfiʿ (d. 785)	Warsh (812)	Qālūn (835)
Mecca	Ibn-Kathīr (737)	al-Bazzī (854)	Qunbul (903)
Damascus	Ibn-ʿĀmir (736)	Hishām (859)	Ibn-Dhakwān (856)
Basra	Abū-ʿAmr (770)	ad-Dūrī (860)	as-Sūsī (874)
Kufa	ʿĀṣim (744)	Ḥafṣ (805)	Shuʿba (809)
Kufa	Ḥamza (772)	Khalaf (843)	Khallād (835)
Kufa	al-Kisā'ī (804)	ad-Dūrī (860)	Abū-l-Ḥārith (854)

While Ibn-Mujāhid's system of seven readings came after a time to be generally accepted in theory, only one of the fourteen versions, that of Ḥafṣ from ʿĀṣim, is now widely used in practice. The new standard Egyptian edition reproduces this version and thus gives it a certain canonical supremacy. The restriction to seven readers was not immediately approved by all Muslim scholars. Some spoke of ten readers (with two versions each), while others had fourteen, though with only one version of at least the last four. The 'three after the seven' were:

Medina	Abū-Ja'far (d. 747)
Basra	Ya'qūb al-Ḥaḍramī (820)
Kufa	Khalaf (also *rāwī* of Ḥamza) (843).

The 'four after the ten' were:

Mecca	Ibn-Muḥayṣin (740)
Basra	al-Yazīdī (817)
Basra	al-Ḥasan al-Baṣrī (728)
Kufa	al-A'mash (765).

These different lists are a reflection of fierce discussions among scholars of different schools and the struggle of divergent tendencies in the Islamic community; but a detailed history of these matters from a modern standpoint remains to be written. There have been Muslim scholars who prided themselves on knowing the Qur'ān according to every one of the seven readings. The existence of variants, however, has been found inconvenient, especially in modern times. The ordinary Muslim is mostly unaware of the existence of the seven sets of readings; and the modern heretical sect of the Aḥmadiyya appears to deny, in the interests of propaganda, even the existence of the pre-'Uthmānic variants.

4. The authenticity and completeness of the Qur'ān

If one asks what guarantee there is that the Qur'ān as 'collected' in the caliphate of 'Uthmān is a correct record of the revelations as they were originally received and proclaimed by Muḥammad, the modern scholar will seek an answer first of all in the Qur'ān itself and in a comparison of its contents with what he takes to be reliably known about the Prophet's life.

It may be noted to begin with that 'Uthmān's revision was based on written documents previously existing. The official collection by express authority of the caliph Abū-Bakr is, as has been seen, somewhat doubtful. A mass of written documents of some kind, however, was in Ḥafṣa's possession. If we reject the assumption that they were an official collection made by Zayd, we must find some other explanation of what they were. It is clear that they were regarded as authoritative, and were used in producing ʿUthmān's Qur'ān. Other 'collections' of the Qur'ān were in existence, and there must have been a considerable number of people who knew these, or parts of them, by heart. If any great changes by way of addition, suppression or alteration had been made, controversy would almost certainly have arisen; but of that there is little trace. ʿUthmān offended the more religious among Muslims, and ultimately became very unpopular. Yet among the charges laid against him, that of having mutilated or altered the Qur'ān is not generally included, and was never made a main point. The Shīʿa, it is true, has always held that the Qur'ān was mutilated by the suppression of much which referred to ʿAlī and the Prophet's family. This charge, however, is not specially directed against ʿUthmān, but just as much against the first two caliphs, under whose auspices the first collection is assumed to have been made. It is also founded on dogmatic assumptions which hardly appeal to modern criticism. On general grounds then, it may be concluded that the ʿUthmānic revision was honestly carried out, and reproduced, as closely as was possible to the men in charge of it, what Muḥammad had delivered.

Modern study of the Qur'ān has not in fact raised any serious question of its authenticity. The style varies, but is almost unmistakable. So clearly does the whole bear the stamp of uniformity that doubts of its genuineness hardly arise. The authenticity of a few verses has indeed been questioned. The great French scholar Silvestre de Sacy expressed doubts regarding 3.144/38.[18] This speaks of the possible death of Muḥammad, and is the verse said in a well-known tradition to have been quoted by Abū-Bakr, when 'Umar refused to believe the report of the death of the Prophet, which had just taken place. Gustav Weil extended these doubts to a number of other passages which imply the mortality of the Prophet: 3.185/2; 21.35/6f.; 29.57; 39.30/1.[19] Abū-Bakr, however, is hardly likely to have invented 3.144/38 for the occasion; nor does the statement that ʿUmar and others professed never to have heard such a verse, weigh very much. The complete Qur'ān was not circulating among Muḥammad's followers in written form for them to study, and a verse once delivered might easily have been forgotten in the course of years, even by one who happened to hear it. If the verse does not fit smoothly into the context, that is probably because it is a substitution for the one which follows, as the recurrence of the same rhyme-phrase suggests. It fits admirably into the historical situation, for it is a reference, put into an address delivered before Uḥud and re-delivered after the defeat, to the report which had spread during the battle and had no doubt contributed to the rout, that Muḥammad had been killed. There is no reason to question the authenticity of a verse so suited to the circumstances.

As for the other verses which imply the mortality of the Prophet, Schwally[20] has pointed out how they fit well into their contexts and are quite in accord with the rest of the Qur'ān. The humanity and mortality of the Prophet were part of the controversy between him and his opponents, and to take that out of the Qur'ān would be to remove some of its most characteristic portions.

Weil[21] also questioned the authenticity of the famous verse in which reference is made to the night journey to Jerusalem [17.1]. He argued that there are no other references to such a night journey in the Qur'ān, that it is contrary to Muḥammad's usual claim to be simply a messenger and not a wonder-worker, that so far as there is any basis for the later legend in Muḥammad's life, it is merely a dream or vision, and that the verse has no connection with what follows. As matters of fact these arguments are correct; but they hardly bear the inference based on them. If we take the verse by itself, without the structure of later legend built upon it, there is nothing in it very much out of keeping with other claims made for Muḥammad; and there are so many unconnected verses in the Qur'ān that we can hardly make that an argument against this one in particular.

Finally, Weil[22] questioned 46.15/14 on the ground that Tradition makes it refer to Abū-Bakr, and that presumably it was invented in his honour. No one who knows the traditional exegesis of the Qur'ān, however, will pay much attention to such a statement. Tradition is full of guesses about the particular person to whom a verse refers. This verse is quite general, and simply develops an injunction several times repeated in the Qur'ān.

Hirschfeld[23] has questioned the authenticity of certain other verses, in which the name Muḥammad occurs, on the ground that this was not the Prophet's real name but was bestowed upon him later. There may be something suspicious in such a name, meaning 'Praised', being borne by the Prophet; but even if it were an assumed name, it might have been adopted in his own lifetime. It occurs, not only in the Qur'ān but in documents handed down by Tradition, notably the constitution of Medina,[24] and the treaty of al-Ḥudaybiya[25]; in the latter the pagan Quraysh are said to have objected to the title *rasūl Allāh*, and to *ar-Raḥmān* as a name of God, but raised no question about the name Muḥammad. Further, though it does not appear to have been common, there is evidence that Muḥammad was in use as a proper name before the time of the Prophet. There is therefore no reason to doubt that it was his real name.

The most serious attack upon the reliability of the book and the good faith of the collectors was that made by the French scholar, Paul Casanova, in his book, *Mohammed et la fin du monde* (Paris, 1911–24). His thesis is a development of the view that Muḥammad was moved to undertake his mission by the impression made on him by the idea of the approaching Judgement. Casanova thinks that he must have come under the influence of some Christian sect which laid great stress on the near approach of the end of the world. He considers that this formed the main theme of his early deliverances and was an essential part of his message from beginning to end of his prophetic activity; but that when no event occurred to substantiate his prophecy, the leaders of early Islam so manipulated the Qur'ān as to remove that doctrine from it, or at least conceal its prominence.

This thesis has not found much acceptance, and it is unnecessary to refute it in detail. The main objection to it is that it is founded less upon study of the Qur'ān than upon investigation of some of the byways of early Islam. From this point of view, the book still has value. When Casanova deals with the Qur'ān itself, however, his statements often display incorrect exegesis and a failure to appreciate the historical development of Qur'ānic teaching. As to his main thesis, it is true that the Qur'ān proclaims the coming Judgement and the end of the world. It is true that it sometimes hints that this may be near; for example, in 21.1 and 27.71/3f. In other passages, however, men are excluded from knowledge of times, and there are great differences in the urgency with which the doctrine is proclaimed in different parts of the Qur'ān. All this, however, is perfectly natural if we regard the Qur'ān as reflecting Muḥammad's personal problems and the outward difficulties he encountered in carrying out a task to which he had set his hand. Casanova's thesis makes little allowance for the changes that must have occurred in Muḥammad's attitudes through twenty years of ever-changing circumstances. Our acceptance of the Qur'ān as authentic is based, not on any assumption that it is consistent in all its parts, for this is not the case; but on the fact that, however difficult it may be to understand in detail, it does, on the whole, fit into a real historical experience, beyond which we discern an elusive, but, in outstanding characteristics, intelligible personality.

The question whether the Qur'ān, as we have it, contains all that Muḥammad delivered, is more difficult to answer. It is difficult to prove a negative; and we cannot be certain that no part of the Qur'ān delivered by Muḥammad has been lost.

The Qur'ān itself speaks of the possibility of God causing Muḥammad to forget some passages [87.6f.]; and further states that when this happens other verses as good or better will be substituted for those forgotten [2.106/0]. It should be noted, however, that some Muslims found difficulties in such an interpretation of 2.106/0, and tried to avoid these by adopting other readings and interpretations.[26] There would seem, however, to be no good reason for rejecting the standard reading and the obvious interpretation of it, and this course has the advantage of giving an assurance that no revelation of permanent value has been omitted. There is also a Tradition which describes how Muḥammad heard a man reciting the Qur'ān in a mosque, and realized that the passage recited contained a verse (or verses) which he had forgotten.[27]

Tradition again gives a number of verses as belonging to the Qur'ān although they do not stand in our present book.[28] The most famous of them is the 'verse of stoning', a verse in which stoning is prescribed as punishment for persons of mature age guilty of fornication. The caliph ʿUmar is said to have been very positive that this was laid down in the Qur'ān, until he was convinced of the contrary by lack of evidence to support his opinion. The verse is assigned either to sura 24 or to sura 33; but the rhyme does not fit sura 33, while the prescription of stoning contradicts 24.2 where flogging is ordered. On the whole it seems unlikely that the punishment of stoning was ever prescribed in the Qur'ān, since in certain tribes in pre-Islamic times loose forms of polyandry appear to have been normal practice, and it would have been difficult to distinguish some of these from fornication. The story about ʿUmar and certain Traditions about Muḥammad himself are probably attempts to meet the criticism that the Qur'ān differs from the Old Testament on this point.[29] Interesting also is the addition to 98.2 said to have been read by Ubayy, which began 'religion in God's sight is the moderate Ḥanīfiyya'.[30] It is noteworthy that in 3.19/17, which normally runs 'religion in God's sight is Islam', Ibn-Masʿūd read 'Ḥanīfiyya' instead of 'Islam'.[31] Since there appears to have been a time when a follower of Muḥammad was called a *ḥanīf* by preference, and his religion the Ḥanīfiyya, it may well be that these readings reflect an older form of the text.[32] Of the other verses preserved by Tradition, two or three may simply be variants of verses in the standard text; but apart from such variants there are no good reasons for thinking any of these verses from Tradition belonged to the Qur'ān, while there are grounds for holding that some did not belong.

In a different category are the so-called 'satanic verses', two (or three) verses which came after 53.19, 20 when these were originally proclaimed in public in the precincts of the Kaʿba at Mecca. Muḥammad is said to have been hoping for a revelation which would have led the Meccan merchants to accept his religion, when there came to him the passage:

Have you considered al-Lāt and al-ʿUzzā
and Manāt, the third, the other?
These are the intermediaries exalted,
whose intercession is to be hoped for.
Such as they do not forget.[33]

Later – but it is not clear how much later – Muḥammad realized that this could not have come from God, for he received an emended revelation in which after the first two verses there came the passage beginning

> Is it the male for you and the female for him?
> That would then be a crooked division.

The first passage permitted intercession to the local deities, presumably regarded as a kind of angelic being who could plead with the supreme God on behalf of their worshippers, while what was substituted was an *argumentum ad hominem* against the belief that such deities were 'daughters of God', and was understood as making such intercession impossible. In essentials it would seem that this account is true, since no Muslim could have invented such a story about Muḥammad. The story has also some support from the Qur'ān, since 22.52/1 (which is said to refer to this incident) states that God 'never sent messenger or prophet before (Muḥammad) but that, as he desired, Satan threw (something) into his formulation', though the satanic addition was afterwards abrogated by God.

Whatever view is taken of the collection and compilation of the Qur'ān, the possibility remains that parts of it may have been lost. If, as Tradition states, Zayd in collecting the Qur'ān was dependent on chance writings and human memories, parts may easily have been forgotten. Yet the conjunction of apparently unrelated verses at certain points in the Qur'ān suggests that the editors preserved absolutely everything they came across which they had reason to believe had once been part of the Qur'ān. The hypothesis that Muḥammad had some way of obtaining a revised form of a revelation would lead one to suppose that he might then have discarded the older form; and something similar might be inferred from the Qur'ānic phrase about God causing him to forget. In this way some revealed passages might be altogether lost. There is no reason, however, to think that anything of importance has gone astray. The very fact that varying and even contradictory deliverances have been preserved is strong proof that, with perhaps minor exceptions, we have the whole of what was revealed to Muḥammad.

FOUR

THE EXTERNAL FORM OF THE QUR'ĀN

1. Its name and liturgical divisions

The book as a whole is usually called (in strict transliteration) *al-qur'ān*. This was represented in Latin by *Alcoranus*, and in English formerly by 'Alcoran' and still popularly (as also in German) by 'Koran', while French prefers 'Coran'. Muslims often out of reverence speak of *al-qur'ān al-karīm*, 'the noble or glorious Qur'ān'. In English the title 'The Holy Qur'ān' is sometimes used. This name for the book as a whole is not itself part of the revealed text, and so is often omitted in written or printed copies. The word *qur'ān* occurs in the text of the book in various senses, and these will be discussed later, as will be the other words found in the text which are sometimes used of the book as a whole (chapter 8, sections 3, 5).

For purposes of recitation Muslims divide the Qur'ān, which is of comparable length to the New Testament, into thirty approximately equal portions or 'parts' (*ajzā'*, sing. *juz'*). This corresponds to the number of days in Ramadān, the month of fasting, when one 'part' is recited each day. The 'parts' are usually marked on the margin of copies. A smaller division is the *ḥizb* (plural *aḥzāb*) of which there are two to each 'part'. A yet smaller division is the 'quarter' of the *ḥizb* (*rub' al-ḥizb*). Even this may be marked on the margins. To facilitate recitation in the course of a week, there is also a division into seven *manāzil*. All these are external divisions which take little or no account of the natural sections of the Qur'ān, the suras and groups of suras.[1]

2. The suras and verses

The suras are real divisions in the body of the Qur'ān. The translation 'chapter' is sometimes used, but this is not an exact equivalent. The word *sūra* (plural *suwar*) also occurs in the text, but its derivation is doubtful. The most accepted view is that it comes from the Hebrew *shūrāh*, 'a row', used of bricks in a wall and of vines.[2] From this the sense of a series of passages, or chapter, may perhaps be deduced, but it is rather forced. Besides, it hardly gives the sense in which the word is used in the Qur'ān itself. In 10.38/9 the challenge is issued: 'Do they say: "He has devised it"?; let them come then with a sura like it'. In 11.13/16 it is a challenge to bring ten suras like those which have been produced. In 28.49, however, where a similar challenge is given, it is to produce a book, or writing, from God. Evidently the sense required is something like 'revelation' or 'Scripture'. The most likely suggestion is that the word is derived from the Syriac *ṣūrṭā*, which has the sense of 'writing', 'text of Scripture', and even 'the Scriptures'. The laws which govern the interchange of consonants in Arabic and Syriac are against that derivation, but in Syriac itself the spelling of the word varies to *ṣūrthā*, and even *sūrthā*; and in any case, in words directly borrowed, these philological laws do not necessarily hold.[3]

The suras number 114. The first, known as the Fātiḥa, 'the Opening', is a short prayer, very much used in Islam. The two last are short charms which, as already noted, Ibn-Masʿūd seems not to have included in his collection of the Qur'ān. The rest are arranged roughly in order of length, which varies from many pages to a line or two. Thus in Redslob's edition of Flügel's text sura 2, the longest, occupies 715 lines, or over 37 pages, while several suras near the end, such as 108 and 112, occupy two lines or less. How far this arrangement goes back to Muḥammad himself, and how far it is due to the compilers, scholars will probably never be able to elucidate completely; but, as will be seen later, there is reason for holding that he had more to do with it than the traditional account allows.

Each sura has a name or title, and this – and not the number – is normally used by Muslim scholars in referring to the sura. As a rule, the name has no reference to the subject-matter of the sura, but is taken from some prominent or unusual word in it. Usually this word occurs near the beginning, but this is not always so. Thus sura 16 is entitled 'The Bee', but the bee is not mentioned in it until v. 68/70, more than half-way through; this is the only passage in the Qur'ān, however, which speaks of the bee. Similarly, sura 26 is entitled 'The Poets'; but the only mention of the poets is in v. 224 at the very end of the sura. Here again, however, this is the only reference to poets in the Qur'ān, apart from those passages which reject the suggestion that the Prophet is himself a poet. This passage, too, is a striking one; no Arab who heard that brief, but trenchant, description of his much-belauded poets would forget it. For the choice of a name there seems to be no general rule; men apparently used any word in the sura sufficiently striking to serve as a means of identification. (One may compare the reference in the Gospels to *Exodus* 3 as 'The Bush')[4]. Sometimes a sura has two such titles, both still in use; for example, suras 9, 40, 41; and in early Islamic literature there are references to other titles in use at one time, but later dropped. All this supports the assumption that these titles do not belong to the Qur'ān proper, but have been introduced by later scholars and editors for convenience of reference.

In copies of the Qur'ān, both written and printed, the commencement of each sura is marked by a heading. First comes the name or title of the sura, then a statement about its date, and finally a note of the number of verses. The dating does not go beyond the bare description of the sura as Meccan, or Medinan; and these descriptions do not necessarily apply to the sura as a whole. Muslim scholars have always been ready to admit that suras are composite, and that one marked as Meccan may contain one or more Medinan passages, and vice versa. These descriptions, then, are to be regarded merely as the judgements of the compilers, or of early scholars, about the period at which the main content of each sura was revealed. The modern Egyptian printed edition specifies the verses which are exceptions to the general description, and also indicates the position of the sura in order of delivery. The heading as a whole is thus a piece of scholarly apparatus; and the recent Egyptian additions are no more than the considered views of the most authoritative contemporary Muslim scholars.

After the heading comes the *bismillāh*. At the beginning of all the suras, except one, stands the phrase, *bi-smi llāhi r-raḥmāni r-raḥīm*, 'In the name of God, the Merciful, the Compassionate'. The exception is sura 9. Muslim commentators say that the omission is due to this sura having been revealed shortly before Muḥammad's death, so that he left no instructions on the matter. That cannot be correct, but it implies that in the view of Muslim scholars it was Muḥammad himself who was responsible for the placing of the *bismillāh* at the head of the suras. That it belongs to the original form rather than to the later editing of the suras is confirmed by the fact that in sura 27, where Solomon is represented as sending a letter to the Queen of Sheba, the letter begins with the *bismillāh* (v. 30), as if that were the appropriate heading for a document coming from a prophet (as Solomon is considered in the Qur'ān). So also in sura 96, Muḥammad is commanded to recite in the name of his Lord. It has been suggested that the omission of the phrase at the head of 9 may be due to 8 and 9 having originally formed one sura. Sura 8 is short for its position; on the other hand 8 and 9 together would make a sura too long for the position. The real reason for the omission is that sura 9 begins with a proclamation which is already sufficiently attested as being issued in the name of God; the *bismillāh* was therefore superfluous. The exception thus confirms the conclusion that the *bismillāh* is not a mere editorial formula but belongs to the time of Muḥammad. That need not, of course, be taken so strictly as to exclude the possibility of its having in some cases been added by the compilers or editors.

The suras are divided into verses, which are termed *āyāt*, singular *āya*. This word is also used in the text. It is only in passages of later date, however, if at all, that it has the sense of 'verses'. More commonly it has the sense of 'sign', 'wonder'. It is related to the Hebrew *'ōth* and Syriac *'āthā*, and 'sign' is evidently its basic meaning. The verse-division is not artificially imposed, as the verse-divisions of the Christian Bible frequently are. It belongs to the original form of the Qur'ān, and the verses are distinctly marked by the occurrence of rhyme or assonance. Differences in the division into verses, and the consequent differences in the numbering of the verses, occur in the various sets of readings of the Qur'ān; and unfortunately the verse-numbering of Flügel's edition, which is the one generally used in the West until recently does not exactly correspond to that most generally adopted by Muslims, or in fact to that of any of the Oriental recensions. The differences are due to the occurrence of cases in which it can be doubted whether the rhyme marks the end of a verse or comes in accidentally; and this results from the fact that the rhymes or assonances are largely produced by the use of the same grammatical forms or terminations.

The length of the verses, like the length of the suras, varies much. In some suras, and these generally the longer ones, the verses are long and trailing; in others, especially the shorter ones near the end of the book, the verses are short and crisp. This, however, is not an invariable rule. Sura 98, which is comparatively short, consists of 8 long verses; sura 26, which is long, has over 200 short verses. It may be noted, however, that as a rule the verses in the same sura, or at least in the same part of a sura, are of approximately the same length. There are exceptions even to this generalization, but on the whole it remains valid, particularly where the verses are short.

The verses are in prose, without metre, though in some passages there is a kind of rhythm or metre of stresses [for example 74.1-7; 91.1-10]. This feature is due to the shortness of the rhyming verses and the repetition of the same form of phrase rather than to any effort to carry through a strict metrical form. Where the verses are of any length, and the form of phrase varies, no fixed metre, either of syllables or of stresses, can be traced. The Qur'ān is thus written in rhymed prose, in verses without metre or definitely fixed length, whose ends are marked by the occurrence of a rhyme or assonance. (The rhymes are discussed more fully in chapter 5, section 1.)

3. The mysterious letters

At the beginning of 29 suras following the *bismillāh* stands a letter, or a group of letters, which are simply read as separate letters of the alphabet. These letters are a mystery. No satisfactory explanation of their meaning, if they have one, has ever been given, nor has any convincing reason been found for their occurrence in this position. If reference is made to pp. 206-13, it will be seen that some occur once only, singly or in combination, and before isolated suras, but that there are other combinations which occur before several suras, and that the suras having the same combination of letters stand in groups. Thus the suras in front of which the letters *ḥā'*, *mīm* stand, including the one where these letters are combined with others, form a solid block (40-46) and are known in Arabic as the *ḥawāmīm*. The suras with *alif*, *lām*, *rā'*, including 13 which has *mīm* in addition, form a block from 10 to 15. The *ṭā*,' *sīn*, and *ṭā'*, *sīn*, *mīm* suras form another little group, 26-28. The *alif*, *lām*, *mīm* suras are separated; 2 and 3 stand together, sura 7, which has *ṣād* in addition, stands by itself, sura 13 is included in the *alif*, *lām*, *rā'* group, and then there is the block 29-32. Altogether the impression is given that groups of suras, similarly marked, have been kept together when the Qur'ān was put in its present order.

Consideration of the lengths of the suras tends to confirm this. A glance at the table will show that on the whole the suras stand in order of decreasing length, and this almost looks like the principle on which the suras have been arranged. It is equally evident that there are many deviations from the strict sequence, and it is necessary to guard against laying too much stress on a mechanical rule of this kind, which is not likely to have been carefully carried through. Some of the deviations from the rule of decreasing length, however, seem to be connected with these groups of suras. Thus, if we take the group 40-46, we find that the first is a little longer than 39, while 45, and especially 44, are short for their position. It looks as if the order of decreasing length had been departed from in order to keep the *ḥawāmīm* group as it stood before the final arrangement was undertaken. Again, taking the *alif*, *lām*, *rā'* group, we find that 10, 11, 12 stand approximately in their proper position according to the length, but 13, 14, 15 are short, and with 16 we return again to something like the length of 10. It looks as if this group had been inserted as a solid block. On the other hand, the *alif*, *lām*, *mīm* suras are placed in different positions, suras 2 and 3, the longest, at the very beginning, 29-32 in a group much farther on, as if the deviation from the rule would have been too great, and the group had therefore been broken up. These facts give some support to the supposition that, when the present order of the suras was fixed, the groups marked by these mysterious letters were already in existence.

That, of course, throws no light on the meaning of these symbols. But founding on this assumption and on the tradition that Zayd ibn-Thābit collected the Qur'ān after Muḥammad's death, some European scholars have regarded these letters as abbreviations of the names of persons who had previously for their own use collected, memorized, or written down certain suras, and from whom Zayd had obtained them. Thus the *ḥawāmīm* would have been obtained from somebody whose name was abbreviated to *ḥā' mīm*; and so on. This is a plausible theory; but the difficulty is to suggest names of possible persons who might be so indicated. No one has satisfactorily solved the problem. Hirschfeld, for instance, who tried to work it out, takes *ṣād* as standing for Ḥafṣa, *kāf* for Abū-Bakr, *nūn* for ʿUthmān.[5] Again it is difficult to see why, for important suras like 2 and 3, the collectors should have been dependent upon one person, denoted by *alif*, *lām*, *mīm*, whom Hirschfeld takes to be al-Mughīra, while other less important suras had no letters at their head, and were thus presumably general property.

Even greater difficulty attaches to the suggestion of Eduard Goossens that these letters are contractions for disused titles of the suras.[6] It may well be that a title which had acquired wide usage, but was not finally adopted, was retained in an abbreviated form. If so, however, it is necessary to find some word or phrase in the sura for which the letters at the head of it may be accepted as a contraction. Goossens succeeded in a number of cases, but in others his solutions were impossible or based on some drastic rearrangement of contents and change of the division of suras. Further, he did not succeed very well in explaining why several suras should have had the same title, as the groups with the same letters at their head would imply.

These suggestions go on the assumption that the letters belong to the collection and redaction of the Qur'ān, and are therefore later than the texts before which they stand. It makes no real difference if we suppose them to have been marks used by Muḥammad or his scribes to identify or classify the suras. These letters always follow the *bismillāh*, and reasons have been given for thinking that the *bismillāh* belongs to the text and not to the editing. It seems almost certain, therefore, that these letters also belong to the original text, and were not external marks added either in Muḥammad's lifetime or by later compilers. That is the view of all Muslim interpreters. Most try to explain the letters as contractions for words or phrases, but their suggestions are just as arbitrary as those of European scholars, and there is no agreement among them on details. Others again reject the idea that the letters are contractions but take them as indicating numbers with special significance or in various other ways. The divergence of views shows the intractability of the problem.

Nöldeke, to whom the suggestion that these letters were indications of names of collectors was originally due,[7] in his later articles departed from it, and adopted the view that they were meaningless symbols, perhaps magic signs, or imitations of the writing of the heavenly Book which was being conveyed to Muḥammad.[8] A somewhat similar view has recently been put forward by Alan Jones.[9] On the basis of statements by Ibn-Hishām and in Tradition to the effect that on certain occasions the Muslims used the watchword or battle-cry '*Ḥā mīm*, they shall not be aided', he argues that the letters are mystical symbols, suggesting that the Muslims have God's help. While there may be something in this view, its very nature prevents it being worked out in detail and argued for in a convincing fashion.

Some further points may be made. That the letters belong to the revealed text receives further confirmation from the fact that the majority of the suras at the head of which they stand begin with some reference to the Book, the Qur'ān or the revelation. Of the 29 suras to which they are prefixed only three have no such reference immediately following [19, 29, 30]. Considering how often the Book is referred to later in it, sura 19 can hardly be counted an exception. Analysis also shows that suras marked by such letters are of either late Meccan or Medinan composition, or at least have traces of late revision; they belong to the time when Muḥammad was consciously 'collecting' a revelation similar to the revelation in the hands of previous monotheists. It is possible that the letters are imitations of some of the writing in which these scriptures existed. In fact, in some of these combinations of letters it is possible to see words written in Syriac or Hebrew, which have been afterwards read as Arabic. This suggestion, however, like others is impossible to carry through. We end where we began; the letters are mysterious, and have so far baffled interpretation.

4. The dramatic form

It has been seen that Muḥammad believed that his message came to him by prompting from without, and drew a clear distinction between what came to him in this way and his own thoughts and sayings. The Qur'ān, therefore, is cast mainly in the form of someone addressing Muḥammad, and not of Muḥammad addressing his fellow-men directly, though he is frequently ordered to convey a message to them. This question of who speaks and who is addressed, that is, of the dramatic form, is worthy of consideration.

It is usually assumed, in accordance with Islamic doctrine, that throughout the Qur'ān the speaker is God, and that the Prophet is addressed as the recipient of the revelation. This corresponds to the setting in many passages. God speaks sometimes in the first person singular. A clear example of this is 51.56f., 'I have not created jinn and men but that they should serve me; I desire not any provision from them, nor do I desire that they should feed me'. Others are 67.18, 74.11-15, and even distinctly Medinan passages such as 2.40/38, 47/4 (where God makes, as it were, a personal appeal to the Children of Israel) and 2.186/2. Much more frequently, however, we find the first person plural used where God is without doubt the speaker. As creation is, in the doctrine of the Qur'ān, the prerogative of God, passages in which the speaker claims to have created may be taken as certainly spoken by God; e.g. 15.26f., 17.70/2, 21.16-18, 23.12-14, and many other passages. If one takes passages in which the creation is not mentioned but which are in the same form, it will be found that much of the Qur'ān is thus placed in the mouth of God speaking in the plural of majesty.

It is also clear in many passages that the Prophet is being

addressed. The well-known verses, usually considered the two earliest revelations 'O thou clothed in the *dithār*, arise and warn, thy Lord magnify...' [74.1-7] and 'Recite in the name of thy Lord...' [96.1-5] are evidently addressed to the Prophet. The use of the second person singular is very common in the Qur'ān, and the individual addressed must be Muḥammad himself. Many passages are indeed personal to the Prophet: encouragements, exhortations, assurances of the reality of his inspiration, rebukes, pieces of advice on how to act. On the other hand, many passages thus addressed to the Prophet have no special reference to him, but contain matter of interest to others as well. That is, in fact, frequently stated, in such phrases as: 'Surely in that is a lesson for those who fear'. Even when not stated, it is the evident intention that the communication should be made public; the Prophet is exhorted to 'recite', and that was no doubt the method by which these revelations were made known to the people. Sometimes the Prophet is addressed as the representative of the people, and after a direct address to him the passage may continue with the second person plural, as in 65.1: 'O prophet, when you (pl.) divorce women,...'

The assumption that God is himself the speaker in every passage, however, leads to difficulties. Frequently God is referred to in the third person. It is no doubt allowable for a speaker to refer to himself in the third person occasionally, but the extent to which we find the Prophet apparently being addressed and told about God as a third person, is unusual. It has, in fact, been made a matter of ridicule that in the Qur'ān God is made to swear by himself.[10] That he uses oaths in some of the passages beginning, 'I swear (not)...' can hardly be denied [e.g., 75.1, 2; 90.1]. This was probably a traditional formula.[11] 'By thy Lord', however, is difficult in the mouth of God. 'The Lord' is, in fact, a common designation of God in the Qur'ān, as in the two early passages quoted above. Now there is one passage which everyone acknowledges to be spoken by angels, namely 19.64/5f.: 'We come not down but by command of thy Lord; to him belongs what is before us and what is behind us and what is between that; nor is thy Lord forgetful, Lord of the heavens and the earth and what is between them; so serve him, and endure patiently in his service; knowest thou to him a namesake?' In 37.161-6 it is almost equally clear that angels are the speakers. This once admitted, may be extended to passages in which it is not so clear. In fact, difficulties in many passages are removed by interpreting the 'we' of angels rather than of God himself speaking in the plural of majesty. It is not always easy to distinguish between the two, and nice questions sometimes arise in places where there is a sudden change from God being spoken of in the third person to 'we' claiming to do things usually ascribed to God, e.g. 6.99b, 25.45/7.

In the later portions of the Qur'ān, it seems to be an almost invariable rule that the words are addressed by the angels, or by Gabriel using the plural 'we', to the Prophet. God is spoken of in the third person, but it is always his will and commands which are thus communicated to men. This is the case even where the people or the believers are directly addressed. In some of these passages it might at first sight appear that Muḥammad was addressing his followers in his own words; but in many of them the indications that the angel speaks are so clear that we must assume that this is the form in them all. Muḥammad is the mouthpiece of the divine will, which is communicated to him by Gabriel, and thus, like a confidential official, he stands on the border-line between the king's court and the subjects. Subject he is always. Sometimes he receives messages to convey to the people, or he receives commands and exhortations intended for them; sometimes he is directly addressed as the representative of the people; at other times special exhortations and directions for his own conduct are addressed to him; at times he steps, as it were, across the line, and facing round upon the people conveys the divine commands and exhortations directly to them. Thus in these late passages the dramatic setting remains fairly constant: God is a third person in the background, the 'we' of the speaker is the angel (or angels); and the messages are addressed to the Prophet; even where the people are directly addressed and the words come through him, he is mouthpiece only.

The dramatic setting of some earlier passages must be considered in the light of this result. There are a few passages where it might be thought that Muḥammad was speaking in his own person. Thus in 27.91/3f., there is a declaration of his position: 'I have been commanded to serve the Lord of this region ...'. In 26.221, 'Shall I tell you on whom the demons come down?' the pronoun would naturally be taken as referring to Muḥammad, but it could also be interpreted of God. Other dubious instances are: 81.15-29; 84.16-19; 92.14-21. Some of the lists of 'signs' adduced as instances of God's power might be regarded as spoken by the messenger, and also descriptions of the Last Day like 91.1-10. With regard to all these passages it may be noted that declarations similar to 27.91/3f., are often preceded by the command (presumably addressed to Muḥammad himself), 'Say'. Yet, even where this word does not occur, the passages must have been regarded as part of what Muḥammad was commanded to proclaim to the people, following on the 'Recite!' of 96.1. Thus the principle that the messages came to Muḥammad from beyond himself is not infringed.[12]

FIVE

FEATURES OF QUR'ĀNIC STYLE

1. Rhymes and strophes

There is no attempt in the Qur'ān to produce the strict rhyme of poetry. In an Arabic poem each verse had to end in the same consonant or consonants surrounded by the same vowels – an interchange of *ī* and *u* was allowed, though considered a weakness. Short inflectional vowels following the rhyme-consonant were usually retained, and, if retained, were pronounced long at the end of the line. Only in very exceptional cases is it possible to find this type of rhyme in the Qur'ān. What one finds rather is assonance, in which short inflectional vowels at the end of a verse are disregarded, and for the rest, the vowels, particularly their length, and the fall of the accent, that is the form of the end-word of the verse, are of more importance than the consonants. Of course the consonant may remain the same, but that is not essential. Thus in sura 112 the four verses rhyme in *-ad*, if one disregards the inflections; in 105 the rhyme is in *-īl*, if one disregards end-vowels and allows *ū* in place of *ī* in the last verse. In sura 103 *r* is rhyme-consonant, but the inflections vary and have to be disregarded, though, for pronunciation, we require a short vowel sound of some kind after the *r*, or, alternatively, a short vowel before it which is not in the form. In sura 54, where *r* as a rhyme-consonant is carried through 55 verses, we have not only to disregard the end-vowels but to accept variations of the preceding vowel, *i* and *u* and even *a* occurring in that position; the assonance is technically described as *-faʿil*, that is, an open syllable with short vowel which takes the accent, followed by a syllable with short vowel closed by *r* which thus becomes a rhyme-consonant. On the other hand, the accusative termination *-an* is often retained, being probably pronounced as *-ā*; for example in suras 18, 72 and 100, where the accusative termination seems to be essential to the rhyme. Further, the feminine termination *-atun* loses not only its inflections but also its *t* sound, as in sura 104 where, if one drops end-vowels and pronounces the feminine termination as *ā* or *a*, there is a consistent assonance formed by an accented syllable followed by a short unaccented syllable and the ending (technically fa'ala) in which both vowels and consonants are variable, but the place of the accent and the ending *-a* remain the same. The actual rhyme-words are: *lúmaẓa*, *'addada*, *ákhlada*, *al-ḥúṭama*, *al-ḥúṭama*, *al-mūqada*, *al-áf'ida*, *mú'ṣada*, *mumáddada*; this illustrates the retention of the same sound formation with variation of consonant, and even of vowel. In sura 99 we have a similar assonance, formed by a long accented *ā*, followed by a short syllable, and the feminine suffix *-hā*, that is *-ālahā*, the *-hā* being in one verse replaced by the plural suffix *-hum*. The assonance of sura 47 is the same, but with greater variation of suffix.

The structure of the Arabic language, in which words fall into definite types of forms, was favourable to the production of such assonances. Even in the short suras, however, there is a tendency to rely in part for the assonance on grammatical terminations, such as the suffix *-hā* in suras 99 and 91. In the longer suras this tendency increases. Thus in 55 the assonance depends largely upon the dual-ending *-ān*. Often in the longer suras, though seldom carried through without a break, the assonance is *-ā(l)*, that is, a long *ā* vowel followed by a (variable) consonant; so in parts of suras 2, 3, 14, 38, 39, 40 and sporadically elsewhere. In the great majority of the suras of any length, however, and even in some short ones, the prevailing assonance is *-ī(l)*, that is, a long *ī* or *ū* sound (these interchange freely) followed by a consonant. This is formed largely by the plural endings of nouns and verbs, *-ūn* and *-īn*, varied by words of the form technically known as *fa'īl*, one of the commonest forms in Arabic. By far the greater part of the Qur'ān shows this assonance.

With an assonance depending thus upon grammatical endings there may occasionally be doubt as to whether it was really intended. The varying systems of verse-numbering depend to some extent, though not entirely, upon varying judgement as to where the rhyme was intended to fall in particular cases; but it cannot be doubted that there was assonance at the end of verses. In passages with short verses and frequently recurring assonances this is unmistakable. Yet even in suras in which the verses are long, there are special turns of phrase employed in order to produce the assonance. Thus the preposition *min* with a plural participle is often used where a participle in the singular would have sufficiently given the sense; so that we get phrases like 'one of the witnesses' instead of simply 'a witness' (*min ash-shāhidīn* instead of *shāhid*) because the former gives the rhyming plural-ending, while the latter does not [3.81/75; cf. 60/53; 7.106/3]. *Kānū* 'were', with an imperfect or participle in the plural often takes the place of a simple perfect plural; for example in 2.57/4 and 7.37/5. Or an imperfect plural may be used where a perfect might have been expected, as in 5.70/4. Occasionally a phrase is added at the end of a verse which is really otiose as regards sense but supplies the assonance, as in 12.10 and 21.68, 79, 104. Sometimes the sense is strained in order to produce the rhyme, for instance in sura 4, where statements regarding God are thrown into the past by the use of *kāna*, 'was', in front of them and are thereby given the accusative ending on which the rhyme depends. The form of a proper name is occasionally modified for the sake of rhyme, as *Sīnīn* [95.2] and *Ilyāsīn* [37.130].

Statements regarding God occur frequently at the end of verses, especially in the long suras where the verses also are of some length. Where the verses are short, the word or phrase which carries the rhyme forms as a rule an integral part of the grammatical structure and is necessary to the sense. In a few passages it appears that the phrases which carry the rhyme can be detached without dislocating the structure of what remains [e.g. 41.9/8-12/11]. Usually the phrase is appropriate to the context, but stands apart from the rest of the verse. These detachable rhyme-phrases – most of which carry the assonance in *ī(l)* – tend to be repeated, and to assume a set form which recurs either verbally or with slight changes in wording. Thus *inna fī dhālika la-āyatan li-l-mu'minīn* 'truly in that is a sign for the believers', often closes the account of a 'sign'. *'Alā llāhi fa-l-yatawakkal il-mu'minūn* (*il-mutawakkilūn*) 'in

God let the believers (the trustful) trust' occurs 9 times. *Wa-llāhu 'alīm ḥakīm* 'and God is all-knowing, wise' occurs 12 times, or, if we include slight modifications, 18 times. Other combinations of adjectives referring to God are frequently used in the same way. Perhaps the most frequent of all such phrases is *inna llāha 'alā kulli shay'in qadīr*, 'verily God over everything has power', which is used 6 times in sura 2, 4 times in sura 3, 4 times in sura 5, and some 18 times in other suras. There is a certain effectiveness in the use of these sententious phrases regarding God. Mostly they close a deliverance, and serve at once to press home a truth by repetition and to clinch the authority of what is laid down. They act as a kind of refrain.

The use of an actual refrain, in the sense of the same words occurring at more or less regular intervals, is sparse in the Qur'ān. One is used in sura 55, where the words 'Which then of the benefits of your Lord will you two count false?' occur in verses 12, 15, 18, 21, and from there on in practically each alternate verse, without regard to the sense. The same tendency to increasing frequency and disregard of sense appears in the use of the words, 'Woe that day to those who count false!' as a kind of refrain before sections of sura 77. More effective didactically is the use of the refrain in the groups of stories of former prophets which occur in various suras [e.g. 11, 26, 37, 54]. The stories in these groups not only show similarities of wording throughout, but are often closed by the same formula.

In addition to the rhymes which occur at the end of the verses, we can occasionally detect rhymes, different from the end-rhymes, occurring in the middle of verses. These give the impression of a varied arrangement of rhymes. Rudolf Geyer pointed out some of these, and argued that stanzas with such varied rhymes were sometimes deliberately intended in the Qur'ān.[1] If that were so, we should expect the same form to recur. In going through Geyer's examples, however, we do not get the impression that any pre-existing forms of stanza were being reproduced, or indeed that any fixed forms of stanza were being used. There are no fixed patterns. All that can be said is that in some passages there is such a mixture of rhymes, just as, within a sura there are often breaks in the regular recurring rhyme at the end of the verses. As will be seen, however, these facts may be otherwise explained.

A similar argument applies to the contention advanced by D. H. Müller.[2] He sought to show that composition in strophes was characteristic of prophetic literature, in the Old Testament as well as in the Qur'ān, and even in Greek tragedy. From the Qur'ān he adduced many passages which appear to support such a view, such as sura 56. If we are to speak of strophic form, however, we expect some regularity in the length and arrangement of the strophes; but Müller failed to show that there was any such regularity. What his evidence does show is that many suras of the Qur'ān fall into short sections or paragraphs. These are not of fixed length, however, nor do they seem to follow any pattern of length. Their length is determined not by any consideration of form, but by the subject or incident treated in each.

Interpreted in this way, Müller's contention brings out a real characteristic of Qur'ānic style, namely that it is disjointed. Only seldom do we find in it evidence of sustained unified composition at any great length. The longest such pieces are the addresses found in some of the later suras. The address before Uḥud appears to have become broken up and it is now difficult to decide which sections from the middle of sura 3 ordinally belonged to it. The address after the Day of the Trench and the overthrow of the clan of Quragza [33.9-27], however, and the assurance to the disappointed Muslims after the truce of al-Ḥudaybiya [48.18-29] may be taken as examples of fairly lengthy pieces relating to a single occasion. Some of the narratives, too, in the Qur'ān, especially accounts of Moses and of Abraham, run to considerable length; but they tend to fall into separate incidents instead of being recounted straightforwardly. This is particularly true of the longest of all, the story of Joseph in sura 12. In other suras, even where one can trace some connection in thought, this arrangement in paragraphs is evident. In sura 50, for instance, it is arguable that a line of thought governs the collection of the separate pieces, running from the Prophet's dissatisfaction with his cajoling of the wealthy, through the sublimity of the message, which ought to commend itself but is thwarted by man's ingratitude for religious and temporal benefits, up to the description of the final Judgement-day. The distinctness of the separate pieces, however, is more obvious than their unity; and one of them, verses 24-32 bears traces of having been fitted into a context to which it did not originally belong. In the longer suras devoted largely to political and legal matters, one finds, as is natural enough, that subjects vary. Yet, while there exist considerable blocks of legislation devoted to one subject, for example, the rules regarding divorce in 2.228-32, it does not appear that any subject was dealt with systematically in a single sura or lengthy passage. On the contrary one mostly finds that one sura contains passages dealing with many different subjects, while the same subject is treated in several different suras. The Qur'ān itself tells us that it was delivered in separate pieces [17.106/7; 25.32/4]; but it does not tell us anything about the length of the pieces. The traditional accounts of 'the occasions of revelation', however, often refer to passages consisting of a verse or two and this favours the assumption that the pieces were short. Examination of the Qur'ān itself gives further support to this assumption. Not only do many short pieces stand alone as separate suras but the longer suras contain short pieces which are complete in themselves, and could be removed without serious derangement of the context. Consideration of the passages introduced by a formula of direct address exemplifies this. Thus 2.178/3-179/5 deals with retaliation; but though it comes amongst other passages also addressed to the believers and dealing with other subjects, it has no necessary connection with them. Again 5.11/14 stands by itself and is clear enough, if only we knew the event to which it refers, but if it had been absent we should never have suspected that something had fallen out.

The form of these short pieces may be illustrated from 49.13; 'O ye people, We have created you of male and female and made you races and tribes, that ye may show mutual recognition; verily, the most noble of you in God's eyes is the most pious; verily God is knowing, well-informed'. Here, following the words of address, there is an indication of the subject that has called for treatment, then comes a declaration regarding it, and finally the passage is closed by a sententious maxim. This form is found not only in passages with direct address, but in a multitude of others. They begin by stating the occasion; a question has been asked, the unbelievers have said or done something, something has happened, or some situation has arisen. The matter is dealt with shortly, in usually not more than three or four verses; at the end comes a general statement, often about God, which rounds off the passage. Once the reader has caught this lilt of Qur'ānic style it becomes fairly easy to split up the suras into the separate pieces which constitute them, and this is a great step towards the interpretation of the Qur'ān. It is not, of course, to be too readily assumed that there is no connection between these separate pieces. There may sometimes be a connection in subject and thought, and even where this is absent there may still be a connection in time. On the other hand, there may be no connection in thought between contiguous pieces, or the sura may have been built up of pieces of different dates that have been fitted into a sort of scheme.

2. Various didactic forms

It is only when the modern student has dissected the suras into the short units of which they are constituted that he can speak of the style of the Qur'ān. The insistence frequently met with on its disjointedness, its formlessness and its excited, unpremeditated, rhapsodical character, partly rests on a failure to discern the natural divisions into which the suras fall, and to take account of the numerous displacements and undesigned breaks in connection. Since Muḥammad's function as a prophet was to convey messages to his contemporaries, what should be looked for are didactic rather than poetic or artistic forms. One such form, indeed the prevailing one in later suras, has just been mentioned. Various others may also be distinguished.

(a) *Slogans or maxims.* The simplest of these didactic forms is the short statement introduced by the word 'Say'. There are about 250 of these scattered throughout the Qur'an. Sometimes they stand singly; elsewhere groups of them stand together, though distinct from each other (for instance, in 6.56-66); sometimes they are worked into the context of a passage. These statements are of various kinds; there are answers to questions, retorts to the arguments or jeers of his opponents, and clarifications of Muḥammad's own position; there are one or two prayers [e.g. 3.26/5f.]; there are two credal statements for his followers to repeat, the word 'Say' being in the plural [2.136/0; 29.46/5], and to these may be added sura 112, though the verb is singular; finally, there are a number of phrases suitable for repetition in various circumstances, such as: 'God's guidance is the guidance' [2.120/14]; 'God is my portion; on him let the trusting set their trust' [39.38/9].

It is evident that these were separate phrases designed for repetition, and not originally as parts of suras or longer passages. They were thus of the nature of slogans or maxims devised for public use by themselves and only later found their way into suras. Where a context is given, as is usual in the later parts of the Qur'ān, one sees how the formula is revealed to deal with some matter of concern to Muḥammad or the Muslims. Muḥammad is asked about new moons [2.189/5], about contributions [2.215/1], about what is allowable [5.4/6], about 'windfalls' [8.1], and various other matters; or some hostile argument or jeering remark has come to his notice [e.g. 6.37]. The problem or the criticism has led to general concern. Muḥammad may be presumed to have 'sought guidance', and has then received the revelation instructing him what to say. The statement or formula thus becomes a part of one of the paragraphs already described as characteristic of Qur'ānic style.

These slogans or maxims are difficult to date, and it is doubtful if any of those which appear in the Qur'ān are very early, though some of them may well be so. They are so common, however, that the presumption is that they were a constant element in the life of the Muslim community, and that the repetition of such maxims proved an effective way of stabilizing the attitudes and practices associated with Islam.

The use of assonance in these formulae might be expected; but it is not found to any extent. Most of the formulae fall naturally enough into the rhyme of the sura in which they occur, but few of them rhyme within themselves. Possible exceptions are 34.46/5 and 41.44. Though not preceded by 'Say', the early passage 102.1-2 is not unlike a slogan. On the whole, it would seem that the association of rhythmic assonanced prose with the *kāhin* or soothsayer made it inappropriate for formulae and maxims.

(b) *Soothsayer utterances*. The Qur'ān asserts that Muḥammad is not a soothsayer (*kāhin*) [52.29] and that the revelations are not the speech of a soothsayer [69.42]; and this is certainly true of the great bulk of the Qur'ān. The need for such a disclaimer, however, suggests that there were similarities between some of the early passages and the utterances of soothsayers. Among the Semitic peoples there was a deep tradition linking knowledge of the supernatural with unusual forms of verbal expression, such as rhyme. An early example, of this is to be seen in the pronouncements of Balaam in the Old Testament [*Numbers*, 22-24]. Muslim writers give some allegedly pre-Islamic Arabian examples, one of which, foretelling Muḥammad, may be thus rendered in English:

Thou sawest a light
Come forth from night,
Then on lowlands alight
Then all devour in its flight.

The person who foretold the future in this way, the soothsayer or *kāhin*, does not appear to have been specially attached to any sanctuary or god, but to have had his own special prompter, one of the jinn or spirits, who inspired him. Such a person might be consulted on all sorts of matters. He would be called on for prognostications of the future, for the solution of past mysteries, and for decisions on litigious questions. His oracles were often cryptic, frequently garnished with oaths to make them more impressive, and usually couched in the *saj'* or rhythmic rhymed prose of which an example has been given.

Originally, according to the evidence of the Arabic language, there was little difference between the soothsayer, the poet and the madman; and thus it is not surprising that the Qur'ān contains denials that Muḥammad was a poet and a madman [as in 69.41 and 52.29]. The poet or *shā'ir* was etymologically the one who is aware, 'the knower', who had insight into matters beyond the ken of ordinary men; but by AD 600 this connotation had been largely lost, and the poet was conceived much as he is nowadays, though he had greater public recognition. Since both soothsayer and poet were aided to knowledge of the unseen by one of the jinn, they might be described as *majnūn*, 'affected or inspired by jinn'; but this word even by the seventh century had come to have its modern meaning of 'mad'.

At least five passages in the Qur'ān [37.1-4; 51.1-6; 77.1-7; 79.1-14; 100.1-6] are suggestive of the utterances of soothsayers. In each there are a number of oaths by some female beings, which form a jingle and lead up to an assertion which does not rhyme with the oaths. In Arabic the last of these runs:

wa-l-ʿādiyāti ḍabḥan
wa-l-mūriyāti qad'ḥan
wa-l-mughīrati ṣubḥan
fa-atharna bi-hi naqʿan
fa-wasaṭna bi-hi jamʿan
inna l-insāna li-rabbi-hi la-kanūd

The following verses may be part of the original assertion or may have been added later; and this may also be the case in sura 79. The sense of the first five verses here is uncertain, but the passage (which is usually interpreted of war-horses) might perhaps be rendered:

By the runners panting,
By the kindlers sparking,
By the raiders early starting,
Then they raised up a dust-cloud,
Then they centred in a crowd –
Truly man to his Lord is ungrateful.

In the other passages the feminine participles are mostly taken to refer to angelic beings, and for this suggestion some slight support is claimed from the Qur'ān, since the participle of 37.1 is used of angels (but in the masculine) in 37.165. It may be doubted, however, whether those who first heard Muḥammad recite these passages attached any definite meaning to the asseverations. If there was one unequivocal interpretation, it would seem to have been forgotten by later Muslims. Even without a definite meaning, however, the oaths would serve to make the final assertion more impressive; and this was doubtless in line with the traditional methods of soothsayers.

The utterances of the soothsayers which were rhythmic but not in a fixed metre, and which were assonanced but not always exactly rhymed, are said to be in *saj'*, which is thus distinct from both poetry and prose.[3] The whole of the Qur'ān is often said to be in *saj'* because of the assonances at the end of verses; but Muslim scholars have sometimes held that the Qur'ān is not in *saj'* in the strict sense. Certainly the great bulk of it is very different from the utterances of the soothsayers.

(c) *Asseverative and 'when' passages.* These random and mysterious oaths are only impressive when used sparingly. Sura 89 begins with four clauses so cryptic as to be unintelligible – 'By the dawn, By ten nights, By even and odd, By the night elapsing . . .' – and these are followed by a verse [5/4] which is probably to be taken parenthetically, and which may either suggest the efficacy of the asseverations (as in Paret's translation) – 'is that not for a man of understanding an (effective) oath?' – or may (with Bell's translation) question their value – 'is there in that an oath for a man of sense?' Yet even the former interpretation must have left men wondering. In a passage like 52.1-8, while there is the same device of making the statement stand out by change of assonance, the oaths, though still difficult to interpret, seem to have had a clear sense for the first hearers. In other asseverative passages, of which there are not a few,[4] the oaths are chosen as having some bearing on the statement to which they lead up, and this statement in the same assonance makes an effective close to the passage. The best example is perhaps 91.1-10, where four pairs of oaths by contrasted things (sun and moon, day and night, heaven and earth, and what formed the soul and implanted in it its wickedness and piety) lead up to an assertion of the contrast between him who purifies his soul and him who corrupts it. This asseverative style tends to be less frequent in later revelations. Passages occur where a single oath comes at the beginning, but in the Medinan period oaths hardly appear at all.

A modification of the asseverative passage is the use of a number of temporal clauses, introduced by *idhā* 'when', or *yawma* 'the day when' leading up to a statement pressing home the fact of the Judgement upon the conscience. In

75.26-30, a death-scene is described in the temporal clauses, but usually it is the Last Day which is conjured up by a selection from its awe-inspiring phenomena. In 84.1-6 the statement of the main clause is left unrhymed, but in all the others it has the same rhyme as the clauses which lead up to it. The longest of these passages is 81.1-14, where twelve *idhā*-clauses lead up to the statement: 'A soul will know what it has presented', that is, the deeds laid to its account. The effectiveness of such a form is even more evident in some of the shorter pieces, and there can be no doubt that these passages impressed the conscience of the hearers.[5]

(d) *Dramatic scenes.* A homiletic purpose of this kind is evident throughout the Qur'ān. The piling up of temporal clauses did not continue, but at all stages of the Qur'ān the scenes of the Judgement and the future life are evoked, not for any speculative purpose but in order to impress the conscience and clinch an argument. Despite all the details which the Qur'ān gives of the future abodes of the blessed and the damned, there is nowhere a full description. Such a picture seems to have been partially given [e.g. in 55, 76 and 83], but it is not completed. On the other hand there are short well-polished pieces depicting luscious attractions or lurid terrors. The same applies to the descriptions of the Judgement; evidently the interest in these scenes is not for their own sake but for their homiletic value. Only once or twice does the Qur'ān describe the theophany, and then only partially [39.67-74; 89.22-30].

In many of these scenes of Judgement there is a dramatic quality which is often unrecognized, but very effective. Some of the passages are difficult to understand, because they are designed for oral recitation, and do not indicate by whom the various speeches are made; this was left to be made clear by gesture or change of voice as the passage was delivered. As examples may be cited, 50.20/19-26/5 and 37.50/48-61/59; in both of these passages we have to use our imagination to supply the accompanying action of the speeches, but when this is done the result is an intensely vivid and moving picture. Such passages, if recited with appropriate dramatic action, must have been very telling. This dramatic quality is, in fact, a pervading characteristic of Qur'ānic style. Direct speech is apt to be 'interjected' at any point, as the personages mentioned in the narrative express themselves in words. In the story of Moses in sura 20, for example, more space is occupied by the spoken words of the actors than by narrative. Even where narrative predominates, the story is hardly ever told in a straightforward manner, but tends to fall into a series of short word-pictures; the action advances incident by incident discontinuously, and the intervening links are left to the imagination of the hearers.

(e) *Narratives and parables.* In the relatively few narrative passages in the Qur'ān, the homiletic element is again apt to intrude. The longest narrative is the story of Joseph in sura 12, and there every now and then the account of events is interrupted by a parenthesis to make clear the purpose of God in what happened. Another of the didactic forms of the Qur'ān, the parable or *mathal*[6], tends to be dominated by the homiletic element. The best of these parables is that of the Blighted Garden in sura 68. The parable of the Two Owners of Gardens is less clear and more didactic [18.32/1-44/2]. Others are little more than expanded similes: 14.24/9-27/32; 16.75/7f.; 18.45/3f.; 30.28/7; 39.29/30. That of the Unbelieving Town is difficult to classify; [36.13/12-29/8] it is perhaps a simile expanded into a story.

(f) *Similes.* The Qur'ān contains numerous similes. These occur in all contexts. In descriptions of the Last Day, when the heavens are rolled up like a scroll [21.104], when the people are like moths blown about, and the mountains like carded wool [101.4/3, 5/4], the similes sometimes belong to the same traditional framework as the rest of the material; but there is also much that is fresh and original in the Qur'ān by way of vivid and even grimly humorous comparisons. Jews who have the Torah but do not profit by it are compared to an ass loaded with books [62.5]. Some who in the early days in Medina made advances to Muḥammad and then drew back are likened to those who have lit a fire which has then gone out and left them in the darkness more bewildered than ever [2.17/16; cf. 19/18f.]. Polytheists who serve other gods besides God are like the spider weaving its own frail house [29.41/0]. The works of unbelievers, from which they hope to benefit at the Judgement, are like ashes blown away by the wind [14.18/21], or like a mirage which appears to be water, but, when one comes to it, turns out to be nothing [24.39]. People who pray to gods other than God are like a man who stretches out his hand to raise water to his mouth, but no water reaches it [13.14/15]. The prayer of the unbelieving Quraysh of Mecca at the Kaʿba is only whistling and clapping of hands [8.35]. Lukewarm supporters, asked for their opinion and getting up to speak, no doubt hesitatingly, are compared to logs of wood propped up [63.4]. Other comparisons will be found in 2.171/66, 261/3, 264/6, 265/7; 3.117/3; 7.176/5; 10.24/5; 57.19; 74.50/1. Many of these reflect the Arab's experience of life in the desert in a way reminiscent of pre-Islamic poetry. Where a simile is expanded into an allegory or parable, it tends to be further removed from actual experience [as in 30.28/7 and 39.29/30].

(g) *Metaphors*. Metaphors are even more frequent than similes. A modern Arab scholar[7] has collected over four hundred metaphorical uses of words. Many of these, however, were, no doubt, already so common in ordinary speech as to be no longer felt as metaphorical. It is not easy to say how far the Qur'ān added new metaphors to the language. The number of commercial terms transferred to the religious sphere is noteworthy and examples have been given above (p. 4). From bedouin life come the designation of the delights of Paradise as *nuzul*, 'reception-feast', and the application of the verb *ḍalla*, 'to go astray', to those who follow false gods. The use of metaphors from bodily functions to describe spiritual matters is almost unavoidable; thus unbelievers are deaf, unable to hear, blind, unable to see; they cannot discern the truth; they have veils over their hearts, heaviness in their ears; they are in darkness. The revelation is guidance and light, and the task of a messenger is to lead people out of the darkness into the light. Doubtful supporters among the people of Medina are said to have disease in their hearts; after their conduct at Uḥud they are dubbed *munāfiqīn*, 'jinkers', 'those who dodge back into their holes like mice'.[8]

3. The language of the Qur'ān

The Qur'ān itself asserts that the revelation is in 'a clear Arabic tongue' [16.103/5; 26.195], and from this assertion later Muslim scholars developed the view that the language of the Qur'ān was the purest variety of Arabic. Such a view, of course, is a theological dogma rather than a linguistic theory; and modern scholarship tends to leave it aside and to study at a purely linguistic level the relation of the language of the Qur'ān to contemporary varieties of Arabic.

It is now generally accepted even by critical scholars that at least some of the so-called pre-Islamic poetry was genuinely composed before the time of Muḥammad; and it is further agreed that the language of this poetry is not the dialect of any tribe or tribes, but is an artificial literary language, usually called 'the poetical *koinē*', which was understood by all the tribes. Traditional Muslim scholars, influenced by their theological dogma, tended to assume that, since Muḥammad and his first followers belonged to the tribe of Quraysh in Mecca, they must have recited the Qur'ān according to the dialect of Quraysh; and the scholars further assumed that this was identical with the language of the poetry. On the other hand, Muslim scholars preserved a certain amount of information about the dialects of the Arabian tribes in the time of Muḥammad, and this information tends to refute the belief that the dialect of Quraysh was identical with the language of poetry.

European scholars paid some attention to the language of the Qur'ān during the nineteenth century, but the most vigorous discussions have followed on the publication of a novel theory by Karl Vollers in 1906.[9] Vollers held that the dialect of Mecca differed considerably both from the 'eastern' dialects used in Nejd and elsewhere, and from the poetical *koinē*; and he argued that the present form of the Qur'ān with its peculiarities of orthography had come about through scholars assimilating the Meccan dialect in which it was originally recited to the poetical language. In this process of assimilation many dialectical forms were removed, though some are still recorded as variants in the standard 'readings' or from pre-'Uthmānic codices. Vollers' theory received some support at a later date from Paul Kahle,[10] but on the whole was not accepted by scholars. Nöldeke,[11] followed by Becker[12] and Schwally,[13] argued that the language of the Qur'ān could not be identified with any form of Arabic that was ever actually spoken. For these scholars the Qur'ān was written essentially in the poetical *koinē*. More recently the hypothesis of Vollers has been criticized by Régis Blachère[14] and Chaim Rabin.[15] The former holds that Vollers exaggerated the differences between the 'eastern' and 'western' dialects, and that the differences between Qur'ānic forms and those of the poetry are not always what Vollers' theory would lead one to expect. Among other arguments Rabin urges that, if the Qur'ān had originally been revealed in the spoken Arabic of Mecca, it is difficult to see how after a century or two the bedouin poetic language could have become the authoritative form of Arabic. He quotes with approval the suggestion of Johann Fück[16] that in the Qur'ānic phrase 'a clear Arabic tongue' the word 'Arabic' (*ʿarabī*) refers to the *ʿArabiyya* or literary language of the *ʿarab* or bedouin. The final conclusion appears to be that the language of the Qur'ān falls somewhere between the poetical *koinē* and the Meccan dialect. The omission of the *hamza* or glottal stop, which is mentioned as a peculiarity of Meccan speech, has affected the orthography of the Qur'ān. Perhaps one might say that the Qur'ān was in a Meccan variant of the literary language.

The dogma that the Qur'ān was written in pure Arabic also made Muslim scholars unwilling to admit that any of the vocabulary of the Qur'ān had been borrowed from other languages. Reluctantly, however, in course of time they recognized that a number of words in the Qur'ān were not derived from Arabic roots; but their knowledge of other languages was slight and they often failed to elucidate the origin of these words. The view of later Muslim scholars is represented by as-Suyūṭī (d. 1505) and ʿAbd-ar-Raḥmān ath-Thaʿālibī (d. 1468)[17] who very reasonably held that as a result of the Arabs' foreign contacts various non-Arabic words had been incorporated into Arabic, but that, since these words had been arabicized, it was still true that the Qur'ān was in 'a clear Arabic tongue'. Modern scholarship has devoted much attention to the foreign words in Qur'ānic Arabic. The wider knowledge now possessed of the languages and dialects used in pre-Islamic times in the countries surrounding Arabia has made it possible to trace the provenance of most of these words with a degree of accuracy.

The most convenient and accessible treatment of the question for English readers is Arthur Jeffery's work on *The Foreign Vocabulary of the Qur'ān*.[18] After an 'introduction' of some forty pages describing the attempts of Muslim scholars to deal with the question, he lists about 275 words, other than proper names, which have been regarded as foreign, discusses the views of modern scholars about their origin, and either sums up the previous discussion or gives fresh suggestions of his own. About three-quarters of the words in this list can be shown to have been in use in Arabic before the time of Muḥammad, and many had become regular Arabic words. To this extent the view of as-Suyūṭī is confirmed. Of the remaining 70 or so, though there is no written evidence of their earlier use, it may well be true that they were already employed in speech; but no record has come down to us prior to the Qur'ān of the form or special meaning. About half of the 70 come from Christian languages, chiefly Syriac, but a few from Ethiopic; some 25 come from Hebrew or Jewish-Aramaic; the remainder, mostly of slight religious importance, come from Persian, Greek or unknown sources. While this result is roughly correct, there may be variations in detail, since, when there are similar forms in a number of Semitic languages, it may be difficult to say which is the source from which Arabic borrowed.

SIX

THE SHAPING OF THE QUR'ĀN

1. The theory of abrogation and the possibility of revision

According to the Islamic view that the Qur'ān is the speech of God conveyed to Muḥammad by an angel, there can be no revision of the Qur'ān by Muḥammad *of his own volition.* This is made clear in a number of verses:

> When our signs (or verses) are recited to them as Evidences, those who look to no meeting with us say, Bring a different Qur'ān from this, or alter it. Say, It is not for me to alter it of my own accord; I follow only what is revealed to me; if I go against my Lord, I fear the punishment of a mighty day. [10.15/16].

An earlier passage described the punishment more vividly:

> If he were to forge against us any statements
> we should take him by the right hand
> then cut his heart-vein;
> not one of you would protect him (from us). [69.44-47].

Yet the other verses indicate that the pagan Meccans brought pressure to bear on Muḥammad to produce 'revelations' more favourable to themselves, presumably by permitting some recognition of the idols as lesser deities.

> They almost tempted you from what we revealed to you, so that you invented against us something else; and then they would have taken you as a friend. Had we not made you stand firm (Muḥammad), you had almost inclined towards them a little. Then we would have made you taste the double of life and the double of death, and you would not have found against us any helper. [17.73/5-75/7].

Muḥammad must have believed that these were true revelations, and therefore could not have contemplated deliberately producing any verses and passing them off as revelation.

Nevertheless the Qur'ān speaks of various ways in which changes come about by the initiative of God. God may cause Muḥammad to forget some verses; but, if he does so, he will reveal other verses in their place.

> We shall cause you to recite, and you shall not forget
> Except what God wills . . . [87.6f.]
> For whatever verse we cancel or cause (the messenger) to forget we bring a better or the like. [2.106/0]

The following verse probably also refers to this, but it could also refer to the forgetting of matters other than revelations:

> . . . and remember your Lord when you forget, and say: Perhaps my Lord will guide me to something nearer the truth (*rashad*) than this. [18.24/3]

There are also verses which speak of God deleting or otherwise removing and changing certain passages.

> God will delete or confirm what he will; and with him is the 'mother' of the Book. [13.39]
> When we substitute one verse for another – and God knows best what he sends down – they say, You (Muḥammad) are simply an inventor; nay most of them do not know. [16.101/3]

Two other verses which are probably relevant to this topic are:

> We have made changes (?) in this Qur'ān that they might be reminded. [17.41/3]
> If we so will, we shall assuredly take away what we have revealed to you. [17.86/8]

In the light of all these verses it cannot be denied that some revision of the Qur'ān (as it was publicly proclaimed) took place. This was admitted by Muslim scholars in their doctrine of abrogation (*an-nāsikh wa-l-mansūkh*). The idea underlying the doctrine is that certain commands to the Muslims in the Qur'ān were only of temporary application, and that when circumstances changed they were abrogated or replaced by others. Because the commands were the word of God, however, they continued to be recited as part of the Qur'ān. Thus the command to spend a considerable part of the night in prayer, given at the beginning of sura 73 was abrogated or cancelled by the long verse [20] at the end, doubtless because in view of the public reponsibilities of Muḥammad and the leading Muslims at Medina it was undesirable that they should be awake much of the night. The quotations just given, however, if taken at their face value, indicate something more extensive than is contemplated in the doctrine of abrogation. If due attention is also paid to the words in 75.17 spoken by God (or perhaps the angels) to Muḥammad: 'ours it is to put it together and recite it', the process of 'collecting' separate passages to form suras would also be undertaken by Muḥammad as he followed a divine initiative; the word here translated 'put together', *jamʿ*, is the word later used for the 'collection' of the Qur'ān after Muḥammad's death.[1]

To complete this survey of the possibilities of revision another important passage must be quoted [22.52/1f.]:

> We have not sent before you (Muḥammad) any messenger or prophet, but that, when he formed his desire, Satan threw (something) into his formulation; so God abrogated what Satan threw in; then God adjusts his signs (or verses)... that he may make what Satan has thrown in a test for the diseased of heart and the hard-hearted... and that those with knowledge may know that it is the truth from your Lord and believe in it...

This verse is usually illustrated by the story of the 'satanic verses' intruded into sura 53 and later cut out[2]; but there is nothing in the text of the passage to prevent something similar having happened in a number of other cases. The underlying principle is that something once proclaimed and recited as part of the Qur'ān came to be regarded as satanic and then was no longer regarded as belonging to the Qur'ān.

The use of the word 'abrogate' (*yansakhu*) in this passage differs from its usage in the theory of abrogation, for in the latter the abrogated verses are still retained as part of the Qur'ān. In passing it may be noted that the retention of abrogated verses in the text of the Qur'ān as we have it is a confirmation of the accuracy of the text, since it shows that later textual scholars did not remould it in accordance with their own conceptions. The discussion of abrogation in Islam has been voluminous, but belongs primarily to the sphere of jurisprudence. Some of the standard works of the jurists like the 'Epistle' of ash-Shāfiʿī (d. 820),[3] have sections on various questions connected with abrogation, while there are also special treatises on the subject which list and discuss the 'abrogating' and 'abrogated' verses of the Qur'ān.[4] The fifteenth-century scholar as-Suyūṭī in his compendium of Qur'ānic studies known as the *Itqān* devotes about half a dozen pages to the question.[5] Many subtle points were raised by the jurists, and the conception was applied not only to the Qur'ān but also to the Sunna (or practice of Muḥammad), while it was further asserted that the laws of the Jews and Christians had been abrogated by the revelation of the Qur'ān.

If the later theories of jurists and others are distinguished from what the Qur'ān itself says, it would seem that various processes took place which may be comprehended under the term 'revision'. It may be conjectured that Muḥammad carried out this 'revision' in accordance with what he understood to be divine guidance. Perhaps this took the form of a repetition of the revelation in the revised form. There is bound to remain some uncertainty about details, but enough has been said to justify an examination of the text of the Qur'ān to discover detailed evidence of revision.

2. Evidences of revision and alteration

The simplest form of 'revision' is the 'collection' or putting together of the small units in which the revelation originally came. There are grounds for thinking that this process was begun by Muḥammad himself, that is, that it was continuous with his receiving of revelations. This seems to be implied by 75.17 which has already been mentioned. The whole passage runs:

> Move not your tongue in it to do it quickly;
> ours is the collecting of it and the reciting of it;
> when we recite it follow the reciting of it;
> thereafter ours is the explaining of it. [75.16-19]

The most likely explanation here of the word 'collecting' (*jamʿ*) is that passages which had originally come to Muḥammad separately were now repeated for him in combination with one another. This explanation is borne out by other points. When Muḥammad's opponents are challenged to produce a sura [10.38/9] or ten suras [11.13/16] like what has been revealed to him, the implication is that there are already in Muḥammad's possession ten units which may be called 'suras'. The date of the second passage is at latest early Medinan, and that would make it possible for many other suras to have been added before Muḥammad's death. Again, it has always been held by Muslim scholars that the mysterious letters are part of the revealed text and were not added by later 'collectors'; and since there is a certain grouping together of the suras with letters (as will be seen in the Table pp. 206-13), it is probable that these groups already existed as groups in Muḥammad's lifetime. If the *bismillāh* is also part of the original text, this would be a reason for thinking that the commencement of the suras at least goes back to Muḥammad. Moreover, the great variation in the length of the suras is hardly accounted for by differences of subject, rhyme or form – the type of criterion which might have been used by collectors; and this suggests that much of the Qur'ān was arranged in suras before the collectors began their work. Altogether, then, it is likely that much of the work of 'collecting' had been performed by Muḥammad guided by a continuing process of revelation.

Next it may be noticed that not only were passages placed together to form suras but that, when this was done, some adaptation took place. One piece of evidence for this is the occurrence of hidden rhymes.[6] It would seem that sometimes, when a passage with one assonance was added to a sura with a different assonance, phrases were added to give it the latter assonance. As an example of this, sura 23.12-16 may be analysed.

(12) la-qad khalaqnā l-insāna min sulāla / min ṭīn
(13) thumma jaʿalnā-hu nuṭfa / fī qarārin makīn
(14) thumma khalaqnā n-nuṭfata ʿalaqa /
fa-khalaqnā l-ʿalaqata muḍgha /

fa-khalaqnā l-muḍghata ʿiẓāma^{n} /
fa-kasawnā l-ʿizāma laḥma^{n} /
thumma ansha'nā-hu khalqan akhara /
fa-tabāraka llāhu aḥsanu l-khāliqīn
(15) thumma inna-kum baʿda dhālika la-mayyitūn
(16) thumma inna-kum yawma l-qiyāmati tubʿathūn

The translation might run as follows:
(12) We have created man of an extract / of clay
(13) Then we made him a drop / in a receptacle sure
(14) Then we created the drop a clot,
then we created the clot a morsel,
then we created the morsel bones,
then we clothed the bones with flesh,
then we produced him a new creature; /
blessed be God the best of creators.
(15) Then after that you are dead,
(16) then on resurrection-day you are raised again.

In this example it is to be noted that the verses as they stand rhyme in -*ī*(*l*) – in fact -*īn* or -*ūn* – which is the assonance of the sura as a whole. Verse 14, however, is unusually long, and moreover can be broken up into six short verses, five of which rhyme in -*a*, while the sixth, which is superfluous to the sense, gives the rhyme in -*īn*. The same rhyme in -*a* can also be found in verses 12 and 13 by dropping the concluding phrase. With the omission of the rhyme-phrases verses 12 to 14 constitute a little passage of seven verses rhyming in -*a*, describing the generation of man as a sign of God's creative power. It may be noted that the word *sulāla*, translated 'extract' to suit the following phrase, may also mean 'the choicest part of a thing' or 'what is drawn gently out' and so 'semen'; in the only other instance of the word in the Qur'ān it is stated that, while the first man was created from clay, his progeny came 'from a *sulāla* of base water' [32.8/7]. Thus the removal of the rhyme-phrases seems to give a better and clearer sense. It may further be supposed that verses 15 and 16 were added as part of the adaptation of the passage to its place in this sura. The passage which immediately follows, 23.17-22, has marks of having been similarly dealt with; when the concluding phrases with the rhymes are detached, there are traces of an assonance in *fāʿil* (namely, *ṭarāʾiq*, *fawākih*, etc.). A number of other passages appear to have been treated in the same way.[7]

Of special interest are one or two cases where the rhyme of the sura changes. In sura 3, for example, the first part (up to about verse 20/18)[8] rhymes in -*ā*(*l*), and so does the end, from verse 190/87 to verse 200. The large middle section, however, has the rhyme in -*ī*(*l*). Near the point where the first change occurs stands a passage [33/0-41/36] dealing with the story of Mary and Zechariah, in which several of the verses – namely, 37/2, 38/3a, 39a/3b, 40/35, 41/36 – rhyme in -*ā*(*l*), while it seems possible that the other verses have had phrases added to them to carry the rhyme -*ī*(*l*); e.g. the end of 36/1 would be *ash-shayṭān* if *ar-rajīm* is removed.[9] Thus it looks as if a portion with the rhyme -*ī*(*l*) had been inserted into a sura which originally rhymed in -*ā*(*l*) and an attempt made to dovetail the two pieces together. The impression is strengthened when it is noticed that the rhyme -*ī*(*l*) occurs at the end of verse 18/16 carried by a phrase with a difficult construction which leads on to 21/0 rather than to 19/17 and 20/18-19. Other instances of something similar connected with a change of rhyme occur in 13.2-4 and 19.51/2-58/9; but these cases are not so clear.

There are, again, many passages in which the rhyme-phrases can be detached without revealing an older rhyme underneath. In these cases one cannot be certain that revision has taken place, since (as noted above on pp. 70-1) an otiose, and therefore detachable, rhyme-phrase often appears to mark the close of a verse. When, however, such a phrase is found at the end of a number of consecutive verses [as in 6.95-9, 102-4] it is reasonable to assume that it has been inserted into an originally unrhymed passage in order to give it the rhyme of the sura. In two cases [6.84-7; 38.45-8] this seems to have been done with a list of names; and there is something comparable in 19.51/2-57/8.

Another way in which passages have been adapted is illustrated by 6.141/2-144/5. These verses cannot be grammatically construed as they stand, but each verse may be divided into two parts. The first parts by themselves give a list of God's bounties in the produce of the soil and animals; but into this list sentences (the second parts) have been introduced combating pagan food-taboos. Again in 7.57/5, 58/6 the sign of God's goodness in the revival of dead land and the varying response of different soils – perhaps a simile of the varying response of men to the divine message – has been transformed by inserted sentences into a corroboration of the resurrection; the insertions are marked by a sudden change of pronoun from 'he' to 'we', referring to God.

In addition to these changes which seem to have taken place when the passage was adapted to its place in a sura, there are many other evidences of revision and alteration. It should be theoretically possible to revise a passage in such a way that no mark of the patching remains, but in practice a careful reader will often be able to detect the alteration through some unevenness in the style. There are indeed many roughnesses of this kind, and these, it is here claimed, are fundamental evidence for revision. Besides the points already noticed – hidden rhymes, and rhyme-phrases not woven into the texture of the passage – there are the following: abrupt changes of rhyme; repetition of the same rhyme-word or rhyme-phrase in adjoining verses; the intrusion of an extraneous subject into a passage otherwise homogeneous; a differing treatment of the same subject in neighbouring verses, often with repetition of words and phrases; breaks in grammatical construction which raise difficulties in exegesis; abrupt changes in the length of verses; sudden changes of the dramatic situation, with changes of pronoun from singular to plural, from second to third person, and so on; the juxtaposition of apparently contrary statements; the juxtaposition of passages of different date, with the intrusion of late phrases into early verses. So common are these features in the Qur'ān that they have often been regarded as characteristics of its style and in no need of further study or explanation. This is not the case, however. It is here being argued that these features of the Qur'ān are most simply explained by supposing a measure of revision and alteration; but even if this view is rejected, some explanation of these features is still called for. Meanwhile what has been said about the unevenness and roughness of Qur'ānic style may be amplified.

Glosses are a common feature of ancient Greek, Latin and

other manuscripts. They are short explanations of some obscurity, presumably first written on the margin by some reader and then mistakenly incorporated in the text by a later copyist. While it is doubtful if the Qur'ān contains any glosses in the strict sense, there is something approaching a gloss in 2.85/79. Beginning at the previous verse the passage runs:

> (Recall) when we made a covenant with you (on the following terms): You shall not shed your own (*sc.* one another's) blood; and you shall not expel yourselves from your dwellings. Then you confirmed it, yourselves being witnesses.
>
> Then there you are killing yourselves, and expelling a party of you from their dwellings, as you join together against them in guilt and enmity; / and if they come to you as prisoners, you shall ransom them; / and it is forbidden to you, their expulsion. Do you believe . . .

The clause about ransoming prisoners seems an intrusion here. Bell in his *Translation* considers that it belongs to the terms of the covenant in the previous verse, which is possible but not certain.[10] If this clause is removed, the following clause, which may then be translated 'although it is forbidden to you' is perfectly clear without the addition of 'their expulsion', *ikhrāju-hum*. There is thus a strong presumption that 'their expulsion' is a gloss or addition, made after the clause about ransoming prisoners had been intruded. Other possible examples of such additions or explanatory substitutions will be found in: 6.12, 20; 7.92/0; 21.47/8, 104; 27.7; 41.17/16; 76.16.[11]

Explanations of unusual words or phrases are sometimes added in the form of an extension of the passage. There are twelve instances of such extensions beginning with the words: 'What has let you know what . . . is?'[12] A short description then follows. It is clear that some of the descriptions have been added at a later time, since they do not correspond to the sense in which the word or phrase was originally taken. The most striking case is at the end of sura 101 [verses 9/6-11/8]: '. . . his mother shall be *hāwiya*. And what has let you know what it is? A scorching fire.' *Hāwiya* presumably meant 'childless' owing to the death or misfortune of her son; but the addition suggests that it is a name of Hell. A somewhat similar passage is 90.12-16. The addition is seldom an exact definition of what is to be explained.

Additions and insertions of other kinds may be illustrated from the shorter suras. In sura 91 it is evident that the main passage, when first revealed, ended at verse 10; but this is followed by a summary of the story of Thamūd, which may either have been added to illustrate the moral, or simply placed here because of the similar rhyme. Verses 6 and 7 of sura 88 may be marked as an insertion by the different rhyme, and verses 33 and 34 of sura 78 by the breaking of the connection between verses 32 and 35. In sura 87 a sudden change in the dramatic situation at verse 16 marks an addition which might have followed immediately on the original revelation, but is probably much later. In sura 74 the passage 31-31/4 is clearly marked as an insertion by the different style and length of verse. Some of these additions might conceivably be due to a later collector or reader; but this is unlikely.

There are other additions, however, which can hardly have been made without authority. The misplaced phrase of 2.85/79, for instance, though it looks like a gloss written on the margin and taken in by a copyist at the wrong place, makes a real addition to the regulation laid down. There are few such misplacements, but short additions which make substantial alterations to the sense are frequent. In 74.56/5 we have a limitation of the freedom of man's choice which virtually takes back what had been stated in verse 55/4; cf. 76.29, 30; 1.28, 29. This corresponds to the hardening of the doctrine of predestination which took place in Medinan days. Reservations introduced by *illā*, 'except', are specially frequent. We must not, of course, assume that every such reservation is a later addition, but in a number of cases there are independent reasons for such an assumption, as in 87.7, and 95.6, where *illā* introduces a longer verse, which has characteristic Medinan phraseology, into an early passage with short rhythmic verses. Such additions, making as they do a distinct modification of the statement, must have been deliberately introduced. In at least some of them we can discern the grounds for making the exception.

Longer additions can sometimes be easily distinguished.

Thus in sura 73 a long verse occurs at the end which, by containing a reference to Muslims engaged in fighting, is clearly marked as Medinan, and is recognized by everyone as being so. But the rest of the sura, and especially the beginning, is in the short crisp verses characteristic of early passages. The reason for the addition is that the passage at the beginning recommended night-prayer; but since this was being overdone, it became necessary in Medina to counsel moderation.[13]

Additions in the middle of suras are common. A few examples will suffice. The first part of sura 19 has the assonance in *-iyyā*, but this is interrupted by verses 34/5 to 40/1, which have the common *-ī(l)* assonance. These verses follow an account of Mary and Jesus, and, by rejecting the idea of God having offspring, criticize a popular misconception of Christian doctrine. 3.130/25-134/28 warn against the taking of excessive interest, and promise heavenly reward to those who act generously. The passage evidently closed with the rhyme-phrase of 134/28, but two verses follow giving a further description of those who do well by repenting and asking forgiveness, and containing a promise of heavenly reward which is largely a repetition of that already made. Those who have transgressed but are prepared to reform are thus included. Verses 5 to 8 of sura 22 argue for the resurrection as in line with God's power otherwise manifest, and close by scoffing at those who 'without knowledge, guidance, or light-giving book' argue to the contrary. Verses 9, 10 join to this rather awkwardly and threaten not only future punishment but 'humiliation in this life', a Medinan threat, to those who so act. The change of tone and attitude shows clearly enough that these verses did not belong to the original passage. In sura 37.73-132 there are accounts of various Biblical persons, closing in three cases with the refrain: 'Thus do we reward those who do well; verily he is one of our servants believing'. In the case of Abraham, however, this refrain [110f.] is followed by a statement about the posterity of Abraham and Isaac [112f.]. This must have been added after the passage was composed.

Another important feature of Qur'ānic style is that in many cases a passage has alternative continuations, which follow one another in the present text. The second of the alternatives is marked by a break in sense and by a break in grammatical construction, since the connection is not with what immediately precedes, but with what stands some distance back; there may also be the repetition of a word or phrase. Thus 23.63/5, which speaks of men continuing a defective course of conduct, is followed by three passages introduced by *ḥattā idhā*, 'until when', commencing with 64/6, 77/9 and 99/101 respectively. It is possible, with some straining, to join verse 77/9 to 76/8, but verse 99/101 will not join to 98/100. The words *ḥattā idhā*, however, require before them a reference to something continuing. Verses 99/101f. are in fact the proper continuation of 63/5, as is evident if we read them together; the other verses introduced by *ḥatta idhā* are alternative and presumably later continuations of 63/5. Again, 5.42/6 begins with a phrase *sammāʿūna li-l-kadhib*, which is entirely out of connection with what precedes. The same phrase occurs in 41/5, however; and, if the part of 41/5 from this phrase to the end is omitted, 42/6 fits perfectly to the earlier part of 41/5. Here also then, there are alternative continuations. Another example will be found at the end of sura 39 where there is a verse which appears isolated [75]. It follows a Judgement-scene and evidently belongs to it; but the scene is already finished; judgement has been given, the unbelievers have been sent to Gehenna, the pious have entered the Garden; then we find ourselves back at the scene of Judgement where judgement will be given with truth. This phrase, which has already occurred in verse 69, indicates what was the original position of verse 75; it followed the first phrase of 69 and completed the scene; at some later stage it was displaced by the much longer description in verses 69-74.[14]

Occasionally a change of rhyme may accompany such a substitution. Thus 80.34-37 have their assonance in *-īh*, while verses 38-42, which join equally well to verse 33, have the *-a* assonance which runs through the whole of the rest of the sura. More frequently the occurrence of the same rhyme-word or -phrase is a sign that such a substitution has been made, since the new version ends with the same rhyme as that which it replaced. Thus in sura 2 verses 102/96 and 103/97 both end in *law kānū yaʿlamūna*, 'if they had known', which gives a presumption that the latter verse was intended to replace the former. In sura 3 the similar ending indicates that verse 144/38 is a substitute for verse 145/39. A similar phenomenon is to be found in 9.117/8, 118/9; 34.52/1, 53/2; 45.28/7, 29/8; 72.24/5, 27-8. In such cases the alternative continuations often stand in reverse order of date, the later coming first, but this is not an invariable rule.[15]

Further evidence of alteration and revision may be obtained by approaching the Qur'ān from the standpoint of the subject-matter and considering passages dealing with the situations which presented special difficulties or problems to Muḥammad and the Muslims. In these passages there is often much confusion. A simple case is that of the ordinance concerning fasting. When he removed to Medina, Muḥammad hoped for support from the Jews and showed himself willing to learn from them. Tradition says that he introduced the Jewish fast of the 'Āshūrā, which consisted of the Day of Atonement preceded by some days of special devotion. Later, the month of Ramaḍān was prescribed. Now, in 2.183/79-185/1 these two things lie side by side; verse 184/0 prescribes a fast of a certain number of days, verse 185/1, the month of Ramaḍān. The two verses are, of course, read consecutively, and the 'certain number of days' of the former verse is held to be made more precise by the mention of the month of Ramaḍān in the latter. But 'a certain number of days' is not naturally equivalent to a month, and the repetition of phrases in the two verses shows that the one was intended to replace the other. The verses are, in fact, alternative continuations of 183/79.[16]

The marriage laws in sura 4 are another clear case of alternative continuations. Verse 23/7 lays down the forbidden degrees of relationship, and reproduces the Mosaic list with some adaptation to Arab custom. That this was deliberate is shown by 26/31, which states that 'God desires . . . to guide you in the customs of those who were before you'. At a later time, however, some relaxation became necessary, and 25/29-30 and perhaps 27/32a were substituted for 26/31, allowing marriage with slaves. Finally 24/8, which gives ample liberty, was substituted for 25/29-30, and 28/32b was added to give a verse-ending. The similar endings of 26/31, 27/32a and 28/32b show that substitutions have been made.

The change of *qibla* (the direction to be faced in prayer)

affords another example. The passage dealing with it is very confused [2.142/36-152/47]; the portion from 141/39 especially is unintelligible as it stands. When analysed, however, the verses turn out to contain (*a*) a private revelation to the Prophet of the solution to his problem [144/39a, 149/4]; (*b*) a public announcement, using part of (*a*) accompanied by an appeal for obedience based on gratitude [144/39a, 150/45-152/47]; and (*c*) the final form of the ordinance [144/39a, 144/39b].

The process of the introduction of the religion of Abraham is outlined for us in 2.130/24-141/35. It takes the form of answers to the assertion of Jews and Christians [135/29a]: 'They say: "Be ye Jews or Christians and ye will be guided"'. This is followed by three retorts introduced by 'Say'. Verses 139/3-141/35 claim that the Prophet and his followers have a perfect right to serve God in their own way, as did Abraham and the patriarchs; these constituted an independent religious community long since passed away. This passage was cut off and replaced by 136/0, 138/2, in which it is claimed that Muḥammad and his followers stand in the line of Abraham and the patriarchs, Moses, Jesus and all the prophets. It was again modified by the insertion of 137/1 in place of 138/2. Finally, the short retort of 135/29b was written in, professing the creed of Abraham, who was a *ḥanīf* and no polytheist. Verses 130/24 to 134/28 are a further addition.

The question of the pilgrimage, which was part of the religion of Abraham, also caused difficulty. The ceremony was recognized and Muḥammad's followers were counselled to take part in it, but as *ḥanīfs*, followers of the religion of Abraham, not as polytheists [22.31/2]. Sacrificial animals were to be sent to Mecca [22.34/5a, 33/4]. When, however, Muslim attacks on Meccan caravans, and especially the battle of Badr, led to bloodshed, it became dangerous for any Muslim to visit Mecca. It was therefore laid down that the animals dedicated for sacrifice might be slaughtered at home and their flesh given to the poor. This can be deduced from 22.29/30-37/8.[17]

Fighting in the sacred months also caused difficulty. Muḥammad's attitude is made clear by the analysis of sura 9. These months were at first recognized as a period of truce, by a deliverance which consisted of 9.36a, 2, 5; but since the intercalary month, which kept the Arab lunar year in conformity with the seasons, was decreed from Mecca, misunderstandings about which months were sacred would soon arise. Hence the deliverance was issued which now stands as 9.36, 37, abolishing the intercalary month and decreeing that war with the polytheists was to be carried on continuously. The discarded verses dealing with the sacred months now appear as verses 2 and 5, linked up with a renunciation of agreements with polytheists, probably the treaty of al-Ḥudaybiya. As the heading informs us, however, this is also a proclamation to be made at the pilgrimage; and it was presumably altered and added to for this purpose after the fall of Mecca.[18]

The defeat of the Muslims at Uḥud was a severe blow to the confidence of the Muslims. The passage dealing with the battle is in great confusion [3.102/97-179/4]. Analysis shows that there was an address intended for delivery before the battle, which consisted of verses 102/97, 103/98-9, 112/06a, 115/1-117/3, 123/19, 139/3-143/37, 145/39-151/44, 158/2, 160/54. Part of this, perhaps from 139/3 onward, was re-delivered, with a few alterations, some time after the battle. Reactions to the defeat appear in a reproof to the Prophet himself for having, without authority, promised the assistance of angels [verses 121/17, 124/0, 125/1 and parts of 126/2-129/4]. That was later revised as an explanation and rebuke to his followers. That he had been inclined to speak angrily to them is indicated in the private verse [159/3]. Part of this 'rough' speech may be embedded in 152/45-154/48, a passage which has been revised and added to in a milder sense later. In fact, we can see the attitude to the defeat growing gradually calmer and more kindly towards the faithful. Finally, when the set-back had been overcome, part of the original address was used again, with a new continuation added after 110/06a, in preparation probably for the attack on the Jewish tribe of an-Naḍīr [110/06b-114/0].[19]

The great volume of evidence, of which what has been presented here is only a sample, shows that the Qur'ān is far from being a straightforward collection (out of chronological order) of short passages of a revealed text. The matter is too complex for any simple explanation of this kind. The vast number of dislocations and the roughness of some of them cannot simply be ascribed to 'the Qur'ānic style'. The modern scholar may seldom be able to give a correct solution of the problems raised by the dislocations, but it can surely be no longer denied that there are problems of this kind. My personal view is that in the working out of solutions to these problems in his *Translation* Richard Bell was often successful. The following section, however, presents a small part of his view which has not met with the same degree of approval.

3. Bell's hypothesis of written documents

(a) *The hypothesis.* The critical literary analysis of the Qur'ān, besides producing the kind of evidence given in the last section, led Richard Bell to formulate a particular theory about the place of written documents in the 'collection' of the Qur'ān. This theory was not simply that parts of the Qur'ān had been written down at a fairly early stage in Muḥammad's career, but more particularly that the occurrence in the middle of a sura of a passage wholly unrelated to the context was to be explained by the supposition that this passage had been written on the back of the 'scrap of paper' used for one of the neighbouring passages which properly belonged to the sura. Bell used the word 'paper' as a convenient term for any kind of writing material.

As examples of such passages out of relation to the context Bell selected 75.16-19, 84.16-19, and 88.17-20. The argument may be presented most clearly in the case of the latter. The sura begins with a description of the Judgement and the fate of the wicked, and then continues with a picture of the righteous

(10) in a garden lofty (*'āliya*)
(11) wherein they hear no babbling; (*lāghiya*)
(12) therein is a spring running; (*jāriya*)
(13) therein are couches upraised (*marfū'a*)
(14) and goblets set out (*mawḍū'a*)
(15) and cushions in rows (*maṣfūfa*)
(16) and carpets spread. (*mabthūtha*)
(17) Will they not look at the camels, how they have been created (*khuliqat*)
(18) at the heaven, how it has been uplifted; (*rufi'at*)

(19) at the mountains, how they have been set up; (*nuṣibat*)
(20) at the earth, how it has been laid flat? (*suṭiḥat*)
(21) So warn. You are only a warner . . . (*mudhakkir*)

The argument here is as follows. The passage 17-20 has no connection of thought either with what goes before or with what comes after; and it is marked off by its rhyme. It is thus difficult to know why it has been placed here. If one assumes that its position has been given to it by a collector, one may still ask whether a responsible collector could not have found a more suitable place for it. Bell's hypothesis is that verses 17-20 have been placed here because they were found written on the back of verses 13-16. He further holds in this particular case that 13-16, which are marked off by rhyme from the preceding verses, were a later addition to these, and happened to have been written on the back of a 'scrap' which already contained 17-20.

Something similar is true of 75.16-19. Verses 13-16 (partly distinguished by rhyme, partly by length) seem to have been added to 7-12, which deal with the Last Day, and to have been written on the back of the early 'scrap' containing 16-19 (quoted above on p. 89). In sura 84 there is no abrupt change of rhyme, but verses 13-15 destroy the balance of the preceding piece, verses 7-12, which is complete as it stands. In each case, then, an addition has been made, and the addition occupies approximately the same space as the extraneous passage which follows. A simple explanation of the position of the extraneous passage would thus be to suppose that it stood on the scrap of paper on which the addition was later written, and that the two sides of the paper had been read and copied consecutively when the Qur'ān came to be made up in the form of a codex.

Similar examples may be found throughout the Qur'ān. To take an example from near the beginning: 2.15/16 compares those who have accepted the Prophet's guidance and then gone back upon it to people who have lit a fire, which has then gone out, leaving them blinded in the darkness. Verse 18/17, 'Deaf, dumb and blind, they do not return', evidently closes the passage, but verses 19/18, 20/19 contain another simile: they are like people in a thunder-storm, the rain pours down, the thunder deafens them, the lightning blinds them. Evidently this is a parallel to 17/16 and should have preceded 18/17. It has been added later. There follows a passage, 21/19b, 22/20, unconnected with the context, appealing for the worship of God and adducing signs of his power and bounty. This appears to be continued, after a break, in 28/26, 29/27. Now 27/25, while not evidently an addition, is probably so, for 26/24 finishes with a reference to the 'reprobate', which is conclusive enough. But 27/25 proceeds to describe a special class of 'reprobates', who violate a covenant after having made it. Further, we find in verses 163/58-165/oa a passage which, by the use of the rather unusual word *andād*, 'peers' is marked as almost certainly a continuation of 21/19b, 22/20, 28/26, 29/27. Here we have, not preceding but following, a passage 165/ob-167/2, which returns to the theme of 161/56, 162/57, and must have been intended as an addition to that passage. This whole section is an interesting example of how a passage has been expanded by additions. The point, however, here is that we find a passage originally dealing with the worship of God apparently cut up, and the back of the pieces used for making insertions into other passages.

An interesting example of the same kind is found in sura 9. The last two verses of this sura are traditionally said to have come to the knowledge of Zayd ibn-Thābit when he had almost completed his task of collecting the Qur'ān, and were placed here as the most convenient position at the time. This is evidently an attempt to account for the fact that there is a break in connection between verses 127/8 and 128/9, and another between 128/9 and 129/30. These two verses seem to stand isolated, but 129/30 will connect well enough with 127/8, though the latter verse ends as if nothing more were to be said. It is a case of something having been later added to a passage, and we may suppose that the back of 128/9 was used to write it on. By some accident (127/8 had itself been used for the writing of another passage) the back was read by the compilers before the addition. But this is not all; verse 40 of the same sura stands isolated, though it evidently requires something in front of it. The pronoun 'him' must evidently refer to the Prophet of whom there has been no mention in the context, but verse 128/9 speaks of the Prophet, and if we read verses 128/9 and 40 together we get a moving appeal for loyalty to the Prophet addressed to his followers. This has evidently been cut in two, one part being added to 127/8 and the other placed after 39.

The reverse seems also to have taken place; scraps of paper were somehow pasted together to form a sheet. Sura 14.8-14/17 – an evident addition to the account of Moses – in which he addresses his people in regular Qur'ānic style, is followed by a series of disjointed pieces, 15/18-17/20, 18/21, 19/22, 21/4-22/7, 23/8, which together occupy practically the same space. In fact, it is almost a rule in the later parts of the Qur'ān that an addition or connected deliverance of any length is preceded or followed by a number of disconnected pieces which together make up approximately the same length. An interesting instance of this occurs at the end of sura 2. There we find a long deliverance dealing with the recording of debts [282, 283]. This occupies approximately the same space as verses 278-281, a deliverance forbidding usury, 284 a separate verse, and 285, 286 a profession of faith of the believers. Into this piece two little sentences intrude at the junction of the verses [285b, 286a]; they have no connection with each other or with the context and break the connection of v. 285 and v. 286, which must have originally formed one verse. If now we suppose the deliverance regarding debts [282-3], to have been written on the back of a sheet (or part of a sheet) which contained the deliverance on usury [278-81], and on that of a second sheet containing 284-6, we find that the intrusion into the latter piece comes practically opposite a proviso introduced into the deliverance about debts excepting from its scope transactions in the market where goods pass from hand to hand. This proviso, we may suppose, was written on the back of two scraps and inserted into the deliverance. To do so, the sheet was cut and the proviso pasted in. In this way the two extraneous scraps appear on the other side of the sheet.

The same thing occurs in sura 4, where, if we suppose verses 88/90-91/3 to have been written on the back of 79/81-87/9, a proviso introduced by *illā* [90/2a], will come opposite 82/4 which breaks the connection between 81/3 and 83/5. This part of the sura is further interesting in that the passage 79/81-81/3, 83/5, 84/6 is almost certainly private and was not meant to be publicly recited. A number of private passages of this kind, intended only for Muḥammad himself, are included in the Qur'ān. The most striking of them is 3.159/3, which can hardly have been intended for publication either at the time or later; cf. also 154/48c and 161/55. The passage about fasting discussed above (p. 98) gives a further illustration [2.183/79-187/3]. Verse 186/2 is entirely unconnected; it has no reference to fasting, and while in the preceding verses the believers are being addressed and God is spoken of in the third person, in this verse God is speaking, the Prophet is being addressed, and other men are spoken of in the third person. Verse 187/3 returns to the subject of fasting and the dramatic setting of 183/79-186/2. If we consider the length of 185/1, we shall find that when written out it occupies approximately the same space as 184/0 and 186/2 together. The presence of this latter verse seems to have arisen from the necessity of adding to the space afforded by the back of 184/0 by using the back of a verse from some other context.

(b) *Critique of the hypothesis*. This theory that the order of the Qur'ān is often due to the fact that some passages were written on the backs of others was worked out in detail for the whole Qur'ān by Richard Bell. His results are incorporated in his *Translation* by various typographical devices such as divisions down the middle of pages. The more one studies these results, the more one is impressed by the infinite pains taken and the great ingenuity shown. For a long time to come scholars will have to take account of this detailed work.

The hypothesis certainly cannot be rejected out of hand. For one thing it seems clear that there were written documents from a fairly early period. Even if Muḥammad himself did not write, he could have had them written by secretaries. It is known that he used secretaries in his later years, and there are Traditions in which the secretaries are employed to write down the revelation. The reference to Muḥammad's forgetting in 87.6 could be held to suggest the inference that he came to distrust his memory and wrote out and memorized the revealed messages before proclaiming them publicly. The gibe of the Meccans about 'old-world tales which he has had (?) written for himself' implies that at Mecca he was at least suspected of having things written down [25.6]. If, as is likely, he had some of the Qur'ān written, he may have tried to keep the matter secret. At Medina one would expect that at least the legal deliverances were recorded. The report about the first 'collection' of the Qur'ān after Muḥammad's death by Zayd ibn-Thābit implies that some was already written on pieces of papyrus and other materials. The result of Zayd's work was a 'collection' of the Qur'ān on 'sheets' (*ṣuḥuf*), and these eventually passed into the possession of Ḥafṣa. As was argued above, it is unlikely that there was any official 'collection' such as is described; but it is fairly certain that Ḥafṣa had 'sheets' of some sort. It is thus probable that much of the Qur'ān had been written down in some form during Muḥammad's lifetime. It is even possible that there were several written versions of parts of it in the hands of different individuals.

Bell's distinctive hypothesis, however, is concerned not with the mere existence of written documents, but with a special way of dealing with them which he alleges to be responsible for some aspects of the order of the text. It should at once be admitted that what he suggests may occasionally have happened. On the other hand, there are suras (such as 80 and 96) where unconnected pieces have been brought together; and Bell apparently simply accepts this fact without trying to apply his theory. It may then be inferred that, at least at some periods, whoever was responsible for collecting the Qur'ān was not unduly worried by the absence of continuity of thought; and in so far as this is the case a discontinuity of thought in a sura may easily have come about without the passage having been written on the back of another. This makes some of Bell's elaborate reconstructions (such as the examples from sura 2 and sura 9) all the more dubious.

It may also be urged that little is gained by the hypothesis. The problem before the scholar is the accidental character of the unconnected passages. In effect Bell's hypothesis explains this accidental character by supposing another accident, namely, that one passage was written on the back of another. In particular cases there is bound to be great uncertainty about the precise way in which the hypothesis is to be applied; but, even if the application were known to be correct, little would be added to our understanding of early Islam. In this respect the results produced by the hypothesis are in contrast to the evidence tending to show revision and alteration. If the analysis of the passage about the *qibla* is sound, then it gives us increased insight into the profound re-orientation of the policy of the Islamic state about March 624.

The emphasis on documents in the hypothesis and in Bell's treatment generally requires to be balanced by giving increased weight to the aspect of oral transmission. In the traditional account 'the hearts of men', that is, their memories, was one of the sources drawn on by Zayd ibn-Thābit; and the Qur'ān-reciters subsequently became an important group of men. The possibility that Muḥammad might forget a passage envisaged in 87.6 implies that for at least a time he was relying on his memory. This suggests the further question whether Muḥammad clearly distinguished between proclaiming from memory a message he had previously received and proclaiming at the moment of revelation a message which partly coincided with another message previously received. The reference to God's 'collecting' of the Qur'ān in 75.17 would seem to imply that Muḥammad received revelations combining (and perhaps adapting) previous revelations. This further implies that a revelation may be repeated, perhaps in slightly different terms. This becomes all the more significant when one remembers the numerous repetitions of phrases and verses throughout the Qur'ān. It may also be linked up with the phenomenon of alternative continuations. It seems likely, then, assuming that some passages had been revealed in slightly different forms on different occasions, and remembered by individual Muslims in their different forms, that the 'collectors' had on their hands a formidable problem. They would not want to omit any smallest scrap of genuine revelation, and yet the total mass of material may have been so vast that they could not include it all. This may explain some of the roughnesses in the 'Uthmānic text.

In conclusion one may underline the value of detailed studies of the text of the Qur'ān such as those carried out by Richard Bell. At the same time one may urge on scholars the need for concentrating on those aspects of the subject which are likely to contribute to a deepening understanding of the early life of the Islamic community.

SEVEN

THE CHRONOLOGY OF THE QUR'ĀN

1. Traditional Islamic views of dating

Muslim scholars usually accepted the fact that the Qur'ān had originally been revealed for the most part in short passages. They tended to assume that most of the passages in a sura had been revealed about the same time. On this basis they came to classify the suras as 'Meccan' or 'Medinan', and this description was included in the heading of each sura in the later copies. They were also aware, however, of instances where a few verses had to be classified differently from the rest of the sura. This has now come to be noted in the heading. Thus in the official Egyptian edition the heading of sura 73 reads: 'The sura of Al-muzzammil, Meccan except verses 10, 11 and 20, which are Medinan; its verses are 20; it was revealed after Al-qalam.' The last statement is part of the attempt to arrange all the suras according to the order in which the main part of each was revealed.

The chief basis for the dating of passages and verses in the eyes of Muslim scholars consists of Traditions about Muḥammad and statements by later students of the Qur'ān. The older Muslim scholars, though presumably they sometimes paid attention to internal evidence, seldom used it explicitly in their arguments. The Traditions in question here are usually to the effect that such and such a passage was revealed in connection with such and such an event. Thus sura 80.1-10 is said to have been revealed when a blind man called 'Abd-Allāh ibn-Umm-Maktūm came up to him as he was talking to some leading men of Quraysh and hoping to win them over. Stories of this type are said to deal with 'the occasions of revelation' (*asbāb an-nuzūl*). There is a well-known book on this subject by al-Wāḥidī (d. 1075). Unfortunately this traditional material suffers from several defects. For one thing it is incomplete, and specifies the 'occasion' for only a relatively small part of the Qur'ān. Again, many of the 'occasions' are incidents, unimportant in themselves, whose precise date is unknown. Such is the anecdote just mentioned about the blind man. Finally, there are inconsistencies. Thus it is usually said that the first passage to be revealed was the beginning of sura 96 (Al-qalam); but there is another story according to which the first revelation was the beginning of sura 74. There are also stories trying to harmonize the two accounts, e.g. by saying that 74 was the first after a gap. In fact neither of these may be the first extant revelation, and the stories may be only the guesses of later Muslim scholars, since there are grounds for selecting each as first. Sura 96 begins with 'recite', and this is appropriate for a book which is called 'the recitation' or Qur'ān; and sura 74 after addressing Muḥammad has the words 'rise and warn' – an appropriate beginning to the work of a messenger or warner.

Despite these deficiencies the traditional dating of passages by Muslim scholars is by no means valueless, and indeed forms the basis of all future work. In so far as it is consistent it gives a rough idea of the chronology of the Qur'ān; and any modern attempt to find a basis for dating must by and large be in agreement with the traditional views, even if in one or two points it contradicts them.

2. European theories of dating

European attempts to work out the chronological order of the suras have usually taken internal evidence into account as well, that is, apparent references to known public events, especially during the Medinan period of Muḥammad's career. Attention has also been paid to considerations of style, vocabulary and the like. In short, the Qur'an has been subjected to severe scrutiny according to the methods of modern literary and historical criticism.

Several nineteenth-century scholars made useful contributions to the study of Qur'ānic chronology; but the most important book by far was Theodor Nöldeke's *Geschichte des Qorāns*, first published in 1860.[1] A second edition, revised and enlarged by Friedrich Schwally and others, appeared in three volumes in 1909, 1919 and 1938, and was reprinted by a photocopying process in 1961. In respect of chronology Nöldeke assumed a progressive change of style from exalted poetical passages in the early years to long prosaic deliverances later. He followed the Islamic tradition in recognizing a division into suras mainly revealed at Mecca and those mainly revealed at Medina, but further divided the Meccan suras into three periods.

The suras of the First Meccan Period are mostly short. The verses also are short, and the language rhythmic and full of imagery. Groups of oaths often occur at the beginning of passages. The suras of this period, in the order assigned to them by Nöldeke are: 96, 74, 111, 106, 108, 104, 107, 102, 105, 92, 90, 94, 93, 97, 86, 91, 80, 68, 87, 95, 103, 85, 73, 101, 99, 82, 81, 53, 84, 100, 79, 77, 78, 88, 89, 75, 83, 69, 51, 52, 56, 70, 55, 112, 109, 113, 114, 1.

In the Second Meccan Period there is a transition from the sublime enthusiasm of the first period to the greater calmness of the third. The fundamental teaching is supported and explained by numerous illustrations from nature and history. There are also discussions of some doctrinal points. In particular emphasis is placed on the signs of God's power both in nature and in the events which befell former prophets. The latter are described in a way which brings out their relevance to what was happening to Muḥammad and his followers. Stylistically, the period is distinguished by new modes of speech. Oaths are seldom used. The suras grow longer and frequently have formal introductions, such as: 'This is the revelation of God...'. Passages are often preceded by *qul*, 'say', as a command to Muḥammad. God is frequently referred to as *ar-Raḥmān*, 'the Merciful'. The suras of the period are: 54, 37, 71, 76, 44, 50, 20, 26, 15, 19, 38, 36, 43, 72, 67, 23, 21, 25, 17, 27, 18.

In the Third Meccan Period the use of *ar-Raḥmān* as a proper name ceases, but other characteristics of the second period are intensified. The prophetic stories are frequently repeated with slight variations of emphasis. The suras of this period are: 32, 41, 45, 16, 30, 11, 14, 12, 40, 28, 39, 29, 31, 42, 10, 34, 35, 7, 46, 6, 13.

The suras of the Medinan Period show not so much a

change of style as a change of subject. Since the Prophet is now recognized as such by a whole community, the revelations contain laws and regulations for the community. Often the people are directly addressed. Some contemporary events are mentioned and their significance made clear. The suras of the period are: 2, 98, 64, 62, 8, 47, 3, 61, 57, 4, 65, 59, 33, 63, 24, 58, 22, 48, 66, 60, 110, 49, 9, 5.[2]

As a first approximation to the historical order of the Qur'ān Nöldeke's arrangement is useful. The criterion of style plays too large a part in it, however. The style of the Qur'ān undoubtedly changes through the years, but it should not be assumed that the change was a steady progression in one direction, for example, towards longer verses. It may well be that the style of different passages of about the same date varied according to their purposes, as indeed is suggested in the Qur'ān (e.g. 47.20/2; cf. 62.2). It is doubtful, too, whether the use of *ar-Raḥmān* as a proper name can be restricted to a few years. It may have been introduced in the Second Meccan Period, but there is no record of it having been explicitly dropped. It continued to be used in the *bismillāh*, and the Meccans who objected to this as a heading for the protocol of the treaty of al-Ḥudaybiya seem to have regarded *ar-Raḥmān ar-Raḥīm* as proper names.

The chief weakness of Nöldeke's scheme, however, is that he mostly treats suras as unities. Occasionally he admits that passages of different dates have found their way into the same sura, but this is exceptional. Subsequent scholars, while retaining the sura itself as the ultimate unit and showing reluctance to admit breaks in its composition, have allowed more intrusion of later passages into earlier suras. If, as has been argued above, however, the original unit of revelation was the short passage, and such passages were afterwards 'collected' to form suras, then the date of the separate passages becomes a prior question. There may be a slight presumption that passages of about the same date would be 'collected' into the same sura, but it is at least possible that some suras contain passages originally revealed at different dates. If both the unit passages and the suras have been subject to revision during Muḥammad's lifetime, the problem becomes even more complicated. Thus it may well be doubted whether it will ever be possible for scholars to produce a complete arrangement of the Qur'ān in chronological order.

Other proposed solutions of the problem by European scholars may be mentioned briefly. In his biography of Muḥammad Sir William Muir, working independently of Nöldeke, suggested an arrangement of the suras that was broadly similar; but a number of passages dealing with the wonders of nature were placed before Muḥammad's call to be a prophet and before the suras traditionally accepted as the first revelations [96 and 74].[3] An order different from Nöldeke's resulted from Hubert Grimme's attempt to arrange the suras on the basis of doctrinal characteristics.[4] He distinguished two main groups of Meccan suras. The first proclaims monotheism, resurrection, the Last Judgement and a future life of bliss or torment; man is free to believe or not; Muḥammad is spoken of as a preacher only, not a prophet. The second group introduces God's *raḥma*, 'mercy' or 'grace', and with this the name of *ar-Raḥmān* is associated; the revelation of 'the Book' becomes prominent, and stories of former recipients of revelation are recounted. Between these two groups are some intermediate suras in which the Judgement is represented as near, and stories are told of punishments falling on unbelieving peoples. While Grimme is right in looking to the sequence of ideas, this criterion by itself is insufficient and must be combined with others.

A radical departure from Nöldeke's scheme came at the beginning of the twentieth century with Hartwig Hirschfeld's *New Researches into the Composition and Exegesis of the Qoran*.[5] He based his dating on the character of separate passages as original revelation, confirmatory, declamatory, narrative, descriptive or legislative. His position is interesting in that he recognizes that it is passages rather than suras with which we have to deal; but his detailed arrangement has not found much acceptance. A recent treatment of the subject is that of Régis Blachère in his French translation.[6] The suras are printed in a chronological order which deviates from Nöldeke's only at a very few points, and fully accepts his idea of three Meccan periods. In the actual arrangement two suras have been divided into two; the opening verses of suras 96 and 74 come first of all (in accordance with Islamic tradition), while the remainder of each sura is put considerably later. Even where a sura is all printed consecutively, however, it may be divided into separate sections and different dates assigned to these. When Blachère's dating and structural analysis is compared with Bell's, it appears that, while he is prepared to accept many of the latter's presuppositions, he is less radical in working them out. Though he refers to Bell, the impression is given that he became familiar with the *Translation* only after his own work was virtually complete – something for which the Second World War may be chiefly responsible.

The most elaborate attempt so far to discover the original units of revelation in the Qur'ān and to date these is that incorporated by Richard Bell in his *Translation*, published in 1937 and 1939. He set out from the position, accepted in a general way by Muslim scholars, that the original unit of revelation was the short passage. He further held that much of the work of 'collecting' these into suras had been done by Muḥammad himself under divine inspiration, and that both in the process of 'collecting' and at other times – always under divine inspiration – he had revised passages. The arguments Bell used are roughly those given in the first two sections of the previous chapter. These points seem to be accepted by Blachère, though he is much more hesitant in claiming that he is able to detect revisions. Beyond that Bell put forward the hypothesis explained and criticized in the last section of the previous chapter. Though the hypothesis has greatly influenced the physical appearance of the printed translation, its rejection does not invalidate to any appreciable extent his dating of particular passages. This dating was based on a careful analysis of each sura, which was in effect a dissection of the sura into its component parts. This analysis, though making the work of dating more complex, in itself yielded certain results, for example, through the recognition of alternative continuations of a verse or phrase. Bell also made a resolute attempt not to read into any passage more than it actually says. This meant setting aside the views of later Muslim commentators in so far as these appeared to have been influenced by theological developments which came about long after the death of the Prophet, and endeavouring to understand each passage in the sense it had for its first hearers.

Like all those who have attempted to date the Qur'ān Bell accepted the general chronological framework of Muḥammad's life as this is found in the *Sīra* or biography by Ibn-Hishām (d. 833) and other works. This is chiefly a chronology of the Medinan period from the Hijra or emigration to Medina in 622 to Muḥammad's death in 632. For the previous period the dates are few and uncertain. Where passages of the Qur'ān can be linked up with events like the battles of Badr or Uḥud or the conquest of Mecca, they can be dated fairly exactly. This chronological framework may be supplemented by the sequence of ideas in the Qur'ān. About this, of course, there is some disagreement. On this point Bell had definite views, some already worked out in his book on *The Origin of Islam in its Christian Environment*. These views were similar to those about to be given in the next section, but not identical with them. Bell also regarded style as being to some extent a criterion of relative date, and agreed with Nöldeke in holding that the short crisp verse and studied rhyme usually belong to an earlier stage than the loose trailing verse and rhyme mechanically formed by grammatical terminations. Now some thirty years after the appearance of Bell's *Translation* it is clear that he did not solve all the problems, but he nevertheless made a contribution of supreme importance by calling the attention of scholars to the complexity of the phenomena.

3. The sequence of ideas as a guide to chronology

Islamic scholarship, regarding the Qur'ān as the eternal Word of God, is unwilling to admit any development of thought in it. Clearly, in so far as God is eternal and unchanging, his thought cannot change. Yet in so far as the Qur'ān is God's Word addressed to men, there is nothing inconsistent in supposing a change of emphasis according to the needs of the original hearers at any given time and according to what they were able to accept and understand. Some such idea is indeed implicit in the doctrine of abrogation. It is no easy matter, of course, to establish a sequence of ideas or of emphases, and in details there are bound to be divergences between scholars. Yet by noting the ideas emphasized in the suras or passages about whose date there is some agreement, an approximation may be made to the sequence of ideas. The study of phraseology sometimes helps, since certain words and turns of phrase are associated with the introduction of a new emphasis in doctrine. The use of a word or phrase tends to continue indefinitely, however, and in its later instances it does not necessarily indicate a special emphasis.

During the last century there has been considerable discussion among European scholars about which points were given prominence in the earliest revelations. For long it had simply been assumed that, in so far as Muḥammad's mission had had a genuinely religious aim, it was to proclaim the unity of God and to attack idolatry. In 1892 in a biography of Muḥammad[7] the German scholar Hubert Grimme tried to show that he was primarily a socialistic reformer who made use of religion in order to carry out his reforms. This hypothesis was vigorously criticized and demolished by a Dutchman, C. Snouck Hurgronje,[8] who argued not only that Muḥammad was primarily a religious leader but also that the motive which drove him on had been the thought of the Day of Judgement and its terrors. This view was accepted favourably in certain circles, especially where eschatology was in fashion. It is prominent, for example, in the life of Muḥammad by Tor Andrae, a Swede.[9] There were also opponents, however, and among these was Richard Bell who suggested rather that the earliest revelations were appealing to men to recognize 'God's bounties in creation' and to show gratitude to him. Bell admitted that the idea of Judgement was in some sense present from the first, but maintained that the descriptions of the terrors of Hell came only later, and indeed after accounts of special punishments on those who disbelieved in prophets.[10]

The question is best answered by a careful examination of the passages generally agreed to be early. It may also be assumed that before opposition appeared to Muḥammad, he had proclaimed some positive message which had annoyed some men; and from this it follows that among the early passages those in which the existence of opposition is mentioned or implied are likely to be later than those where it is not. If one then considers the passages which are regarded as early by both Nöldeke and Bell, and where there is no mention of opposition, one finds that the following points are most prominent:

(1) God is all-powerful and also good or well-disposed towards men; all that is best in men's lives is due to him and also life itself.

(2) God will judge men on the Last Day, and assign them to Heaven or Hell according to their conduct in this life.

(3) Man is to recognize his dependence on God and to show gratitude to him and worship him.

(4) Man's recognition of his dependence on God must also express itself in his attitude to wealth – no niggardly hoarding, but generosity to those in need.

(5) Muḥammad has a special vocation to convey knowledge of these truths to those round him.[11]

In the early passages these points are of course elaborated in various ways; but it is perhaps worth remarking that on the practical side (point 4) there is virtually nothing apart from the different aspects of the attitude to wealth.

There seems to be some connection, though its precise nature is not clear, between the appearance of opposition to Muḥammad and the revelation of passages criticizing and attacking idol-worship. At a very early date in Surat Quraysh (106) there is an appeal to the people of Mecca to worship 'the Lord of this house', that is, the Kaʿba at Mecca. This phrase has puzzled some European scholars, since they assumed that at this period the Lord of the Kaʿba was an idol. The explanation of the verse is simple, and rests on two points.[12] One is that the Arabic word *allāh*, like the Greek *ho theos*, may be understood either as 'the god' worshipped at a particular sanctuary (and so one god among many) or as 'God' in the sense of the purest monotheism. Thus while some Arabs may have thought of *allāh* as 'the god' of the Kaʿba in a polytheistic sense, Muslims could believe that it was God, the source of the revelations to Muḥammad, who was worshipped there. The transition from one interpretation to the other was made easier by the second point for which there are several pieces of evidence in the Qur'ān. This is that among the Arabs of Muḥammad's time there were many who believed that above the deities represented by the idols there was a 'high god' or supreme deity, *Allāh*. One passage apparently describing such a view is 29.61, 63, 65:

> If you ask them who created the heavens and the earth and made the sun and moon subservient, they will certainly say, 'God' . . . And if you ask them who sent down water from the heaven and thereby revived the earth after its death, they will certainly say, 'God' . . . And when they sail on the ship, they pray to God as sole object of worship, but when he has brought them safe to land they 'associate' (*sc.* other beings with God).

Sometimes the lesser deities were apparently regarded as interceding with the supreme God.[13] The temptation in the 'satanic verses' intruded after 53.19, 20 was probably to regard God as a supreme deity of this type besides whom there were lesser deities–perhaps to be identified with angels–who might intercede with him on behalf of those who showed honour to them.

Whatever the precise form of the pagan beliefs of those who opposed Muḥammad, and whatever non-religious motives they may have had, it is clear that at some point the Qur'ān began to attack all forms of polytheism with the utmost vigour. In some passages the pagan deities are not denied all reality, but are spoken of as a species of inferior beings, possibly angels or jinn, who have no power to thwart or even influence God's will though popularly supposed to be able to intercede with him. In other passages all reality is denied to them, and they are said to be mere names invented by the ancients. In yet other passages belonging to the Medinan period and perhaps with Christians in view, it is stated that messengers sent by God have wrongly had worship rendered to them, but that they will deny their worshippers at the Judgement. Chronologically the emphases probably came in the order in which they are described here.

After the appearances of opposition a change is also found in the statements about God's punishment of unbelievers and wrongdoers. On the one hand, it is frequently asserted that God will destroy or otherwise punish unbelieving peoples in this world. This theme is illustrated from a number of actual stories, the 'punishment stories' to be considered in chapter 8, section 2. On the other hand, the doctrine of the Last Day is further developed, and the torments of Hell and joys of Paradise are described in greater detail. In connection with this, however, several other matters seem to make their first appearance or to receive greater emphasis. It may be that the angels were first mentioned in connection with the Judgement. Certainly it is towards the end of the Meccan period that they are often spoken of as agents, either alone or with 'the spirit' (*ar-rūḥ*), of God's providence and revelation. About the same time the name of *ar-Raḥmān*, 'the Merciful', is introduced, and is perhaps accompanied by a deeper sense of *raḥma* or 'mercy'. It is presumably because of the deepening spiritual understanding of the believers that the Qur'ān begins to employ such terms expressive of their relation to God as *tawba*, 'repentance', *maghfira*, 'forgiveness', *kaffāra*, 'absolution', and *riḍwān*, 'approval'. Some of these may first have come after the Hijra.

The Hijra brought the Muslims into close contact with Jews. Muḥammad seems at first to have expected that the Jews would recognize the identity of the revelation given to him with what they had in the Hebrew Bible, and was prepared to be friendly with them. It soon became evident, however, that the Jews were not prepared to accept the Qur'ān as revelation, and relations between them and the Muslims deteriorated. The Muslims learnt too of the differences between Judaism and Christianity and were greatly puzzled, since they regarded both as based on genuine revelations from God. Gradually an understanding of the solution of this problem was provided by the Qur'ān. It was linked with fresh emphasis on the figure of Abraham, especially on the fact that he was neither a Jew nor a Christian.[14] Though Jews and Christians believe that they worship 'the God of Abraham, Isaac and Jacob' and there is some continuity with the religion of these men, it is also a fact that the Jewish religion can be said at earliest to begin with Jacob (Abraham's grandson), though the main revelation only came with Moses. In the Qur'ān Abraham is connected with Mecca, but the contemporaries of Muḥammad do not seem to have thought of Ishmael (Abraham's son) as their ancestor, though the descent of many Arabs from Ishmael (as alleged in the Old Testament) was accepted by later Muslim scholars.

The religion of Abraham, then, according to the Qur'ān, was a pure monotheism identical with the revelation given to Muḥammad. Similar, too, was the revelation given to Moses and Jesus, the prophets from whose work came the Jewish and Christian religions respectively. These religions were now different because their followers had perverted them through presumption, disobedience and jealousy. (Once again a more elaborate theory was developed by later Muslim scholars.) The adherent of this pure religion was called at first a *ḥanīf*, a new word apparently in Arabic, whose plural unfortunately resembled the word for 'pagans' in Syriac. Later he was also called a *muslim*, 'one surrendered (to God)', and the religion of Abraham and of Muḥammad became correspondingly *islām* 'surrender (to God)'. One effect of this conception was to give Muḥammad a position as an independent prophet and his followers as an independent community, and thereby to remove the sting from Jewish criticisms of the Qur'ān.

The process of ideological and political adjustment to the hostility of the Jews of Medina culminated about March 624, just before the battle of Badr, in what is called 'the break with the Jews'; and this led to the appearance in the Qur'ān of new words and phrases which may be useful as an indication of date. Passages which appeal to the testimony of earlier monotheists, or which speak of the confirmation of previous revelations, are either Meccan or – perhaps more frequently – early Medinan. Those which speak of more than one messenger to the same people imply a growing awareness of the Jewish religion among Muslims, and are thus late Meccan or Medinan. The word *nabī*, 'prophet', and most words derived from Hebrew, are Medinan. Abraham is spoken of as a prophet only in Medina, and his close association with Ishmael probably belongs to the same time. The word *ḥanīf* and the phrase *millat Ibrāhīm*, 'the religion of Abraham', first come just before 'the break with the Jews'. The use of *islām*, *muslim* and the verb *aslama* (in a religious sense) do not occur earlier than that, and may well be later. It was probably about the same time that the Qur'ān began to speak of Muḥammad receiving 'the Book', but since the word 'book' has other meanings, it is not always helpful in dating. After 'the break with the Jews' there seem to have been few changes of emphasis in Qur'ānic teaching on doctrinal matters.

Some miscellaneous words and ideas which give an indication of date may be briefly mentioned. All passages which recommend fighting or speak of the Prophet's followers being engaged in fighting are necessarily Medinan. It was at Medina too that the maintenance of the morale of the community became of concern to Muḥammad and the Muslims, so that condemnation of *fasād*, 'corruption', 'treason', must be Medinan. The word *fitna* which may have a similar meaning is too ambiguous to be a safe guide, but most of its occurrences are probably Medinan; the same is true of *shiqāq*, 'schism'. Medinan too are the demand to obey the Messenger, the use of the phrase 'God and the Messenger', and the threat of 'humiliation in this world' directed against Jews and other opponents.

The designations applied to opponents vary from time to time. *Kāfir*, 'unbeliever', with the plural *kāfirūn*, is often used throughout the Qur'ān, though it perhaps refers specially to the early emphasis on God's bounty, since in its non-technical use the verb *kafara* means 'to be ungrateful'. The alternative plural form *kuffār* is Medinan only. *Al-mushrikūn*, 'those who ascribe partners (to God)', is a general name for idolaters at all periods. *Alladhīna kafarū*, 'those who have been ungrateful' or 'who have disbelieved', is a frequent designation of the Meccans (though not restricted to them) and continues into Medinan times. *Al-mushrikūn ... Al-mujrimūn*, 'the sinners', seems to be late Meccan and early Medinan. *Alladhīna ẓalamū*, 'those who have done wrong', is Medinan and seems to be often applied to the Jews. *Muhājirūn*, 'Emigrants', and *anṣār*, 'Helpers', are of course Medinan. Uncertain supporters in Medina were at first referred to as *alladhīna fī qulubi-him maraḍ*, 'those in whose hearts is disease'; their conduct at the battle of Uḥud earned them the nickname of *munāfiqūn*, usually rendered 'Hypocrites'. Towards the close of Muḥammad's life this word is applied to a different group of opponents.

EIGHT

THE NAMES OF THE REVEALED MESSAGE

The matters to be considered in this chapter rise out of the use of certain words in the Qur'ān to describe the book as a whole or parts of it. The words in question are: *āyāt*, 'signs' or 'verses'; *mathānī*, 'oft-repeated' (?), and perhaps to be interpreted as 'punishment-stories'; *al-qur'ān*; *al-kitāb*, 'the book'; and *tanzīl*, 'sending down', *dhikr*, etc., 'admonition', and *al-furqān*. In respect of the last three it is only the meaning and interpretation of the terms which will be discussed; but the others suggest further lines of investigation and further problems. Thus one may ask whether these terms occur throughout the period when the Qur'ān was being revealed or only at certain times within the period. Richard Bell has argued that there was a point at which the use of the term *al-qur'ān* ceased, and that in the latest revelations only the term 'the book' is used of the whole corpus of revelation. It is also to be asked whether the 'signs' of God's goodness and power belong to the earlier years only or to the whole of Muḥammad's prophethood. This line of investigation then opens out into another, namely, the extent to which the different terms indicate different types of material. This question applies chiefly to the first two terms. Punishment-stories, whether called *mathānī* or not, constitute a special type of material, and presumably do not belong to the earliest period of all. With these points in mind we may proceed to examine the use of the various terms.

1. Signs

There are many references in the Qur'ān to *āyāt* (sing. *āya*), which are normally to be understood as 'signs' in a variety of connected senses. For the purposes of exposition four usages or applications of the word may be distinguished: (1) natural phenomena which are signs of God's power and bounty; (2) events or objects associated with the work of a messenger of God and tending to confirm the truth of the message; (3) signs which are recited by a messenger; (4) signs which are part of the Qur'ān or of the Book.

(1) In some passages which are probably early Meccan there are said to be signs for men 'in the earth . . . and in yourselves' [50.20f.], or 'in the heavens and the earth . . . and in your (mankind's) creation and the beasts he spreads abroad' [45.3/2f.]. Various phenomena are likewise said to be among God's signs [41.37, 39; 42. 29/8, 32/1]. Apart from the specific mention of phenomena as signs, however, there is a great number of passages in which phenomena of nature and human life are described as evidences of God's power or of the benefits he has bestowed on men. Although these passages do not contain the word 'sign' they may properly be considered 'sign-passages' in view of the verses quoted. Such sign-passages are an important type of Qur'ānic material. The phenomena most frequently cited are: the creation of the heavens and the earth, the creation or generation of man, the various uses and benefits man derives from the animals, the alternation of night and day, the shining of sun, moon and stars, the changing winds, the sending of rain from the sky, the revival of parched ground and the appearance of herbage, crops and fruits, the movement of the ship on the sea and the stability of the mountains. Less frequently cited are: shadows, thunder, lightning, iron, fire, hearing, sight, understanding and wisdom. In four passages [2.28/6; 10.4; 22.66/5; 30.40/39] belonging to the Medinan or late Meccan period, the resurrection of men is included as one of the signs.

The enumeration of these signs in nature and in men serves various purposes. In some cases they embody a call for gratitude to God [16.14; 30.46/5; 36.73] or an invitation to worship him [6.104; 10.3]. Sometimes they are used as evidence of God's creative power as contrasted with the impotence of the false gods [16.10-20]. Sometimes they are used as evidence of God's power to raise the dead [22.5], or to inflict punishment. In general these passages set before us the idea of a powerful and exalted but beneficent deity. They are incompatible with the view that the Qur'ān attempted to bring men to accept Islam by describing the terrors of the coming Judgement. In such passages there is rather an appeal to men to respond to God's bounty.

Sign-passages occur in each of the periods into which the revelation may be divided. Since they refer to permanent objects and constant natural processes, no growth is to be traced in the list of phenomena mentioned as signs. Gardens and palms, vines and pomegranates were doubtless more common in Medina than in Mecca, and it would seem that they are not mentioned in the earlier sign-passages; but to argue that all passages mentioning these were revealed at Medina would be to go beyond the evidence. Another feature of the sign-passages is that there is the semblance of a fixed order in which the signs are mentioned, and there are certainly frequent repetitions. Careful examination, however, shows that there is no one definite order, and that therefore no significance can be attached to the rough semblance of an order. In each passage the signs mentioned are presumably those appropriate to the occasion of revelation.

Richard Bell, who gave much attention to the sign-passages, suggested that some of them were older than the suras in which they stand, such as: 2.21/19, 22/20, 28/6f.; 80.25-31; 88.17-20. Many of them, too, had been revised and adapted to their present position, such as: 6.95-99, 141/2-144/5; 10.102; 13.2-4, 12/13-15/16; 16.3-16; 41.37-40. Occasionally these revisions introduced a reference to resurrection, as in 23.12-16 and 35.9/10-14/15. The latter passage, like 7.57/5f., brings resurrection into connection with the sign of the revival of dead land by the coming of rain, a sign peculiarly apt in Arabia, where the effect of rain is almost miraculous. Other passages where the mention of resurrection was thought by Bell to have been added in the course of revision are 43.11/10, where a detachable rhyme-phrase seemed to have been inserted, and 30.48/7-51/0, where he thought that there was an addition in 49/8 and that the latter half of 50/49 had also been added. If the hypothesis of revision at these points is accepted, it would probably follow that the sign of the revival of dead land had first been used independently of the question of resurrection as a sign of God's power and bounty. It is the case that most passages including this sign use it in this latter way; e.g. 2.164/59; 16.65/7; 25.49/51; 32.27; 36.33; 43.11/10; 45.5/4. The use of the word *raḥma* for 'rain' in 7.57/5 tends to support the view that this sign-passage is early, since *raḥma* acquires a different meaning in later revelations which speak of Judgement and future reward.

Another sign frequently mentioned is that God originates a creature and then restores it [10.4, 34/5; 17.51/3; 21.104; 27.64/5; 29.20/19; 30.11/10, 27/6; 34.49/8; 85.18]. In most of these passages the reference to resurrection is clear, though in one or two it is doubtful. Thus in 29.19/18f. the natural interpretation of the phrase is of the return of vegetation without any reference to resurrection. Similarly in the recurring phrases 'he gives life and causes to die' and 'he brings the dead from the living and the living from the dead' the reference may originally have been to purely natural events.

There is bound to remain an element of hypothesis in the view that passages speaking of the revival of dead land as a sign of God's power and bounty have been revised to bring in a reference to the resurrection. If the arguments are sound, they add to the evidence for the existence of revision. For most purposes, however, the point to be emphasized is that the revival of dead land is *both* a sign of God's power and bounty *and also* an argument for the possibility of resurrection. It should also be emphasized that, while sign-passages are an important part of the contents of the Qur'ān, the word 'sign' is also used in other senses. Until the other senses have been discussed it is best to defer considering the question whether sign-passages were first made public as independent units.

(2) The word 'sign' is also applied to events or objects associated with the work of a messenger of God and tending to confirm the message he bears. Thus in 43.46/5 Moses is sent to Pharaoh and his nobles with God's signs. These are presumably the changing of the rod into a serpent and then the plagues, for it is said [43. 48/7] that every sign God showed them was greater than the previous one. The production of the sign is God's doing, and another verse [40.78] plainly asserts that to no messenger is it given to produce a sign. In this sense of the word signs are far from showing God's goodness, but may be described as being 'sent only to frighten'

[17.59/61]. The signs of Moses are also mentioned in 20.17/18-24/5 (combined in verses 47/9 to 56/8 with the signs in nature of God's bounty), 27.12-14, 7.130/27-136/2 and other passages. Other messengers had special signs accorded to them as a confirmation of the truth of their message; with Ṣāliḥ was sent a she-camel as a sign to Thamūd [7.73/1; etc.], while Jesus brought as a sign the miracle of the bird of clay which became alive [3.49/3]. The destruction of unbelieving peoples is a sign [15.73-5; etc.], and similarly the deliverance of the believers [29.24/3; etc.]. In 54.15 Noah's ship (or, less probably, his story) is left as a sign to warn men that unbelievers and the disobedient are destroyed.

When Muḥammad's opponents demanded of him a sign it was presumably something of this kind that they wanted [6.37; 13.7/8; 21.5]. As already noted, the Qur'ān insisted that only God produced signs, and that no messenger could do this of his own volition. Such is the obstinacy of the opponents that, even if Muḥammad brought them a sign (presumably of this type) – so it is asserted in 30.58 – they would still not believe. In the later years of Muḥammad's life some of his external successes could be referred to as signs, such as the anticipated gaining of spoils in 48.20 about the time of the treaty of al-Ḥudaybiya, and above all the victory of Badr [3.13/11]. The discussion below of the meaning of Furqān is also relevant here. It was probably this demand for a sign during the Meccan period that led to the shift of meaning of the word *āya* to something like 'revealed message'. The messages which came to Muḥammad by the mysterious process of *waḥy* or revelation were the real signs of his truth. This process and the messages he received through it were the evidence (*bayyina*) on which he took his stand [6.57; 47.14/15]; at the same time the evidence was something to be recited [11.17/20].

In so far as the signs are events connected with previous messengers from God they are not far removed from the category of punishment-stories to be discussed in the next section. Signs in contemporary events like the battle of Badr are hardly in this category, though in a sense the underlying principle is the same, namely, God's punitive action in history. In what follows the term 'sign-passages' will be restricted to those which speak of signs in natural phenomena, but it must be insisted that these are not the only signs of which the Qur'ān speaks.

(3) There are many verses which speak of signs being recited. When God's signs are recited, the faith of the believers increases [8.2]. This reciting of signs is the work of messengers sent by God [as in 39.71]; but in most instances in which the phrase is used the reference is to Muḥammad himself [e.g. 31.7/6; 45.25/4; 46.7/6; 62.2; 65.11]. In 45.6/5 the signs are recited to Muḥammad by God himself or by the angels as his envoys. In a number of passages [8.31; 68.15; 83.13], when Muḥammad recites the signs, his opponents criticize them as 'old-world fables' (*asāṭīr al-awwalīn*). By itself this phrase suggests punishment-stories [especially 8.31 and 68.15]. On the other hand, there are a number of passages where the phrase is applied to 'what God has promised', that is, resurrection and judgement [e.g. 23.83/5; 27.68/70; 46.17/16;] and in these it might rather be interpreted of sign-passages. It is also possible there, however, that resurrection and judgement are thought of together, and punishment-stories would then be more appropriate. Thus the presumption is that 'the reciting of signs' is chiefly of punishment-stories, but sign-passages cannot be wholly excluded. Whatever the precise reference in the 'reciting of signs', the idea of reciting leads on to the next usage of the word *āya*.

(4) The signs may be part of the Qur'ān or of 'the book', and will then come close to having the meaning of 'verses'. The word *āya*, of course, regularly means 'verse' in later Arabic, but the modern scholar is justified in asking whether it ever has this meaning in the Qur'ān itself, or whether it has been read into the Qur'ān by later Muslims. The strongest evidence for the meaning of 'verse' in the Qur'ān itself is in passages which speak of an *āya* being cancelled or forgotten and a better or the like given instead [2.106/0] and one *āya* being substituted for another [16.101/3]; but even there the meaning might conceivably be a whole passage. The same may be said about 24.1 ('a sura in which we have sent down signs as evidences') and 31.2/1 ('the *āyāt* of the wise book'). A further problem is raised by such a phrase as 'a book whose *āyāt* have been made distinct' [41.3/2]. Some Muslim scholars

thought that the last part, translating the word *fuṣṣilat*, should rather be rendered 'have been marked with *fawāṣil* or rhyme-phrases', and there are several passages where *āyāt* are connected with some part of *faṣṣala*; the agent is God if any is mentioned. This rendering seems unlikely, however, in the light of such a verse as 6.119 where it is said of God *faṣṣala la-kum mā ḥarrama 'alay-kum*, 'he has made distinct for you what he has forbidden to you'. The word *bayyana* and its derivatives are also frequently connected with *āyāt*, presumably with the sense of 'making clear or distinct'. Thus apart from – at most – one or two instances the word *āya* in the Qur'ān means 'sign' and not 'verse'.

It may well be that sign-passages, where natural phenomena are described as signs of God's power and goodness, were an important element in the early revelations. On other grounds these aspects are known to have been emphasized in the early period. On the other hand, many sign-passages tend to be dated 'late Meccan' or 'early Medinan', and they presuppose a measure of scepticism. The punishment-stories presuppose opposition, but are not clearly later in date than most of the sign-passages. In general the signs come to be spoken of as revealed messages which may be recited and are parts of 'the book', but are seldom, if ever, single verses.

2. Stories of punishment; *al-mathānī*

In dealing with the second usage of 'sign' it has been noted that punishment-stories constitute a definite type of material found in the Qur'ān. In the present section the punishment-stories will first be examined as a distinct category. Then the question will be considered whether they may be identified with 'the seven *mathānī*'. The stories under this head are as follows.

(A) The story of 'Ād. The name of this people occurs in pre-Islamic poetry, but no definite details are given. According to the Qur'ān, they were a great people of old, perhaps giants [7.69/7], who built 'signs' on eminences [26.128]; their buildings were still to be seen. Whether they are to be identified with Iram of the pillars, mentioned in 89.7/6, is a moot point which depends upon the reading and construction of that passage, and cannot be settled. It is, however, the simplest and most natural interpretation. To them the messenger Hūd was sent; but they disbelieved and were destroyed by a wind which blew for seven nights and days and wiped out everything except the buildings. (See Index).

(B) The story of Thamūd. Thamūd was a real people of ancient Arabia. They are mentioned in an inscription of Sargon, in Ptolemy, Pliny and other classical writers, as well as in pre-Islamic Arab poetry. They seem to have been associated with the North West of Arabia, particularly with al-Ḥijr (Medā'in Ṣāliḥ). They are spoken of as having bored the rock in the wadi [89.9/8], having built castles in level places and hewn out the mountain for houses [7.74/2] – presumably a reference to the remains of buildings and rock-hewn tombs to be found there. Their buildings were still to be seen [27.52/3; 29.38/7]. To them a messenger, Ṣāliḥ, one of themselves, was sent, and as a proof of the truth of his message a she-camel and a foal were miraculously produced, which were to be respected and given a share of the water. Thamūd, however, disbelieved, and hamstrung the camel. They were destroyed by an earthquake [7.78/6], by a thunderbolt of punishment [41.17/16; 51.44], or by a 'shout' sent upon them [54.31]. The unspecified people of 23.31/2-41/3, who were destroyed by the 'shout', are probably Thamūd, if they are to be identified at all, and are not merely a type.

(C) The men of al-Ḥijr are probably Thamūd. Though the tribe and place are never definitely associated in the Qur'ān, in 15.80-84, the only passage in which they are mentioned, they are said to have hewn out houses from the mountains, and to have been overwhelmed in the morning by the 'shout' for having turned away from the 'signs'. This corresponds to what is said of Thamūd.

(D) The people of Midian. Of them little definite information is given. The only special item in their story is that Shu'ayb, the messenger sent to them, exhorts them to give full measure and just weight. Like other disbelieving peoples, they were destroyed – by an earthquake or by a 'shout'.

(E) The men of the Grove or Thicket referred to in 15.78f., 38.13/12 and 50.14/13, seem, from the only account given of them, 26.176-91, to be identical with the people of Midian, for their messenger is Shu'ayb, and they also are exhorted to give full measure and just weight.[1]

(F) The men of ar-Rass are referred to in lists of disbelieving peoples who were destroyed, but no details are given [25.38/40; 50.12]. Rass is a word meaning 'well', but it is impossible to identify the place or the people.

(G) The people of Tubba' no doubt were a South Arabian people, since the title is held to be that of the kings of the Ḥimyarites. They are included in a list of peoples punished for unbelief [50.13], and are cited in 44.37/6; but no details of what happened to them are given.

(H) Sabā' (Sheba). Whether this is the same people under another name, we cannot say. A long account of Solomon and the Queen of Sheba is given in sura 27, but, as a punishment-story, the fate of Sheba is dealt with only in 34.15/14-19/18, and it does not conform to the usual type. No messenger is mentioned as having been sent to them, but they had a sign given them – two gardens, evidently fruitful. They turned away, and the flood of the dam (*sc.* of Ma'rib) came upon them and apparently ruined the fertility of their gardens. In the latter part of the story, there seems to be a reference to the decay of the Sabaean caravan trade; and this is apparently regarded as a punishment for the lengthening of the daily stages to be covered by the caravans.

(I) Noah. Something may have been known in pre-Islamic Arabia of the story of Noah and the Flood, though the references in early Arab poetry are doubtful. In the Qur'ān, the people of Noah are frequently referred to as having been destroyed for unbelief. As a developed story it is repeated in some ten places. Usually Noah is sent as a messenger to his people; and they disbelieve and are drowned, while he and those who believe are saved in the Ship (Ark). In some of the passages, however, particularly in 11.25/7-48/50, the story is expanded so as to include details of the Old Testament story and elements from extra-Biblical Jewish tradition. In another set of passages (e.g. 4.163/1) Noah appears as a prophet, and the punishment side of the story falls into the background.

(J) Abraham. As a *ḥanīf*, a prophet, and founder of the religion of Abraham, he is frequently mentioned. The story of his attacking the idol-worship of his father and people, and, when disbelieved, withdrawing from them is related in 19.41/2-49/50; 21.52/1-72; 26.69-102; and 37.83/1-101/99. This last passage comes nearest to the form of a punishment-story, but though his people are twice referred to in lists of earlier unbelievers, who presumably were destroyed, their destruction is never stated. The most that is said is that they were made 'the worst losers' [21.70] or 'the inferior' [37.98/6]. The story is found in Jewish tradition.

(K) Lot. The story of Lot appears in several passages without any connection between him and Abraham being mentioned. It is possible that there may have been a local tradition of this sort, for in several passages it is indicated that the locality of the story is known and can be seen [15.76; 37.137; ?25.40/2]. It conforms to the type of the punishment-story in that Lot is said to have been sent to his people. He accuses them of indecency and sodomy. When they oppose and threaten to expel him, he and his household are delivered, all except his wife, who 'lingered'. The town was then overwhelmed by an evil rain sent upon it, or by a gravel-storm [54.34]. Where the story is associated with the angels' visit to Abraham, it departs from the usual form in that Lot is no longer a messenger to his people, but is troubled when the messengers come to him. In 29.26/5 Lot is one of those who believe in Abraham, and in 21.71 he is delivered along with Abraham. In 21.74f. he is given jurisdiction and knowledge, so becoming a prophet rather than the messenger in a punishment-story.

(L) Al-Mu'tafikāt, the overwhelmed or subverted cities referred to in 9.70/1, 53.53/4f., and 69.9 are probably to be identified with the cities of the Plain, Sodom and Gomorrah, since they seem to stand in place of the people of Lot. The Arabic word is probably, as Hirschfeld suggested,[1a] adapted from the Hebrew *mahpēkhā*, which, in the Old Testament, is associated with the destruction of Sodom.

(M) Pharaoh is sometimes referred to, without mention of Moses, as an example of one who suffered for his unbelief (e.g. 54.41f.). In two passages he is described as *dhu l-awtād*, 'possessor of the pegs' or 'stakes' [38.12/11; 89.9]. What this refers to is unknown. It is improbable that, as Horovitz suggests,[2] it should refer to his buildings, and there seems to be nothing in Jewish tradition to explain it. It may be that some story about Pharaoh was current in Arabia, but the evidence is slender. Usually the Qur'ānic version accords with the Biblical story of Moses and Pharaoh. Sometimes it is reduced to the type of a punishment-story as in 23.45/7-48/50, but more often it is extended and has further details parallel to the Biblical account or to extra-Biblical Jewish tradition. In some of the versions the punishment of Pharaoh is a mere side-issue, the main object being to give an account of Moses and the Children of Israel.

(N) In 29.39/8f. and 40.23/4-25/6 Korah and Haman are associated with Pharaoh. In 28.76-82 Korah figures as one of the people of Moses who is given great wealth, but because of his pride and arrogance is destroyed through the earth sinking with him and his dwelling.

When these stories are examined, it will be seen that A to H inclusive belong to Arabian tradition, and perhaps also details from the others, especially M. Midian, of course, is mentioned in the Bible, and in two suras of the Qur'ān [20.40/2; 28.22/1-28, 45] is connected with Moses; but the stories in D and E are Arabian and not Biblical, though 28.45 may be taken as connecting the two. Other Arabian material is referred to in 105 (the repulse of the expedition of the elephant) and perhaps also in 85.1-9, if that is interpreted of the massacre of Christians in Najrān. Since no messenger is present in these cases, however, they do not have the form of a punishment-story. The remaining stories, I to N, are parallel to Bibilical stories but differ from these at various points. The Qur'ān usually presupposes some knowledge of its stories among the first hearers, and so the presumption is that the stories were current in Arabia in the form implied by the Qur'ān.

When one further considers the manner in which the stories are employed in the Qur'ān, it appears that there are seven main stories; and these are in fact included in a list in 22.42/3-44/3. They are: Noah (I), ʿĀd (A), Thamūd (B), the people of Abraham (J), the people of Lot (K), Midian (D), the people of Moses (M). It may further be noted that C is a duplicate of B, E of D and L of K. For F and G there are only references, not a story. There is only one occurrence of H; and N, though not a duplicate of M, may be called an outgrowth from it, since it is also connected with Moses. The case for considering the punishment-stories a separate element in the Qur'ān is strengthened when it is noticed that they commonly occur together in groups, though the constituents of the group vary. This is clearest if set out in tabular form; to make the relative lengths more obvious only the Flügel verse-numbering is given.

Sura 7: Noah [57-62]; ʿĀd [63-70]; Thamūd [71-77]; Lot [78-82]; Midian [83-91].
Sura 9: [list, v. 71] Noah, ʿĀd, Thamūd, Abraham, Midian, the Mu'tafikāt.
Sura 11: Noah [27.51]; ʿĀd [52-63]; Thamūd [64-71]; Abraham and Lot [72-84]; Midian [85-98].
Sura 14: [brief reference, v. 9] Noah, ʿĀd, Thamūd.
Sura 21: Moses and Aaron [49-51]; Abraham [52-73]; Lot [74f.]; Noah [76f.]; David and Solomon, Job, Jonah, Zacharias, Mary, etc. [78-94; not punishment-stories].
Sura 23: Noah [23-31]; unnamed, perhaps Thamūd [32-43]; others unnamed [44-46]; Moses [47-50].
Sura 25: Moses, Noah, ʿĀd, Thamūd, ar-Rass [37-42].
Sura 26: Moses [9-68]; Abraham [69-104]; Noah [105-22]; ʿĀd [123-40]; Thamūd [141-59]; Lot [160-75]; Midian [176-91].
Sura 27: Moses [7-14]; Sheba [15-45]; Thamūd [46-54]; Lot [55-59].
Sura 29: Noah [13f.]; Abraham [15-26]; Lot [27-34]; Midian [35f.]; ʿĀd, Thamūd [37]; Moses [38f.].
Sura 37: Noah [73-79]; Abraham [81-113]; Moses [114-22]; Elias [123-32]; Lot [133-38]; Jonah [139-48].
Sura 51: Abraham [24-37]; Moses [38-40]; ʿĀd [41f.]; Thamūd [43-45]; Noah [46].
Sura 53: ʿĀd, Thamūd, Noah, the Mu'tafikāt [51-54].
Sura 54: Noah [9-17]; ʿĀd [18-21]; Thamūd [23-32]; Lot [33-40]; Pharaoh [41f.].
Sura 69: Thamūd, ʿĀd, Pharaoh, the Mu'tafikāt [4-10].
Sura 89: ʿĀd, Thamūd, Pharaoh [5-13].

It is interesting to look at the slight differences in the versions of a single story, but space does not permit this here. It is more apposite to note that in some suras (e.g. 26) the stories with the exception of those of Moses and Abraham are assimilated to one another, and may also be marked off from one another by a refrain. The triad of Noah, ʿĀd and Thamūd appears nearly everywhere. In so far as any conclusions can be based on the dating of the suras, it would seem that 53, 54, 69 and 89 are early; and these contain besides this triad the stories of Pharaoh (without Moses) and that of Lot or the Mu'tafikāt. It would also seem that the fuller stories of Abraham and Moses occur only in later passages. That is to say, stories current in Mecca or in Arabia preponderate in the earlier passages and suras, and it is only at a later date that Biblical material is introduced. A further point to note is that the stories are almost exclusively of temporal and not of eschatological punishment. Exceptionally in sura 11 there are references to 'the day of resurrection' in some of the stories, namely, in that of ʿĀd [60/3] and of Pharaoh [98/100f.], while the series of stories is followed by a passage on the Last Judgement [103/5-108/10]. Resurrection and Judgement are also mentioned in the story of Abraham and his people (for whom there is no obvious temporal punishment) in 26.82-5.

At certain points the details of the stories appear to be adapted to the experiences of Muḥammad and his followers. The stories were presumably already familiar to the Muslims, and the main points are told briefly. In many suras the stories are then filled out by accounts, varying from version to version (but often similar in the same sura), of what was said by the messenger and by his opponents. In these accounts there are parallels to what is elsewhere set down as having been said by Muḥammad and his Meccan opponents. There is thus some justification for thinking that other details in the stories may reflect what was happening to Muḥammad. When Ṣāliḥ, for example, is said by his opponents to have been one of whom they had good hopes [11.62/5], this may be taken as confirming the statements that Muḥammad, before beginning to receive revelations, had a respected position in Mecca. The account [in 27.48/9-51/2] of the plot against Ṣāliḥ has features which are probably parallel to those of the Meccan plot to assassinate Muḥammad which is described in Tradition. Again, the account of Noah's preaching to his people in 71.1-20/19, especially the promise of rain as a blessing in 11/10, is more appropriate to the case of Muḥammad than to that of Noah; the distinction between proclaiming publicly and speaking secretly [8/7f.] would then confirm the Tradition that for a time he communicated revelations privately before 'proclaiming publicly',[3] and the passage would also support the suggestion that Muḥammad's early appeals were accompanied by the promise of material prosperity.

After this examination of the punishment-stories the question of the interpretation of the *mathānī* may be considered. The word occurs twice in the Qur'ān. In 15.87 God says to Muḥammad that he has bestowed on him 'seven of the *mathānī* and the mighty Qur'ān', while in 39.23/4 it is stated that 'God has sent down the best discourse, a book, self-resembling (consisting of or containing) *mathānī*, at which (book) the skins of those who fear their Lord do creep, but afterwards their skins and their hearts grow soft to the remembrance of their Lord'. There has been much discussion about the interpretation of these passages.

The Muslim commentators mostly take *mathānī* as the ordinary Arabic plural of *mathnā*, a word which occurs several times in the Qur'ān with some such meaning as 'twofold'. In the two instances of the plural they hold the meaning to be 'things doubled' or 'things repeated'. The favourite interpretation is then that the seven *mathānī* are the seven verses of the Fātiḥa, which are frequently repeated in formal worship and other occasions. Alternatively they may be the seven long suras, namely, suras 2 to 7 along with another whose identity is disputed. These two interpretations – the Fātiḥa and the seven long suras – may also be justified by taking a singular (*muthnī* or *muthnā*) from the fourth stem of the root with the idea of 'praise'; the *mathānī* are then recited to God's praise or contain it. These interpretations by Muslim scholars, though giving some sense to the number seven, do not explain the rest of the description of the *mathānī*.

Some European scholars inclined to the view that the Arabic word was borrowed, either from the Hebrew *mishnā*,[4] or more probably from the Syriac or Jewish-Aramaic *math-nīthā*.[5] The Jewish oral law as a whole is called *mishnā*, and the term may also be applied to any particular part of it; but this does not explain why the skins of those who fear the Lord should creep, and only explains the number seven on the assumption that *mishnā* can mean 'verse'. The majority opinion, however, has favoured the interpretation of 'punishment-stories', either on the ground that *mathānī* means 'things repeated'[6] or because it represents *mishnā* in the sense of 'story'.[7]

There is thus much to be said for the view that the *mathānī* are to be understood as the punishment-stories. It was noted above that there were seven main ones; and the existence of other minor ones is exactly in accordance with the implication of the phrase 'seven of the *mathānī*' that these were not all. The punishment-stories also fit the description in sura 39, for the punishments cause fear, while the deliverance of the messengers and their followers may be said to soften the heart. Some scholars (e.g. Horovitz) have hesitated to accept this interpretation because 15.87 distinguishes the *mathānī* from the Qur'ān. It is not impossible, however, that the punishment-stories originally had a separate existence. The assumption that this was so gains some support from the Tradition that a Meccan called an-Naḍr, wanting to bring Muḥammad into derision, procured stories of Persian kings and recited them in opposition to him. The Persian stories, if compared with most of the contents of the Qur'ān, would be inept; but if they were contrasted with the punishment-stories, they would be more interesting and more varied. The Qur'ānic stories resemble one another in two ways. Firstly, the general scheme is the same: a messenger is sent to a people; he delivers his message, but is disbelieved and the message rejected; the punishment of God then falls upon the people for their unbelief. Secondly, the form of words is often similar. If this point is thought important, 39.23/4 may be translated 'a book where the *mathānī* resemble one another'.

3. The Qur'ān

The word *qur'ān* occurs frequently in the text and has several distinct meanings. It may be the verbal noun of *qara'a* and then denotes the act of reciting, presumably from memory as in 17.78/80; 75.17f. The sense of 'reading' given in dictionaries is not appropriate to the conditions of Mecca in Muḥammad's day. It is probable that at first no attempt was made to write down the revealed messages, and writing presumably became the rule only after the Hijra to Medina. Even if the messages were written down, the writing of the time appears to have been little more than a mnemonic device to supplement the memory. The word *qur'ān* may also denote a single passage recited, as in 10.61/2 and 13.30/1, and perhaps also 10.15/16 and 72.1. Mostly, however, it seems to refer to some larger whole containing a collection of such passages already delivered or in process of being delivered. It should not be assumed, nevertheless, that this collection is identical with the Qur'ān as we now have it. It has just been noted that at one point the *qur'ān* is distinct from the *mathānī*, while its relation to 'the book' will be considered in the next section.

'This Qur'an', then, in whatever sense is to be given to the word when it denotes a collection, has been revealed by God [12.3] and sent down from him [4.82/4; 16.102/4; 27.6; 76.23]. It could not have been produced otherwise [10.37/8; 17.88/90]. It is to be recited by the Messenger [10.61/2; 16.98/100; 17.45/7; 27.92/4; 87.6; 96.1, 3], and to be listened to with respect [7.204/3; 47.24/6; 84.21]. It was sent down not all at once, but in separate pieces [17.106/7f.; 25.32/4]. High claims are made for it: it is glorious [50.1; 85.21], mighty [15.87], noble [56.77/6], and clear [15.1; 36.69].

It is evident from such assertions that the Qur'ān referred to had a special position and was of great importance. The implications of some passages should be noted, however. The frequent phrase 'this Qur'ān' must often mean not a single passage but a collection of passages, and thus seems to imply the existence of other Qur'āns. Similarly the phrase 'an Arabic Qur'ān' seems to imply that there may be Qur'āns in other languages. (The phrases occur in proximity in 39.27/8f.) When it is further remembered that the verb *qara'a* is probably not an original Arabic root, and that the noun *qur'ān* almost certainly came into Arabic to represent the Syriac *qeryānā*, meaning the scriptural reading or lesson in church, the way is opened to the solution of the problem. The purpose of an Arabic Qur'ān was to give the Arabs a body of lessons comparable to those of the Christians and Jews. It is known, too, not only from Tradition and continuing practice, but also from the Qur'ān itself that it was thus used liturgically [17.78/80; 73.20]. It is also implied that this Arabic Qur'ān was not merely comparable but essentially identical with the previous revelations, for it confirmed these [10.37/8]. Its teaching was to be found in them [26.196; 53.36/7; 87.18f.], and this agreement was a proof that Muḥammad was a messenger [20.133].

On the basis of his general Qur'ānic studies and an examination of the passages where the word itself occurs Richard Bell put forward the hypothesis of what he called 'the Qur'ān period', which followed 'an early period', from which only a few sign-passages and fragmentary exhortations to worship God have survived, and preceded the final or 'Book period'. The Qur'ān-period included the latter part of Muḥammad's residence at Mecca and his first year or so at Medina; and it is characterized by the fact that the revelations received or revised during this time envisage the production of an Arabic Qur'ān giving the gist of previous revelation.[8] The detailed account of the Qur'ān-period is derived from a list of passages and suras which Bell regarded as belonging to this period.[9]

He considered that the Qur'ān-period began about the same time as the institution of the *ṣalāt* or formal worship, or at least after Muḥammad had gained some adherents. This was a point marking a new orientation in his religious activity, and it was with this point and not with the beginnings of his mission that the passages traditionally regarded as early should be associated. Such are: the command to recite [96.1-5], the command to rise and warn [74.1-7], the exhortation (in Bell's interpretation) to compose the Qur'ān carefully [73.1, 2, 4b-8], and the assurance of aid in reciting [87.1-6, 8, 9]. These passages, Bell considered, were originally for Muḥammad himself, but exemplified the style in which the Qur'ān was to be composed. Founding on the reference to 'the coming wrath' in 74.5 (and the implications of 96.4f. and 73.5), Bell held that the early passages of the Qur'ān-period consisted mainly of proclamations of coming Judgement to be followed by rewards or punishments in the future life.

A feature of the Qur'ān-period is the appearance of edifying Biblical stories, such as that of Joseph. It is suggested in 12.3 that Muḥammad had previously been neglectful of these, presumably in the sense of not realizing their relevance. These stories of religious personalities differ from the punishment-stories, since their point is not the overthrow of unbelieving peoples but the example and consequent reward of the person. Even where persons from punishment-stories are referred to the emphasis is different; in 37.75/3-82/0 the transformation of the story of Noah from one type to the other may be observed. These personality-stories may also be grouped together and linked by introductory phrases or closing refrains (e.g. 21; 38).

The process of grouping might also be applied to short didactic-pieces, sign-passages and even punishment-stories. Bell considered sura 80 a good example of this, since it consisted of five pieces separate in origin yet when put together forming a unity. In sura 55 and the latter part of sura 77 refrain is used to unify the material. It was probably to the results of this process of grouping that shortly before or after the Hijra the word *sūra* came to be applied [cf. 24.1]. If, as suggested above (p. 58), sura is derived from a Syriac word meaning 'writing' or 'text', this would imply that the grouped material was written. The mysterious opening letters also imply something written, and it is curious that in several cases the next words are a phrase such as 'by the glorious Qur'ān' [50; cf. 36, 38]. Following the letters other forms of reference to the Qur'ān are found in suras 15, 20, 27 and 41; and it is an important fact, noted by Bell but perhaps not emphasized sufficiently, that in nearly all the suras where there are letters the first verse or two of the sura contains a reference to the Qur'ān or 'the book' or something similar. This suggests that the letters are somehow connected with the process of grouping short passages which Bell postulated.

Bell further held that the Qur'ān was 'definitely closed' about the time of the battle of Badr. One piece of evidence is that the word *qur'ān* is seldom found in revelations dated after this period. Where the word occurs in a passage which appears to be of later date [such as 9.111/2 and 73.20] the meaning can be taken to be 'a collection of recitations already completed' and not 'a collection of revelations still in process of being received'. This would apply also to the refrain in 54.17, 22, 32, 40, if these verses are late. This collection of recitations is not something to be communicated by the Messenger, but something to be used by the Muslims in the ritual of prayer. While it is conceivable that the passages mentioned may refer to a Qur'ān still in process of delivery, it is difficult to interpret 2.185/1 in this way. It is a command to fast during 'the month of Ramaḍān, in which the Qur'ān was sent down as guidance for the people, and as evidence of the guidance and of the *furqān*'. Muslim commentators take this to refer either to the beginning of the revelation to Muḥammad or to the sending down of the heavenly Qur'ān from the presence of God to the nearer heaven so as to be available for transmission to him.

There are other passages, too, in which, though the Qur'ān is not specifically mentioned, something seems to be sent down or revealed as a whole: 'we have sent it down on a blessed night' [44.3/2] or 'on the night of the *qadr*' [97.1]; 'what we sent down to our servant on the day of the *furqān*, the day the two parties met' [8.41/2]. The last phrase refers to the day of Badr, and the Furqān is thus associated with the victory. The battle took place in Ramaḍān, and the fast is probably to be regarded as one of thanksgiving.[10] 'What was sent down' was doubtless some form of the Qur'ān. The admonition to Muḥammad in 20.114/3 not to be in a hurry with the Qur'ān 'until the revealing of it to him is completed' may also refer to this event. Perhaps a written form of the collection of recitations was now produced as 'evidences of the guidance and of the *furqān*'; but if this had been so, it is strange that it has left not even a passing trace in Tradition.

Bell's hypothesis of a 'Qur'ān-period' is worthy of fuller consideration from scholars than it has so far received. It is based on careful scrutiny of the Qur'ān in minute detail and contains many acute observations. Even if the hypothesis as a whole is not accepted, scholars must still come to terms with the underlying facts. The points of strength in Bell's view may be summarized as follows. (1) There is certainly a move from the general use of *al-qur'ān* in earlier passages to the almost exclusive use of *al-kitāb* in the latest passages. (2) There is much to commend the suggestion of a gradual change in the meaning of *al-qur'ān*. Some change of meaning is universally admitted, since the word may mean either a single short passage or the complete collection of revelations. It is by no means impossible that there was also an intermediate meaning, namely, a collection of passages suitable for liturgical use. (3) There are certainly passages which speak of the sending down of the Qur'ān as a whole, and it is improbable that the original meaning was that it was sent down to the lowest heaven. It is perhaps worth asking whether this sending down in the month of Ramaḍān could refer to a series of revelations in which there was a repetition of previous revelations now collected into groups or suras; such a repetition, even with modifications or additions, could easily have come in a single day or within a few days. (4) Also to be commended is the view that originally isolated passages were grouped together with some measures of adaptation. This grouping need not have been by Muḥammad's conscious effort, but could have come about through *waḥy* or revelation.

The chief weakness in Bell's hypothesis is that it makes a sharp distinction between the Qur'ān-period and the book-period without showing precisely in what the distinction consists (apart from the name). Some of the evidence rather suggests that there was a gradual transition from the one usage to the other. Bell allows that the period when opening letters appeared spanned the change-over; and some of the verses following the letters have both words, e.g. 'Ḥā', Mīm. A revelation from the Merciful, the Compassionate, a Book whose *āyāt* have been made separate (or distinct) as an Arabic Qur'ān for a people who have knowledge' [41.1-3/2; cf. 15.1; 27.1; 28.85f.; 58.77/6f.]. A gradual change would also explain how *al-qur'ān* could always be interpreted as equivalent to 'the Book', except where it clearly means a single passage or the act of reciting. Another point in which some might find difficulty is the assertion that from an early date the Qur'ān spoke of eschatological punishment, whereas Bell usually insisted that eschatological punishment was not early. This difficulty is more apparent than real; it presupposes that the punishment-stories, which speak of temporal punishment, belong to the period before the Qur'ān-period. There is also some difficulty about the idea of an early period, but this is lessened when it is realized that the view that 96.1-5 is the first revelation is probably only the conjecture of a later Muslim scholar, based on the appropriateness of the opening word *iqra'*. The real difficulty about the conception of an early period is the tentative character of most of the assertions about it.

4. The Book

Whatever view is taken of the hypothesis of a distinct Qur'ān-period, it is a fact that the word *qur'ān* is seldom used in the latest passages. Instead there are references to 'the Book' (*al-kitāb*), and it is implied that this is still in process of being revealed. Perhaps the contrast between 'the Book' and 'the Qur'ān' or 'recitation' also implies that the revelations were now written down shortly after they came to Muḥammad. Certainly his function is now represented not as that of warning people of punishment but as that of producing a book. Thus in sura 19 he is commanded: 'in the Book mention Mary . . . Abraham . . . Moses . . . Ishmael . . . Idrīs' [verses 16, 41/2, 51/2, 54/5, 56/7].

The special sense just mentioned must be distinguished from other meanings of the word *kitāb*. It may simply mean 'something written', 'a letter' [24.33; 27.28f.]. In connection with the Last Judgement it may mean the record of a man's deeds, no doubt suggesting to the hearers the kind of account that was kept in Meccan business circles. Thus each man is given his *kitāb* in his right or left hand according as it shows a credit or a debit balance [17.71/3; 69.19, 25; 84.7, 10]. What is written may also be a kind of ledger kept by the angels who watch over the actions of men [82.10-12]. On the Day of Judgement the book will be produced [18.49/7], and the pages spread open [81.10]. The word is also specially associated with God's knowledge, perhaps in a metaphorical sense; e.g. 'there is no beast on earth but God provides its sustenance; he knows its lair and its resting-place (or its resting in the womb and its time of birth); all is in a clear book' [11.6/8].[11] The dead are said to remain in the book of God until the resurrection [30.56]. What God has decreed is in a book before it happens [57.22].

It has been suggested that the application of the word *kitāb* to the written scriptures of Jews, Christians and Muslims is derived from this conception of the book of God's knowledge, and in some Medinan passages it is difficult to say whether the reference is to God's knowledge or to actual written scriptures [8.75/6; 17.4; 33.6]. It is unlikely, however, that this suggestion is correct. When *al-kitāb* is used in connection with Jews or Christians, it always refers not to any heavenly book, but to the scriptures actually in their hands in written form. Confirmation of the truth of Muḥammad's revelations is to be sought from those who 'recite the Book' [10.94], or 'have knowledge of the Book' [13.43]. The phrase is indeed parallel to *hak-kāthūbh* among the Jews and *hē graphē* among Greek-speaking Christians. This is doubtless what is intended when those who hold that angels are female are asked to produce 'their Book' [37.157; 43.21/0; cf. 35.40/38]. The Book is thus the source and authority for religious belief [cf. 22.8].

In the case of the religion of Islam the term 'the Book' became more appropriate at Medina when the revelations to Muḥammad came to include appeals, exhortations and regulations which were not so suitable for recitation in public worship. At the same time the Muslims were doubtless learning more about the contents of the Book in the hands of the Jews. The controversy with the Jews and the assertion that Islam was a religion distinct from Judaism and Christianity further made it essential that the Muslims should have a Book comparable to that of the other monotheists. This is implicit in such a verse as: 'He has sent down to you (Muḥammad) the Book with the truth, confirming what was before it; and he sent down the Torah and the Evangel previously as guidance for the people...' [3.3/2; cf. 2.89/3; 3.7/5; 4.105/6; 5.48/52; 6.92; 16.64/6; 46.12/11, 30/29].

The point at which the function of the messenger came to be spoken of as the production of a Book cannot be precisely determined, since the word *kitāb* is frequently used in various ways, and the transition from *qur'ān* to *kitāb* may have been gradual. In so far as 'the Book' came into existence, the beginning of it may have been sura 2, which opens with the words:

'Alif, Lām, Mīm. That is the Book, in which there is no doubt, guidance for the pious. . . .' After an introduction of a general nature addressed to believers, and mentioning unbelievers and Hypocrites, the story of Adam is given, followed by an appeal to the Israelites (that is, the Jews of Medina). This would be appropriate as the commencement of the Book. It is also to be noted that in suras, 3 7, 10, 11, 12, 13, 14, 15 – all those up to this point which have opening letters – the letters are immediately followed by an assertion about 'the Book'. It may well be, then, that these suras were given something like their present form as parts of the Book. Sura 2 contains material which must have been revealed before the break with the Jews, and therefore before the battle of Badr. Since the sending down of the Qur'ān is connected with the battle of Badr, it is unlikely that the Book can have been explicitly begun until some time later, unless the Qur'ān and the Book were thought of for a time as distinct and independent of one another. Once the production of the Book was under way, the presumption is that earlier material was incorporated into it.

It can be safely asserted that the Book was never completed. Indeed it is possible that the work of producing it was abandoned, that is, the arranging in an appropriate order of the previously revealed passages. The necessities of a community fighting for its life against external enemies and the constant demand for administrative decisions about its internal affairs and the structure of its social life meant that the rearrangement of earlier revelations could be given only a low priority. It is likely that the larger part of our present Qur'ān was left by Muḥammad in the form in which we have it, as suggested above. The present text would then substantially represent the Book, and so the Book must have contained (in principle) all that had come to Muḥammad by revelation. On Bell's assumption of a Qur'ān limited to certain passages suitable for liturgical recitation, passages which had been included in this limited Qur'ān might have been further revised to fit them for inclusion in the Book. He suggested that this might have happened in the case of suras 13 and 14; in sura 12 he thought that the two openings – verse 3 and verses 1 and 2 – belonged to the Qur'ān and the Book respectively. The Book was thus to be the complete corpus of his revelations, comprising the sign-passages, the punishment-stories, the restricted Qur'ān and any further passages which might be revealed to him. Thus the conception of 'the Book' is in fact the conception of the Qur'ān as we now have it.

5. Other names

Certain other words are also used in the Qur'ān for what is revealed. These emphasize different aspects of the message, but are not so central as the terms already considered.

(a) *tanzīl*. The word *tanzīl* is the verbal noun from *nazzala*, 'to send down', and so means 'the sending down'. It is noteworthy that the phrase *tanzīlu l-kitāb* occurs in the headings of suras 32, 39, 40, 45, 46, all of which except 39 have mysterious letters. The heading of 41, however, runs: 'Ḥā' Mīm, a *tanzīl* from the Merciful ... a Book ...; and *tanzīl* might therefore mean 'what is sent down' or 'a revealed message'. There is something similar in 20.4/3 and 36.5/4 (where it is perhaps an alternative heading) and also in 26.192, 56.80/79 and 69.43. In so far as this word may be regarded as a name for the Qur'ān or part of it, it emphasizes its revealed character. It usually occurs in proximity to the terms 'Qur'ān' or 'Book' or both.

(b) *dhikr*, *dhikrā*, *tadhkira*. These nouns are from the verb *dhakara*, 'to remember, to mention', which in the second stem *dhakkara* has the meaning 'to remind, to admonish'. In several passages Muḥammad is instructed to remind or admonish people, and in 88.21 he himself is called an admonisher, *mudhakkir*. The three nouns cited are often used in association with this sense of the verb; *dhikr* is thus found in 7.63/1, 69/7; 12.104; 38.87; 68.52 and 81.27; *dhikrā* is found in 6.69/8, 90; 11.114/6, 120/1 and 74.31/4; *tadhkira* is found in 69.48; 73.19 and 76.29. In so far as these words are applied to the revealed message or a part of it the aspect intended is obvious and was certainly present. Indeed in 38.1 the Qur'ān is described as *dhū dh-dhikr*, 'having the reminder'. It should be noted, however, that these words have a rich semantic development in Arabic religious writing. Even in the Qur'ān *dhikr* has sometimes [as in 2.200/196; 5.91/3; 62.9; 63.9] the sense of public or private worship. This usage might be influenced by Hebrew or Syriac where words from cognate roots are used to denote parts of or kinds of religious service; but it could be a simple development of one of the meanings of *dhikr Allah* in Arabic, namely, man's remembrance of God.

(c) *furqān*. The word *furqān*, which occurs seven times in the Qur'ān, appears to be derived from the Jewish-Aramaic *purqān* or, more probably the Syriac *purqāna* with the basic meaning of 'salvation'.[12] The Arabic root *faraqa*, 'to separate', however, may have affected the precise connotation of the word. It is mostly associated with revelation, and for this reason has often been regarded as an alternative name for the Qur'ān. The occurrences of the word may be classified as follows:

(1) the Furqān as something given to Moses

2.53/0: ... when we gave Moses the Book and the Furqān.

21.48/9: We gave Moses and Aaron the Furqān and illumination and a reminder for those who show piety.

(2) the Furqān promised to the Muslims (before Badr)

8.29: O believers, if you show piety towards God, he will appoint for you a Furqān and will absolve you from your evil deeds and will forgive you.

(3) the Furqān is sent down to Muḥammad on the day of Badr

8.41/2: ... if you have believed in God and what we sent down to our servant on the day of the Furqān, the day the two parties met.

2.185/1: ... the month of Ramaḍān in which the Qur'ān was sent down as guidance for the people and as Evidences of the guidance and of the Furqān.

(4) other references to the sending down of the Furqān to Muḥammad

3.3/2: he has sent down to thee the Book with the truth, confirming what was before it, and he sent down the Torah and the Evangel aforetime as guidance for the people, and he sent down the Furqān.

25.1: Blessed be he who has sent down the Furqān upon his servant that he may be to the worlds a warner.

These occurrences of the word appear to come in revelations which may be dated shortly before and after the battle of Badr.[13] In 8.29 (which on general grounds is dated about the time of Badr) the Furqān has not yet been received by the

Muslims, whereas 8.41/2 identifies the Day of the Furqān with the Day of Badr. The passage containing 2.53/0 is an appeal to the Jews to prepare for the Last Judgement by accepting the guidance from Muḥammad, and must be much earlier than Badr; and 21.48/9 is probably of similar date. The root *faraqa* is used in 5.25/8 in a prayer to God to 'separate' or 'discriminate' (*fa-fruq*) between Moses (with Aaron) and the reprobate people, where the implication probably is that the brothers are not to suffer for the sins of the people. In another account [7.145/2-156/5] of the giving of the tablets of the Law to Moses and the incident of the calf (with which the Furqān is connected in 2.53/0), the worshippers of the calf are treated differently from those who did evil and repented [151/0-153/2]; and this is a discrimination, even if the root *faraqa* is not used. In view of the words in 156/5 'we have become Jews (in devotion) towards thee', it is further possible that the Furqān is to be thought of as the separation of a community of believers from the unbelievers. Just before Badr the Muslims had been concerned to distinguish themselves from the Jews as a community, and at Badr a 'separation' was made between the Muslims and the Meccan pagans.[14]

In the last resort, however, the meanings suggested, such as 'salvation', 'deliverance' and 'separation' do not wholly fit the last three passages in the above list in that these include the word 'sent down' (*nazzala*, *anzala*). By this time these words had become almost technical terms for 'revelation' of a message by an angel intermediary; and it is difficult to see how an event such as a victory in battle could be 'sent down' in this way. Could it perhaps be the *conviction* of divine approval and acceptance which came to Muḥammad on the day of Badr, though not necessarily in any form of words other than the Qur'ān? If so, it is also possible that it was in the same month of Ramaḍān that the Qur'ān as a whole was 'sent down' in a single night (as discussed above); and this might explain the connection of the Qur'ān and the Furqān. The interpretation of the verses mentioning the Furqān is highly speculative, however, and not altogether relevant to the present subject. In so far as there is a conclusion here, it is that, if the Furqān is a part of the Qur'ān, it is the aspect of it expressing the significance of the victory of Badr – the deliverance of the Muslims and their separation from the unbelievers, the assurance of divine approval, the establishment of the Muslims as a distinct community. It can also be asserted with confidence that the term *furqān* continued in use for only a short period; and the reason for this is presumably that the significance of Badr for the Muslims changed somewhat after the reverse at Uḥud and again after the later successes.

NINE

THE DOCTRINES OF THE QUR'ĀN

1. The doctrine of God[1]

The doctrine of God is central to the Qur'ān. Like the Bible the Qur'ān assumes the existence of God and does not argue for it. In the earlier passages the points that are emphatically asserted are that God is good and that he is all-powerful. These points are supported by calling attention to the 'signs' in nature (as explained in the first section of the previous chapter). All sorts of natural phenomena have been ordered in such a way that they contribute to the maintenance of human life and to the comfort and convenience of individuals. It is in accordance with the emphasis on God's goodness that the suras of the Qur'ān commence with the formula 'In the name of God, the Merciful, the Compassionate'.

God's omnipotence appears above all in his power to create. He is the creator of everything – of the heavens and the earth and what is between them [13.16/17; 50.38/7; etc.]. The alleged deities of the pagans are unable to create anything [25.3; 46.4/3], not even a fly [22.73/2]. The creation of a thing comes about when God says to it 'Be'; 'when he wills a thing, he simply says to it "Be" and it is' [40.68/70 and frequently]. This is not unlike the *fiat* ascribed to God in the Bible – 'and God said, Let there be light; and there was light' [*Genesis*, 1.3]. It should be noted, however, that there is a great difference in emphasis at this point between the Bible and the Qur'ān. The Biblical doctrine of creation is essentially what is found in the first chapter of *Genesis*, that is, the initial or original creation of the universe. The six 'days' of creation are indeed mentioned in the Qur'ān [32.4/3; 41.9/8-10/11; etc.]; but they are given far less prominence than in the Bible. Most of the descriptions of creation in the Qur'ān are of God's continuing activity in the present. What is usually regarded as the first revelation [96.1f.] runs: 'Recite in the name of thy Lord who created – created man from a blood-clot' (or embryo). Thus God's creative power is regarded as being present in the origination of every human being. Moreover it is not restricted to origination, but also manifests itself in the various transformations which occur in the course of development; thus God 'creates' each stage of the embryo from the previous one.[2]

The greater part of the Qur'ān (though not the early passages) emphasizes that God is the only deity and that he has no peers or partners. This insistence is in opposition to the beliefs of the Arab pagans of the time. Among these beliefs three strands may be noticed. Many of the nomads had scant belief in the traditional deities and are rather to be described as humanists of a kind. Then there appear to have been polytheists as these are commonly conceived; that is, they acknowledged a number of gods all roughly equal. It has commonly been assumed by students of Islam that this was the main form of pagansim which was being attacked by the Qur'ān. Careful reading of a number of passages, however, shows that there was a third type of belief among the more thoughtful of Muḥammad's contemporaries. They acknowledged the existence of *Allāh* as the supreme god, but regarded the other 'gods' as lesser divine beings.[3] In some cases they may have held that these lesser deities were intercessors with the supreme god [39.3/4]. The assertions of the Qur'ān about the idols vary in emphasis. Sometimes they appear to be regarded – doubtless because this was the view of the hearers – as angels or even jinn[4]; but at other times they are declared to be mere names employed by men without any authorization.[5] It should also be noted that the term 'daughters of God' applied to certain deities[6] does not imply the type of family relationship found in Greek mythology but stands for a more abstract relationship; the interpretation of the phrase is roughly 'lesser divine beings subordinate to the supreme deity', or 'lesser beings sharing in the quality of divinity'.

That God is one and unique is appropriately the first article of the Islamic Confession of Faith or Testimony (*shahāda*): 'there is no deity but God' (*lā ilāha illā llāhu*). This formula is found in the Qur'ān exactly in 37.35/4 [cf. 47.19/2]; and similar assertions, such as 'there is no deity but he', are frequent. The negative side of this doctrine is the insistence on the heinousness of *shirk*, 'giving partners' (*sc.* to God) or 'associating' (*sc.* other beings with him). In later Islam it was generally agreed that the one sin which excluded a man from the community of Muslims was *shirk*; by it he became a *mushrik*, an 'associater' or 'polytheist'. The word commonly translated 'infidel' or 'unbeliever' is *kāfir*, with the corresponding noun *kufr*. Since *kufr* seems to have meant originally 'ingratitude', it may be that the meaning of 'unbelief' came from the idea that not to acknowledge the signs of God's power and goodness and to worship him was a mark of ingratitude. The opposite of the *kāfir* is the 'believer' or *mu'min* who acknowledges the signs and who has *īmān*, 'belief' or 'faith'. In the Qur'ān the common word for a follower of the Qur'ānic religion is *mu'min*; the word *muslim* meaning 'one who surrenders or submits himself (to God)' is less frequent and only occurs in later passages.

The omnipotence of God is sometimes asserted in what to the European appear to be extreme forms. Man's will is completely subordinate to God's will, so that man cannot do or will anything unless God wills it. With regard to accepting the Reminder or believing men are told that 'you will not so will except it be that God wills'.[7] In other respects also God's will overrides the wills of men. Sometimes it appears to be his previous decree or determination of something, as when it is said of Lot 'we delivered him and his household, except his wife, whom we had decreed (*qaddarnā*) to be of the lingerers' (27.57/8). On the other hand, God may be the real agent of events which appear to be the work of human agents. Thus God is asserted to be the author of the victory at Badr: 'you (Muslims) did not kill them, but God killed them, and you (Muḥammad) did not shoot (*sc.* arrows) when you shot, but God shot' [8.17]. The corollary of this belief in the overriding will of God is that no harm can come to a man except what God wills. When in Muḥammad's later years the Muslims complained if they suffered any misfortune, he was told to say to them: 'nothing will befall us except what God has written (decreed) for us' [9.51; cf. 57.22].

God's overriding control of events is also expressed through various subordinate conceptions such as his guidance, favour or help on the one hand, and on the other his leading astray (*iḍlāl*) and abandoning (*khidhlān*) and placing a seal on the hearts. A few examples may be given:

> If God wills to guide a man, he enlarges his breast for *islām*, surrender (to God), and if he wills to lead a man astray, he makes his breast narrow and contracted ... [6.125]. Had God willed he would have made you one community; but he leads astray whom he will and guides whom he will [16.93/5].
> If God helps you (*yanṣur-kum*), there is none to overcome you; but if he abandons you (*yakhdhul-kum*), who indeed will help you after him? [3.160/54].
> Had it not been for God's bounty and mercy (*faḍl*, *raḥma*) towards you, you would have followed Satan except a few [4.83/5; cf. 24.21].

The teaching of the Qur'ān as a whole, however, maintains human responsibility at the same time as it asserts divine omnipotence. This is really implicit in the doctrine of the Last Judgement; and later Muslim theologians argued that God's justice (which the Qur'ān asserts) would not allow him to punish anyone for an act for which he was not responsible. There are also many passages which show that God's activity of guiding or leading astray follows upon unsatisfactory actions or attitudes on the part of the individuals concerned.

> By this (simile God has coined) he leads astray many and by this he guides many; and he leads astray only the evildoers [2.26/4].
> Those who do not believe in God's signs, God does not guide [16.104/6].
> Truly I (God) am forgiving to him who repents and believes and acts uprightly, and who also accepts guidance (*ihtadā*) [20.82/4].
> How will God guide a people who disbelieved after believing? ... God does not guide the wicked people [3.86/0].

In the end, then, the Qur'ān simply holds fast to the complementary truths of God's omnipotence and man's responsibility without reconciling them intellectually. This is basically also the position of the Bible, though many western Christians have placed the chief emphasis on man's responsibility where most Muslims would have placed it on God's omnipotence.

The names of God have tended to play a large part in later Islamic thought, following on the verses in the Qur'ān which state that to God belong the most beautiful names (*al-asmā' al-ḥusnā*) [7.180/79; 17.110; 20.8/7; 59.24]. A list was later compiled of ninety-nine names, and these were used as the basis of meditations, especially in association with the *subḥa* or 'rosary'. The names are found in the Qur'ān, though some are not in the exact form given in the list; and there are also names in the Qur'ān not usually included in the list, of which there are different versions.[8] A common feature of Qur'ānic style is to have a verse ending with two names of God, such as 'Thou art the Knowing, the Wise' [2.32/0].

While the ninety-nine names are descriptive, there is also a proper or denotative name *allāh*, which is added at the beginning or the end of the list of ninety-nine. It is probably contracted from the Arabic *al-ilāh*, 'the god' or 'the deity', though some modern scholars have preferred to think that it was derived from the Aramaic or Syriac *alāhā*. Inscriptions and pre-Islamic poetry show that the word was in use in Arabia before Islam. It could have stood for 'the god' of a particular tribe, or for 'the supreme god' in which men were coming to believe, or for 'God' in the monotheistic sense.[9] The Qur'ān presupposes that most men already believe in the existence of *Allāh*, and by its teaching restricts the word to its monotheistic interpretation.

One of the other names *ar-Raḥmān*, 'the Merciful', approaches at times in the Qur'ān the status of a proper name. It is also known from inscriptions to have been used in Arabia before Muḥammad's time, and seems to have been employed by at least some of the 'prophets' who appeared at the close of Muḥammad's life. A similar word is common in Jewish writings and is occasionally found in Syriac; but adoption from these sources is unlikely, since the form of the word could be a regular Arabic one. Moreover, the occurrence of the word as a proper name is most frequent not in the earliest passages but in the suras of Nöldeke's second Meccan period, such as sura 19.[10] Hubert Grimme[11] suggested that the use of this name is associated with an emphasis on God's mercy, *raḥma*, and also that this emphasis corresponded to the tensions arising among the Muslims from failure and persecution and indicated a growing knowledge of the Christian scriptures in particular. About this there can be no certainty. The sudden appearance of this name remains something of a mystery; but its disappearance may have come about because ignorant persons tended to think that *Allāh* and *ar-Raḥmān* were two separate gods, as is indeed mentioned as a possibility by Muslim commentators on 17.110:

> Say: Call on God or call on the Merciful; however you call upon him, his are the beautiful names.

2. Other spiritual beings

Even if the ordinary nomadic Arab did not take belief in the gods seriously, he was fully convinced of the existence of jinn (singular *jinnī*, 'genie').[12] These were shadowy spirits who seldom assumed a distinct personality or name. They were associated with deserts, ruins and other eerie places, and might assume such forms as those of animals, serpents and other creeping things. They were vaguely feared, but were not always malevolent. Though created from fire and not, like man, from clay [55.14/13f.; 15.26f.], their end is likewise to serve or worship God [51.56]. Messengers are sent to them from God [6.130], and they may become either believers or unbelievers [72.11, 14; etc.]. It is asserted that on one occasion a company of jinn listened to Muḥammad proclaiming the Qur'ān and that some of them became Muslims [72.1-19; cf. 46.29/8-32/1]. The unbelievers among them may go to Hell [6.128; 11.119/20; 32.13; 41.25/4], but it is not explicitly stated that the believers may go to Heaven.

A madman was *majnūn*, that is, affected by jinn; but jinn sometimes assisted men to special knowledge [cf. 37.36/5]. The word for 'poet', *shāʿir*, seems to imply that he was inspired by some such being, since it means 'one who is aware' or 'one who perceives'. The *kāhin* or 'soothsayer' may have had his own special prompter, a spirit or genie, who inspired him to give answers on all sorts of questions. The oracles which the *kāhin* gave his clients were often cryptic, garnished with oaths to make them more impressive, and usually couched in *saj'* (rhythmic and assonanced prose) resembling the earlier passages of the Qur'ān. The oracles might give prognostications for the future, the solution of past mysteries, or decisions on litigious questions.[13] Superficially Muḥammad was not unlike men of this class, and the Qur'ān therefore finds it advisable to deny that he was a *kāhin* or inspired by jinn [52. 29; cf. 69.42]. Many varieties of jinn were known to the Arabs, but only the *'ifrīt* is separately mentioned in the Qur'ān [27.39].

Angels are frequently mentioned, though not in the earliest passages. The Arabic word, *mal'ak*, and more particularly its plural *malā'ika*, is thought to have been derived from Ethiopic, but was probably familiar to the Arabs before Muḥammad's time. In the popular mind angels and jinn were roughly identified: and it is instructive that at one point the Qur'ān says Iblīs was one of the jinn [18.50/48] whereas elsewhere he is spoken of as a fallen angel [2.34/2; 7.11/10; etc.]. The Qur'ān speaks as if the conception of angels had been accepted by some pagans, since they are said to demand an angel as messenger [41.14/13; cf. 43.53], or had adopted angels as objects of worship or goddesses [43.19/18f.; cf. 37.149-53; 53.28]; but it is also possible that it is only the Qur'ān (and not the pagans) which asserts that the beings worshipped by the pagans are in fact angels.

The angels are subordinate and created beings [21.26]; they are messengers of God [15.8; 35.1] and in particular the bearers of the revelation, a function which sometimes is said to be performed collectively [16.2; 97.4] and sometimes by Gabriel especially [2.97/1; cf. 81.19-25]. The angels are also watchers over men and recorders of their deeds [13.11/12; 82.10-12], and they call in the souls of men at death [16.28/30, 32/4]. It is presumably as recorders that they are present on the Day of Judgement [2.210/06; 39.75; 69.17]. They also surround the throne of God and sing his praises [40.7; 42.5/3]. Apart from Gabriel the only angel named is Michael in 2.98/2. There is also mentioned, however, along with the angels a mysterious being called 'the Spirit', *ar-rūḥ*, or 'the faithful Spirit' [only in 26.193]. Where it is associated with the angels it is best regarded as one of them [as in 16.2; 40.15; 70.4; 78.38; 97.4]. Later Muslim exegetes take the Spirit to be Gabriel, and in view of its special connection with Muḥammad himself and with revelation in general there would seem to be no objection to this identification [42.52]. The Qur'ānic use of the word *rūḥ*, however, raises many problems which cannot be dealt with here.[14]

Contrasted with the angels are the demons or satans (*shayāṭīn*, sing. *shayṭān*). Just as the believers have angels as guardians and helpers [8.9, 12; cf. 6.61], so a demon is assigned to each unbeliever and prompts him to evil [19.83/6; 43.36/5-39/8; cf. 23.97/9f.; 7.27/6; 41.25/4]. There are some references to a contemporary belief that the demons tried to observe the inhabitants of Paradise by stealth and were driven away by stones which appear to men as shooting stars [15.16-18; 37.6-10].

Besides the ordinary demons there is *ash-shayṭān*, who might be taken to be the demon *par excellence*, and so the Devil or Satan. In the Qur'ān *ash-shayṭān* or Satan is apparently the same person as Iblīs. He is an angel deposed for his pride in refusing to worship the man whom God has just created [2.34/2-36/4; 7/11/10-22/1; etc.]; the one who refused to worship is always Iblīs, but Satan is often mentioned in a later verse. After his refusal, however, he is allowed by God to tempt men, to urge them to evil and unseemliness, and to make evil deeds seem fair to them [17.61/3-64/6; 2.168/3f.; 8.48/50; 16.63/5]. He whispers in the breasts of men [7.20/19; 20.120/18; 114.4-6], and may even insinuate something into the messages revealed to prophets [22.52/1]. His footsteps are not to be followed for he is a betrayer of men [25.29/31], and will repudiate their service at the last [14.22/6f.]. There has been much discussion of whether *shayṭān* is an Arabic word or not, and no agreement has been reached. It is clear that the word was in use in Arabic in pre-Islamic times, but it may have meant a snake or a being something like the jinn. Even if the word is Arabic, the singular seems to have been influenced in meaning by the Hebrew *Sāṭān*, probably through the Ethiopic *Shayṭān*. This development may also have been pre-Islamic.[15]

3. Prophethood; other religions

The Qur'ānic conception of the messenger (*rasūl*) and prophet (*nabī*) has already been described in chapter 2, section 3. It was an essential part of this conception that the message brought to Muḥammad from God by the angels was basically the same as messages brought to other prophets, especially those named in the 'punishment stories'. In some passages the impression is given that each messenger is sent to a different community, and that when the community rejects the message and is punished it disappears. This holds in the case of the Arabian prophets, the 'people of Lot', and others. On the other hand it is recognized that there is at least a genealogical continuity in the case of some of the prophets: 'God chose Adam and Noah, the family of Abraham and the family of 'Imrān above the worlds, descendants one of the other ...' [3.33/0]. Further problems arose for the community of Muslims as they had further contacts especially with the Jews of Medina and heard these deny the similarity of the Qur'ān and their scriptures. In the last year or two of Muḥammad's life as his rule expanded northwards the Muslims experienced comparable hostility from Christians.

When Muḥammad first went to Medina he received messages for 'the people of the Book' (that is, primarily the Jews), as in 5.15/18 and 19/22. When it became clear that the Jews were not going to recognize his prophethood, he was encouraged by the thought that they had in the past rejected and killed messengers who had been sent to them [3.181/77-184/1; 5.70/4]. Another point was that the Jews and Christians put themselves in a false position by rejecting one another 'though they both recite the Book' [2.113/07]. The difficulty that there were basic differences between the Qur'ān on the one hand and on the other the scriptures of the Jews and Christians (usually called the Torah and the Evangel or Gospel), and the further difficulty of differences between the Torah and the Evangel, were met apparently by regarding these scriptures as only part of the Book [3.23/2; 4.44/7, 51/4], and even holding that they had divided up the Qur'ān

[15.90f.; cf. 23.53/5]. The Jews in particular were also accused of concealing part of the scriptures [2.42/39, 76/1, 140/34, 146/1, 159/4, 174/69; 3.71/64; 5.15/18; 6.91]. In some cases this seems to have meant that they concealed verses in the Bible foretelling the coming of Muḥammad as a prophet [7.157/6; 61.6]. In other passages the Jews are accused of deliberately 'corrupting' or 'altering' the scriptures [2.75/0; 5.13/16, 41/5], and from the examples given in 4.46/8f. this seems to mean playing with words to make fun of the Muslims.[16] In later times this doctrine of the 'corruption' (*taḥrīf*) of the Jewish and Christian scriptures was developed in such a way that Muslims generally came to regard the existing texts as valueless.

Corresponding to these criticisms of the People of the Book is the positive conception of 'the religion of Abraham'. The essence of this religion is surrender or submission (*islām*) to the Lord of the worlds [2.130/24f.]. The person who practises it is a *ḥanīf* or – which is practically the same thing – a *muslim* (as noted on p. 15 above). Thus it can be said that Abraham was neither a Jew nor a Christian but a *ḥanīf* and *muslim* [3.67/0]. This leads to the conception of three parallel religions [as in 5.44/8-50/5], firstly that of the Torah given to Moses, then that of the Evangel given to Jesus, and then that of the Qur'ān given to Muḥammad. The Evangel 'confirms' the Torah, and the Qur'ān 'confirms' the previous two scriptures; but Jews, Christians and Muslims will each be judged by their own revelation. Apart from the charges of concealment and corruption of the scriptures already mentioned, the Qur'ān seems to be criticizing Jews and Christians for 'dividing up their religion and becoming sects' [6.159/60]. Muḥammad and his followers are certainly following the true religion of Abraham [4.125/4; 6.161/2; 16.123/4; 22.78/7]; and this virtually implies that Jews and Christians are not, though the developed form of the doctrine that they had 'corrupted the scriptures' did not appear until some time after Muḥammad's death.

In general the teaching of the Qur'ān is in accordance with that of the Old Testament. Such differences of detail as there are in the story of Joseph and in ceremonial matters are peripheral. There is no mention of the writing prophets, though their concern for social justice is present. The Biblical title of 'Messiah' (*masīḥ*) is accepted and applied to Jesus, but there appears to be little realization of its original significance. Indeed the chief point of difference between the Qur'ān and the Old Testament is the absence from the former of any profound conception of sacrifice and a sacrificing priesthood.

On the other hand, there are considerable differences between the Qur'ān and the New Testament. It should be noted, however, that so far as the actual statements of the Qur'ān are concerned, the differences are not so great as they are sometimes supposed to be. Modern scholars, Christian and Muslim, tend to read later controversies into the wording of the Qur'ān. Thus the rejection of the doctrine that 'God is one of three' [5.73/7] is usually taken to be a denial of the Christian doctrine of the Trinity; yet strictly speaking what is rejected is a doctrine of tritheism which orthodox Christianity also rejects. Similarly the rejection of the fatherhood of God the Father and the sonship of God the Son is strictly speaking a rejection of fatherhood and sonship in a physical sense; and this Christianity would also reject. The Virgin Birth is taught [19.16-33/4], but is interpreted simply as a miracle. The denial that Jesus died on the cross [4.157/6-159/7] is primarily a denial that the crucifixion was a Jewish victory; but, in line with the absence of the conception of sacrifice, it means that the Qur'ān never speaks of the atonement or saving work of Jesus.[17]

4. The doctrine of the Last Judgement

After the doctrine that God is one the doctrine of the Last Judgement may be reckoned the second great doctrine of the Qur'ān. In essentials this is the doctrine that on the Last Day men will be raised to life and will appear before God to be judged and to be assigned to Paradise or Hell according as their deeds are mainly good or mainly bad. In some respects this Judgement, as affecting the world as a whole, corresponds to the catastrophe which overtakes particular unbelieving communities in the punishment-stories. The designation of Muḥammad as a 'warner' may refer either to the temporal catastrophe or to the eschatological Judgement, but the emphasis varies from time to time. The eschatological Judgement is implied by such early verses as 'to thy Lord is the return' [96.8] and 'rise and warn . . . the Wrath flee' [74.2, 5]; but the vivid pictures of the terrors of the Last Day come first in later Meccan passages, especially in those of what Bell called 'the early Qur'ān period'.

The climax of history, when the present world comes to an end, is referred to in various ways. It is *yawm ad-dīn*, 'the Day of Judgement', *al-yawm al-ākhir*, 'the Last Day', *yawm al-qiyāma*, 'the Day of Resurrection', or simply *as-sā'a*, 'the Hour'. Less frequently it is *yawm al-faṣl*, *yawm al-jam'* or *yawm at-talāqī*, that is, 'the Day of Distinction' (when the good are separated from the evil), 'the Day of the Gathering' (of men to the presence of God) or 'the Day of the Meeting' (of men with God). The Hour comes suddenly [6.31; 7.187/6; 12.107; 22.55/4; 43.66; 47.18/20]. It is heralded by a shout [*ṣayḥa*, 36.53], by a thunderclap [*ṣākhkha*, 80.33], or by the blast of a trumpet [69.13; 74.8; 78.18; in 39.68 a double blast]. A cosmic upheaval then takes place. The mountains dissolve into dust, the seas boil up, the sun is darkened, the stars fall, and the sky is rolled up. God appears as Judge, but his presence is hinted at rather than described. He is in the midst of the angels arranged in ranks [78.38; 89.22/3] or circling his throne and praising him [39.75]. Many of the details mentioned have parallels in Jewish and Christian literature, though there are also specifically Arabian features, like the neglect of the ten-month-pregnant camels in 81.4; but there is nowhere a parallel to the Qur'ānic picture as a whole.

The central interest, of course, is in the gathering of all mankind before the Judge. The graves are opened and human beings of all ages, restored to life, join the throng. The Qur'ān, however, does not assert a natural immortality of the human soul, since man's existence is dependent on the will of God; when he wills he causes man to die, and when he wills he raises him to life again. To the scoffing objection of the Meccan pagans that former generations had been dead a long time and were now dust and mouldering bones, the reply is that God is nevertheless able to restore them to life, though they will have no knowledge of the time that has elapsed. The statements in 2.154/49 and 3.169/3f. that those who died fighting in God's cause are alive and present with him raise some difficulties; but the simplest solution is to suppose that God has willed to restore them to life before the general resurrection and has admitted them to Paradise.

The actual Judgement is also described, and different details are given prominence. The books with the record of a man's deeds will be opened. His account will be handed to him and he will be asked to read it – perhaps as happened in Meccan business practice. The good man is said to be given his book in his right hand and the bad man given his behind his back or in his left hand [84.7-12; 69.19-32]. In the earlier passages the criterion by which men are judged is apparently the relative weight of their good and bad deeds when weighed in the balance [101.6/5-9/6; 7.8/7f.]. The Judgement, too, is passed on the individual and the Judge is not influenced by a man's wealth or powerful kinsmen [82.19; cf. 31.33/2; 35.18/19; 44.41; 53.38/9; 99.6]. In earlier times, indeed, it seems that whole communities have gone to Hell as communities because they have shown solidarity in rejecting the prophet sent to them. In later passages of the Qur'ān, however, the criterion tends to be belief or unbelief, though this is fundamentally a moral and not an intellectual act. To accept a messenger and his message is, in the Qur'ān, a moral act and the gateway to real uprightness of life and conduct.

The result of the Judgement is either everlasting bliss or everlasting torment. There is no intermediate condition. One passage has sometimes been taken to imply a middle state [7.46/4-49/7], but this probably rests on a misinterpretation[18]; and the word *barzakh* [23.100/2], which was given a similar meaning in later times, in the Qur'ān probably only means 'barrier'. Another passage says that all men shall go down to hell-fire and that the pious shall then be delivered from it [19.71/2f.]. While this could imply a Purgatory in which the believers expiated or were purified from their evil deeds before passing to their reward, it might mean only that all men are brought face to face with the pains of Hell, though the pious as a result of the Judgement are exempted from them. There are thus only the two destinations, Paradise and Hell; but it is sometimes hinted that there are distinctions within Paradise. In 56.88/7-95/4 three classes are named: those who are brought near, the people of the right and those who count false (and who are consigned to Hell); and in 8.4 'degrees in the presence of their Lord' are said to await the true believers.

The abode of those who are condemned at the Judgement is *jahannam*, Gehenna or Hell. Other names applied to it are *al-jaḥīm*, 'the Hot Place', *saqar* (meaning unknown), *sa'īr*, 'the Blaze', *laẓā*, perhaps also 'Blaze' [70.15]. Most common of all names, however, is *an-nār*, 'the Fire'. The torments in it of the damned are depicted with a great wealth of imagery. Many of the details can be paralleled in Christian literature, such as the idea that the overseers of Hell and those who administer punishment are angels (good beings commissioned by God to do so), and the idea that the inmates of Hell will ask the inmates of Paradise for water [7.50/48]. On the other hand, there are distinctively Arabian features, such as being given hot water to drink (probably) and being made to eat from the tree of *zaqqūm*; the latter is said to be a tree which grew in the Ḥijāz and had very bitter fruit.

In contrast the abode of the Just is *al-janna*, 'the Garden', often described as 'a Garden through which rivers flow'. It is also designated *jannat 'adn*, 'the Garden of Eden', or *jannat an-na'īm*, 'the Garden of delight', or simply *an-na'īm*. In some late passages *firdaws* occurs, a singular form perhaps derived from the presumed plural *farādīs* representing the Greek *paradeisos*, or perhaps introduced into Arabic directly from Persian which is the ultimate source of the Greek word. In Paradise the blessed enjoy luxuries of many kinds; they recline on couches, they eat fruit, they have wine served to them by ever-youthful boys. The latter point, which has Christian parallels, is interesting in the light of the later Qur'ānic prohibition of wine-drinking. There are also milk and honey and ever-flowing springs. In addition to these material joys the reward of the pious has more spiritual aspects. They experience forgiveness, peace and the satisfaction of the soul in God. Above all they are given the vision of God.[19]

Western thought has made much of the houris (Arabic *ḥūr*) of Paradise, and indeed so also has the Muslim popular imagination. These 'wide-eyed houris' are mentioned only four times in the Qur'ān by name [44.54; 52.20; 55.72; 56.23/2]; but there are one or two other passages [especially 37.48/7;

38.52; 55.56-8; 56.35/4-40/39; 78.33] which describe the maidens who are to be companions of the blessed. They are 'spotless virgins, amorous, like of age', resembling hidden pearls or ruby and coral, with swelling breasts, untouched by men or jinn, who modestly keep their eyes cast down and are enclosed in pavilions. All these references are usually dated in the Meccan period. In the Medinan period there is mention of 'purified spouses' [2.25/3; 3.15/13; 4.57/60], but it is not clear whether these are the houris or the actual believing wives. It is certainly the teaching of the Qur'ān that believing men, women and children shall enter Paradise as families [13.23; 40.8; cf. 36.56; 43.70]. Since these images are attempts to suggest what is essentially beyond man's capacity to conceive it is unnecessary to seek a single consistent picture. The fundamental assertion of the Qur'ān is that the life of Paradise is one which satisfies man's deepest desires and which involves warm human relationships.

5. Regulations for the life of the community

In addition to its doctrinal teaching the Qur'ān contains liturgical and legal or social prescriptions for the life of the community of Muslims. These rules were greatly elaborated by Muslim jurists in later times to constitute what is now known as 'Islamic law' or 'the Sharīʿa'. The present section indicates the general tenor of these rules without entering into details. The first four to be mentioned belong to the fundamental 'religious' obligations which are often called 'the Five Pillars of Religion'. The remaining pillar, usually the first to be named, is the Shahāda or Confession of Faith which has already been described (p. 25, 149).

(a) *Prayer or worship*. Prayers in the sense of formal public worship (*ṣalāt*) seems to have been part of the practice of Muḥammad's followers from the first. Opponents are said to try to stop the practice [96.9f.]. The details of this formal worship were settled by the actual custom of Muḥammad and the first Muslims rather than by Qur'ānic prescription. The worship is essentially adoration and consists of a series of physical acts accompanied by certain forms of words. The climax is when the worshippers touch the ground with their foreheads in acknowledgement of the might, majesty and mercy of God. When the rules were standardized, it became a duty for Muslims to perform the worship five times a day; but the five times are not mentioned clearly in the Qur'ān. Evening, morning, twilight and noon are said to be commanded in 30.17/16f., and the afternoon prayer is held to be intended by the 'middle prayer' in 2.238/9. Daybreak, sunset and night are mentioned in various places [11.114/6; 17.78/80f.; 20.130; 50.39/8f.]. It is known from sura 73 that prayer for a large part of the night was a practice of the Muslims at Mecca, but that this rule was later abrogated (by verse 20) so that rising at night ceased to be obligatory. At first prayer was made facing Jerusalem, but at the time of the break with the Jews the *qibla* or direction of prayer was changed to Mecca.[20] Special emphasis was placed on the midday prayer on Fridays [cf. 62.9]. Prayers are always preceded by ablutions [4.43/6].

(b) *Legal alms or poor-tax.* This prescription, the *zakāt*, was perhaps originally a kind of tithe, as much for the purification of the giver's soul as for the relief of the needy. The practice began at Mecca. In Medina it was made incumbent on Muslims, presumably because of the difficult circumstances of the poorer Emigrants and perhaps also because of necessities of state. The essential demands on nomadic groups and others who wanted to become Muslims and allies of Muḥammad was that they should perform the *ṣalāt* and give the *zakāt*.[21]

(c) *The fast of Ramaḍān.* Fasting is not mentioned in the Meccan passages, but soon after the Hijra to Medina the Jewish fast of the 'Āshūrā' is held to have been prescribed for the Muslims by 2.183/79.[22] This would be part of the process by which the Islamic religion was assimilated to Judaism. After the break with the Jews the fast of the month of Ramaḍān was substituted [2.185/1], possibly as a thanksgiving for the victory of Badr.[23] The fast consists of total abstinence from food, drink, smoking and sexual intercourse from before sunrise until after sunset on each of the thirty days of the month.

(d) *The pilgrimage to Mecca.* A pilgrimage to places in the neighbourhood of Mecca and perhaps also to Mecca itself (*ḥajj*, *'umra*) was a pre-Islamic practice. About the time of the break with the Jews this was taken into 'the religion of Abraham' [22.26/7-33/4; cf. 2.196/2]. After the slaughter at Badr it was presumably dangerous for Muslims to go to Mecca.

Muḥammad was prevented by the Meccans from making the pilgrimage in 628 as he had hoped, but was allowed to do so in 629 by the treaty of al-Ḥudaybiya [cf. 47.27]. Shortly after the conquest of Mecca in 630 the idolaters were forbidden to approach the Ka'ba [9.28]; and Tradition says that they were debarred from the pilgrimage a year later. The detailed regulations for the pilgrimage are not recorded in the Qur'ān.[24]

(e) *Marriage and divorce.* There are several passages in the Qur'ān dealing with marriage and divorce.[25] The matter is complicated by the fact that previously some of the Arabs who became Muslims had followed a matrilineal system of kinship. Associated with this were forms of polyandry in which a woman had several 'husbands' and physical paternity was neglected. Thus the permission for a man to have four wives [based on 4.3] is not the limitation of a previous unlimited polygamy but an attempt to deal with the problem of surplus women (originally after the numerous male deaths at Uḥud) while at the same time limiting a woman to one husband at a time. The Islamic system may be considered a reform in that, when it was observed, the physical paternity of a child was always known. Divorce was easy, but it was enjoined that after divorce a woman should spend a waiting-period (*'idda*) before remarriage, and this enabled one to know whether she was pregnant by the previous husband [2.226; etc.].

(f) *Inheritance.* The rules for inheritance were complex, doubtless because of the complexity of the social situation. It was probably customary among the Arabs, or at least among the Meccans, to give instructions before death about the disposal of the property [cf. 36.50]. In 2.180/76 the making of a will becomes obligatory for Muslims; the will has to be witnessed, but it is not stated that it has to be written. A few verses give succinct rules for the division of estates [4.11/12-14/18, 176/5]. The shares of parents, children, brothers and sisters are laid down. No special privilege is given to the first-born. The right of women to hold property (of which there are instances in pre-Islamic times) is recognized, and shares are prescribed for women – usually half of a man's share. No share is assigned to a widow, but it was a duty to make provision for her [2.240/1]. The aim of these regulations was probably to ensure that property which had hitherto been partly communal was fairly divided among the nearest kin and was not appropriated by a strong individual.

(g) *Food-laws.* Several Meccan passages are directed against pagan food-taboos, and characterize as ingratitude the refusal to partake of the good things provided by God. The Jewish regulations about clean and unclean animals and similar matters must have come to the notice of the Muslims after the Hijra, and were doubtless found irksome. While the accession of the Jews to Islam was hoped for it was laid down that food allowable for the People of the Book was allowable for the Muslims [5.5/7]. Later, as tension with the Jews increased, the Qur'ān asserted that the food-laws were a punishment laid on the Jews by God for their rebelliousness, and so not applicable to the Muslims [4.160/58; etc.]. Muslims were in fact given simple rules (especially 5.3/4) which are reminiscent of those given to Gentile Christians in *Acts*, 15.29, but also include the prohibition of pork.

(h) *Wine-drinking.* Pre-Islamic poets boasted of their feats in wine-drinking. It was conspicuous luxury-consumption, since wine made from grapes had to be brought from considerable distances and was expensive. Apart from the fact that the trade was largely in the hands of Jews and Christians, Muḥammad had disagreeable experiences with followers who came drunk to public worship [cf. 4.43/6]. Though wine had been mentioned as one of the delights of Paradise, its evil effects were also realized [cf. 2.219/6], and it was finally forbidden altogether [5.90/2].

(i) *Usury.* In a commercial centre like Mecca the taking of interest was presumably a normal practice. The Qur'ānic disapproval of interest belongs to the Medinan period and appears to be directed against the Jews rather than against the Meccans. In 4.161/59 the Jews are accused of having taken usury although they had been forbidden to do so. The most natural explanation of this would be to suppose that in the first year or so after the Hijra the Jews had refused to give contributions in response to Muḥammad's appeal but had said they were willing to lend money at interest. By adopting this position they were refusing to acknowledge Muḥammad's claim to be proclaiming a religion identical with theirs; and this was probably a large part of the reason for the prohibition of usury [3.130/25f.; cf. 2.275/6-281].[26]

(j) *Miscellaneous regulations.* There are Qur'ānic prescriptions on many other matters, some important, others apparently of less moment, though none is treated at any length. Slavery, which had been common in Arabia, was accepted as an institution, but it was laid down that slaves should be treated kindly [4.36/40], and provision was made for the liberation of a slave, which was regarded as a pious act [24.33].[27] Contracts are to be fulfilled [5.1], and debts are to be recorded in writing [2.282]. Adultery and fornication are to be severely punished, but a charge of adultery must first be proved by four witnesses [4.2-4, 13]; theft is punished by the cutting off of a hand [5.38/42]. There is the prohibition of the gambling practice called *maysir*, in which lots were drawn for the various portions of a camel which was to be slaughtered [2.219/6; 5.90/2]. Appropriate conduct is indicated for those who meet the Prophet in public audiences or private interviews [49.1-5; 58.12/13; etc.]. There are rules for the division of the spoils after razzias [8.1, 41/2; 59.6-10]. In short the Qur'ān gives, at least in outline, a solution of the practical difficulties of the growing community in so far as previous custom was inapplicable.[28]

When later Muslim scholars worked out a complete system of law, they had to take into consideration Muḥammad's practice as well as the prescriptions of the Qur'ān. In many cases Muḥammad had adopted some practice without any specific revelation as a basis and probably by modifying previous custom. In this way, although there are many legislative passages in the Qur'ān, it is not the sole source of Islamic law.

TEN

MUSLIM SCHOLARSHIP AND THE QUR'ĀN

1. Interpretation and exegesis

The work of Muslim scholars on the text of the Qur'ān was described in a previous chapter and need not be mentioned here. Ignaz Goldziher in his magistral study of the history of the exegesis of the Qur'ān[1] insisted that even work on the text involved a form of interpretation, and of this he gave examples. This stage merges into the 'traditional' interpretation. The Qur'ān is full of allusions, which were presumably clear at the time of its revelation, but were far from clear to later generations. Thus men appeared who claimed to know who was referred to in a particular passage, and what the incident was which occasioned a passage. In such matters it was easy to allow oneself to be carried away by imagination, and there were many unreliable purveyors of stories. Eventually, however, careful scholars sifted out the accounts which might be regarded as authentic, showing how and when a particular passage was revealed. This became a subdivision of the discipline known as 'the occasions of revelation' (*asbāb an-nuzūl*). The standard work on this subject is taken to be that of al-Wāḥidī (d. 1075), of which there are now printed editions. This work is complemented by that of the later Qur'ānic scholar as-Suyūṭī (d. 1505), entitled *Lubāb an-nuqūl fī asbāb an-nuzūl*, which has also been printed. In the early period there was also much irresponsible elaboration of Qur'ānic stories, using Biblical and extracanonical Jewish and Christian material, Arab legend, and often sheer invention.

As time went on, especially after non-Arabs became Muslims, it became necessary to have explanations of verses and phrases of the Qur'ān whose meaning had ceased to be obvious. It was necessary to show the precise meaning of a rare word or the correct way to take a grammatical construction or the reference of a pronoun. The first great name in Qur'ānic exegesis, and indeed the founder of the discipline is held to be Ibn-ʿAbbās, a cousin of Muḥammad's, who was from ten to fifteen years old in 632 and who lived until about 687. Such was his reputation, however, that all sorts of interpretations were falsely ascribed to him to gain acceptance for them, and thus little can be known with certainty about his views. It appears to be the case, however, that he employed the method of referring to pre-Islamic poetry in order to establish the meaning of obscure words.[2] A less sceptical view of early Qur'ānic exegesis has recently been put forward by a Turkish Muslim scholar, Fuat Sezgin.[3] On the basis of the much greater number of manuscripts now known containing a *tafsīr* or Qur'ān-commentary by an early author Sezgin argues that it is possible to form a good idea of the teaching of at least several pupils of Ibn-ʿAbbās. Most of these manuscripts, however, have not yet been carefully studied, and it is too early to know whether they will yield information of much significance.

The earliest important commentary on the Qur'ān which is extant and readily accessible is the great work of the historian Muḥammad ibn-Jarīr aṭ-Ṭabarī (d. 923), first printed in Cairo in 1903 in thirty volumes and reprinted more than once. As the title (*Jāmiʿ al-bayān ʿan ta'wīl al-Qur'ān*) suggests, this is a compendium of all that was best in the earlier 'traditional exegesis'. For most verses of the Qur'ān aṭ-Ṭabarī gives not merely his own interpretation but also quotes the statements of Ibn-ʿAbbās and other early authorities, in each case with the *isnād* or chain of transmitters through whom it has come to him. There may be a dozen authorities or more for a single difficult phrase. At many points the authorities differ; and there aṭ-Ṭabarī, after expounding the opposing views and giving the supporting statements puts forward his own view and his reasons for it.[4] From this vast work it would be possible to gain much information about the interpretations given by earlier commentators such as al-Ḥasan al-Baṣrī (d. 728); but it is not certain that the results would be commensurate to the efforts involved, since the most distinctive points of exegesis might well have been omitted. The manuscripts mentioned by Sezgin with the views of early interpreters may have been compiled by later scholars from works such as that of aṭ-Ṭabarī.

There are numerous other commentaries on the Qur'ān, of which lists will be found in the reference works of Brockelmann and Sezgin. Only a few of outstanding interest need be mentioned here.

A commentary which modern scholars are finding of increasing value is that of az-Zamakhsharī (d. 1143), entitled *Al-kashshāf an ḥaqā'iq at-tanzīl*, 'The unveiler of the realities of revelation'. Officially az-Zamakhsharī has not had much influence in the Islamic world because he belonged to the group of heretical theologians known as the Muʿtazilites, who ascribed greater freedom to the human will than did the Sunnites and denied the hypostatic existence of the divine attributes. Only at a very few points, however, do his theological views affect his interpretation of the Qur'ānic text; and on the other hand he has the great merits of profound grammatical and lexicological knowledge and a sound judgement.

What has often been regarded, especially by European scholars, as the standard commentary on the Qur'ān is that called *Anwār at-tanzīl wa-asrār at-ta'wīl*, 'The lights of revelation and the secrets of interpretation', by al-Bayḍāwī (d. 1286 or 1291). This was intended as a manual for instruction in colleges or mosque-schools, and therefore aims at giving in concise form all that was best and soundest in previous commentaries, including important variant interpretations. To a great extent al-Bayḍāwī follows az-Zamakhsharī, though in his zeal for conciseness he sometimes becomes cryptic. He belonged to the main stream of Sunnite philosophical theology, and therefore removed az-Zamakhsharī's Muʿtazilite errors. A European edition of this work in two volumes was published at Leipzig in 1846 and 1848, edited by H. L. Fleischer; and two sections (those on suras 3 and 12) have been translated into English, although owing to the nature of the material they are barely intelligible to those who are not also studying the Arabic text.[5]

Between az-Zamakhsharī and al-Bayḍāwī came the theologian Fakhr-ad-Dīn ar-Rāzī (d. 1210), who among many other works wrote an extensive commentary of the Qur'ān.

The distinctive feature of this commentary is that it includes long philosophical and theological discussions on many matters in accordance with the writer's standpoint, that of the later Ashʿarite school of Sunnite philosophical theology.

A popular short commentary is that of the Jalālayn or 'the two Jalāls', namely, Jalāl-ad-Dīn al-Maḥallī (d. 1459) who began it, and his pupil, the great scholar Jalāl-ad-Dīn as-Suyūṭī (d. 1505), who completed it. This gives the gist of the accepted views in the briefest possible form.

As a modernizing theological movement has developed in the Islamic world during the last century this has been reflected in a number of new commentaries.[6] In Egypt the most notable is *Tafsīr al-Manār*, the work of a group of scholars associated with the periodical *Al-Manār*[7]; while from the Indian subcontinent comes the impressive work of Mawlana Abul-Kalam Azad.[8]

2. The theologians

As was seen above (chapter 4, section 4) the dramatic form of much of the Qur'ān is that it is the direct speech of God. Even where this is not the case, as in passages spoken by angels, the assumption is that they say what they have been commanded to say by God. In the theological discussions about to be described, however, the case of verses commanded by God but not 'dramatically' spoken by him was not distinguished from the first. Both sides took it for granted that in the Qur'ān God was speaking.

It is not clear how the discussion began.[9] Some European scholars thought that it had grown out of Christian thinking about 'the Word of God'; but, while some ideas may have been suggested from this quarter, it will be shown that the discussions were not academic but related to important intra-Islamic political questions. It might have been considered obvious that, since the Qur'ān had appeared at certain points in time during the last twenty years or so of Muḥammad's life, it could not be regarded as having existed from all eternity. Nevertheless in the caliphate of al-Ma'mūn (813–33) one finds many of the central body of Sunnite theologians maintaining that the Qur'ān is the eternal and uncreated word or speech of God. (The Arabic is *kalām Allāh*, properly 'the speech of God' and to be distinguished from *kalimat Allāh*, 'God's word', a phrase applied to Jesus in 4.171/69.) Other persons, notably the Muʿtazilite theologians who were in favour with al-Ma'mūn, opposed to this the thesis that the Qur'ān was the created speech of God and was not eternal. The opposition between these two points of view became such that before the end of the reign of al-Ma'mūn an Inquisition (*miḥna*) was established, and all persons in official positions like judges and provincial governors were required to affirm publicly that they believed that the Qur'ān was the created and not uncreated speech of God. The Inquisition continued fitfully until shortly after al-Mutawakkil came to the throne in 848.

At first sight it seems strange that an abstruse theological point of this kind should have political repercussions. An examination of the situation, however, shows that it was linked with a power struggle between what may be called the 'autocratic' bloc and the 'constitutionalist' bloc, each of which represented several bodies of common interest grouped together. The theological dispute specially affected the ulema or religious scholars on the constitutionalist side and the secretaries or civil servants on the autocratic side. The latter were inclined towards the views of the Shīʿite sect, part of which at least insisted on the charismatic or divinely inspired quality of the ruler of the community of Muslims. If this point was accepted, it meant that the ruler by his personal inspiration would be able to override the religious law as hitherto understood and practised. At the same time the power of the civil servants and administrators would be increased. The ruler's power would be all the greater if it was also agreed that the Qur'ān was created, since what was created by God was dependent only on his will, and he could presumably have willed to create it otherwise.

On the other hand, if the Qur'ān was the uncreated speech of God and (as they also maintained) an eternal attribute of his being, it could not be changed and could not be set aside even by the ruler of the Muslims (whose special charisma or inspiration was not accepted by those who held this view). It followed that the affairs of the Islamic empire must be ordered strictly in accordance with the provisions of this eternal speech of God. Since the accredited interpreters of this eternal speech of God were the ulema, it further followed that acceptance of the uncreatedness of the Qur'ān enhanced the power of the ulema at the expense of that of the civil servants.

The policy of the caliph al-Ma'mūn and his immediate successors, of which one expression was the establishment of the Inquisition, may be regarded as a compromise. Although belief in the createdness of the Qur'ān was insisted on in opposition to the constitutionalist bloc, the demands of the autocratic bloc were by no means fully accepted. Thus neither bloc was altogether satisfied with the compromise. Most of the ulema weakly submitted to the demand to make a public affirmation of the new doctrine, although Aḥmad ibn-Ḥanbal refused to do so and suffered as a result, and one or two men lost their lives.[10] It was not this protest, however, which led to a change of policy under al-Mutawakkil but the failure of the compromise to remove the tensions within the caliphate. The abandonment of the Inquisition was one of several steps by which the heartlands of the Islamic world were made predominantly Sunnite and have remained so, with the exception of Persia, until the present day. The uncreatedness of the Qur'ān became a central point of dogma, with the practical corollary that the ordering of state and society was based in principle on the Sharīʿa or revealed law as contained in the Qur'ān supplemented by the Traditions about Muḥammad's standard practice. Theological discussion passed on to such ramifications of the dogma as the question whether man's uttering (*lafẓ*) or pronouncing of the Qur'ān was created or uncreated; but such matters belong rather to the history of theology.[11]

ELEVEN

THE QUR'ĀN AND OCCIDENTAL SCHOLARSHIP

1. Translations and studies

The scholarly concern of Europeans with the Qur'ān may be said to have begun with the visit of Peter the Venerable, Abbot of Cluny, to Toledo in the second quarter of the twelfth century. He became concerned with the whole problem of Islam, collected a team of men and commissioned them to produce a series of works which together would constitute a scholarly basis for the intellectual encounter with Islam. As part of this series a translation of the Qur'ān into Latin was produced by an Englishman, Robert of Ketton (whose name is often deformed into Robertus Retenensis) and was complete by July 1143. Unfortunately this translation and the companion works did not lead to any important developments of scholarly Islamic studies. Numerous books were written in the next two or three centuries, but Islam was still the great enemy, feared and at the same time admired, and what was written was almost exclusively apologetics and polemics, sometimes verging on the scurrilous and the pornographic.[1]

The upsurge of energy at the Renaissance, the invention of printing and the advance of the Ottoman Turks into Europe combined to produce a number of works on Islam in the first half of the sixteenth century. These included an Arabic text of the Qur'ān, published at Venice in 1530, and the Latin translation of Robert of Ketton, published along with some other works at Bâle in 1543 by Bibliander.[2] Interest continued in the seventeenth century, and among various books which appeared there may be mentioned the first translation of the Qur'ān into English (1649); this was made by a Scotsman, Alexander Ross, who also wrote a book on comparative religion, and was based on a French translation and not directly on the Arabic.[3] A new standard of scholarship was reached by the Italian cleric Ludovici Marracci who in 1698 at Padua produced a text of the Qur'ān based on a number of manuscripts, accompanied by a careful Latin translation. Marracci is said to have spent forty years of his life on Qur'ānic studies and was familiar with the chief Muslim commentators. A comparable level of scholarship was attained by George Sale, whose English translation, accompanied by a 'Preliminary Discourse' giving a brief objective account of Islam, appeared at London in 1734. Sale's interpretation was based on the Muslim commentators, especially al-Bayḍāwī, and was accompanied by explanatory notes. There have been many subsequent editions of this book, and the translation and notes are still of value.[4]

The nineteenth century saw further advances in Qur'ānic scholarship, beginning with Gustav Flügel's edition of the text in 1834, of which there have been many subsequent editions, some being revised by Gustav Redslob. The chief advances in the study of the Qur'ān were made by persons who were also, and indeed primarily, interested in the life of Muḥammad. The first of these was Gustav Weil whose biography of Muḥammad (1843), unfortunately not based on the best sources, was followed by a *Historische-kritische Einleitung in den Koran* (Bielefeld, 1844; second edition 1878). The two successors of Weil, Aloys Sprenger and William Muir, both spent many years in India and there found older and better sources for the biography. To Sprenger belongs the credit of first discovering these sources and realizing their importance. His first essay in biography appeared in English at Allahabad in 1851, and was not completed, being ultimately replaced by a three-volume work in German, *Das Leben und die Lehre des Moḥammad* (Berlin, 1861–25). Some 36 pages in the introduction to the third volume are devoted to the Qur'ān, discussing the distinction between Meccan and Medinan suras and the collection of the Qur'ān. Muir followed in Sprenger's footsteps, but, as noted on p. 112, went more thoroughly into the chronology of the suras. His conclusions on this question were contained in an essay on the 'Sources for the Biography of Mahomet' which was attached to his *Life of Mahomet* (London, four vols., 1858–61; subsequently abridged and revised in various editions); and they are stated more fully in *The Coran, its Composition and Teaching; and the Testimony it bears to the Holy Scriptures* (London, 1878).

The growing interest in Islamic studies in Europe led the Parisian Académie des Inscriptions et Belles-Lettres in 1857 to propose as the subject for a prize monograph 'a critical history of the text of the Coran'. It was specified that the work was to 'rechercher la division primitive et le caractère des différents morceaux qui le composent; déterminer autant qu'il est possible, avec l'aide des historiens arabes et des commentateurs et d'après l'examen des morceaux eux-mêmes, les moments de la vie de Mahomet aux quels ils se rapportent; exposer les vicissitudes que traversa le texte du Coran, depuis les récitations de Mahomet jusqu'à la récension définitive qui lui donna la forme où nous le voyons; déterminer d'après l'examen des plus anciens manuscrits la nature des variantes qui ont survécu aux récensions'. The subject attracted three scholars: Aloys Sprenger; the Italian Michele Amari, who was beginning to make a name for himself as the historian of Islamic Sicily; and a young German Theodor Nöldeke who in 1856 had published a Latin disquisition on the origin and composition of the Qur'ān. The latter scholar won the prize, and an enlarged German version of the prize-gaining work was published at Göttingen in 1860 as *Geschichte des Qorans*, and became the foundation of all later Qur'ānic studies.

The subsequent history of Nöldeke's book is itself a veritable saga. In 1898 the publisher suggested a second edition; and as Nöldeke himself could not contemplate this, the task was entrusted to a pupil, Friedrich Schwally. Schwally took up the task with traditional German thoroughness; but because of the thoroughness and for various other reasons the publication of the second edition was spread out over many years. The first volume, dealing with the origin of the Qur'ān, eventually appeared at Leipzig in 1909; and the second, on 'the collection of the Qur'ān', in 1919. Schwally, however, died in February 1919, after virtually completing the manuscript, and it had to be seen through the press by two colleagues. Schwally had also done no more than preliminary work for a third volume on the history of the text, but his successor at Königsberg, Gotthelf Bergsträsser, agreed to make himself responsible for the volume. Two sections of the volume (about two-thirds of the whole) were published in 1926 and 1929. A further quantity of important material had come to light by this time and delayed the third section. Next Bergsträsser died unexpectedly in 1933; and it fell to yet another scholar, Otto Pretzl, to bring the work to completion in 1938, sixty-eight years after the first edition and forty years after the first suggestion of a second edition. It is truly a remarkable work of scholarly cooperation, and deservedly maintains its position as the standard treatment of the subject, even though some parts of it now require revision.

Nöldeke's 1860 volume by no means exhausted the problems of Qur'ānic study. He himself made further contributions, notably in the opening section 'Zur Sprache des Korans' (pp. 1-30) of his *Neue Beiträge zur semitischen Sprachwissenschaft* (Strassburg, 1910). Hartwig Hirschfeld after some earlier work on the Qur'ān published in 1902 in London his *New Researches into the Composition and Exegesis of the Qoran*, of which something has been said above (p. 112). The 'socialist' biographer of Muḥammad, Hubert Grimme, in connection with his work on the biography, pursued independent lines of research into the composition and chronology of the Qur'ān as described above (p. 112). While the twentieth century has seen many further books and articles on the Qur'ān, the most notable work of a general kind has been *Koranische Untersuchungen* by Josef Horovitz (Berlin, 1926), which deals with the narrative sections of the Qur'ān and the proper names. Arthur Jeffery's *Foreign Vocabulary of the Qur'ān* (Baroda, 1938) is a useful reference volume, summarizing much previous work and making fresh contributions; there have of course been many advances in the last thirty years. His *Materials for the Study of the Text of the Qur'ān* (p. 44 above) is a mark of his interest in the field in which Bergsträsser was also working. The volume containing Ignaz Goldziher's lectures on *Die Richtungen der islamischen Koranauslegung* (Leiden, 1920) is outstanding in its field (cf. p. 167 above).

In the last half-century three men have devoted a large part of their time to Qur'ānic studies. The oldest of these, Richard Bell, set out the first-fruits of his work on the Qur'ān in the form of lectures on *The Origin of Islam in its Christian Environment* (London, 1926). The major results of his work, though in a slightly incomplete form, are to be found in his translation – *The Qur'ān: Translated, with a critical re-arrangement of the Surahs* (two vols., Edinburgh, 1937, 1939). Unfortunately it has not proved possible to publish the mass of notes which he left, explaining in detail the reasons for his conclusions. This lack is partly made good by his articles (mentioned in the list below) and partly by his *Introduction to the Qur'ān* (Edinburgh, 1953), of which the present volume is a revised version.

In the case of Régis Blachère the study of the life of the prophet, entitled *Le Problème de Mahomet* (Paris, 1952) and based on the premiss that the Qur'ān is the only reliable source, appeared after the other work on the Qur'ān. This latter was focussed on a translation: *Le Coran: traduction selon un essai de reclassement des sourates* (three vols., Paris, 1947–51). The dating and arrangement of the suras has already been discussed (p. 112). The first of the three volumes is entirely devoted to an introduction, of which a second edition was published separately in 1959. This deals with the collection of the text, the variant readings, the history of the text and similar matters. Specially valuable is the section on 'amélioration graphique' or improvement of the script, since this includes the results of the study of existing ancient copies of the Qur'ān.

It is well known to the colleagues of Rudi Paret that he has been working for many years on the Qur'ān. As in the case of Bell a small book of a general kind came first: *Mohammed und der Koran* (Stuttgart, 1957). This is a short account of the life of the prophet which for the most part passes over the military and political aspects and concentrates on the religious aspects, especially those for which there is Qur'ānic material. He has also published some articles, such as 'Der Koran als Geschichtsquelle' (*Der Islam*, xxxvii / 1961, 24-42). At the centre of his work, however, has been the Qur'ān itself; and a complete German translation appeared in four 'Lieferungen' between 1963 and 1966 at Stuttgart. The interpretation of each term has been based on an exhaustive comparison of all the instances of it and of cognate terms throughout the Qur'ān. The reader may thus have a high degree of confidence that he has been given an accurate rendering of what the Qur'ān meant for the first hearers. There is no structural analysis, apart from a division into paragraphs; and there are no notes apart from explanatory additions to the text and footnotes giving a literal rendering where for the sake of style or clarity the main translation is somewhat free. Further publications are promised in the shape of a commentary or discussions of various problems. It is to be hoped that these, which will indeed be the 'crown of a lifeswork' will not be long delayed.

Of English translations of the Qur'ān those by J. M. Rodwell (1861) and E. H. Palmer (1880) were not without merit, but are now passed over in favour of more recent ones. That of Marmaduke Pickthall (*The Meaning of the Glorious Koran, an explanatory translation*; London, 1930), though it does not read well, is interesting as the work of an Englishman who became a Muslim and had his translation approved by Muslim authorities in Cairo. Another translation by a Muslim is that in the Penguin Classics (1956), *The Koran*, by N. J. Dawood, an Iraqi with an excellent command of English. His translation is very readable, since his aim is that it should always be meaningful to a modern man, but this leads to some departures from the standard interpretations. The most satisfactory English translation so far is that of Arthur J. Arberry of Cambridge. He first published *The Holy Koran, an Introduction with Selections* (London, 1953), which was an experimental translation of selected passages using various methods. This was followed in 1955 by a complete translation entitled *The Koran Interpreted* (two volumes, London). The method adopted for this was to put the whole into short lines, regardless of the length of the Arabic verses but varying to some extent according to the subject-matter. The diction is carefully chosen; and the translation as a whole has managed to suggest something of the grace and majesty of the original Arabic. The present writer's *Companion to the Qur'ān* (London, 1967), based primarily on the Arberry translation, is intended to provide the English reader with a minimum of explanatory notes.

The following is a small selection of useful books and articles not otherwise mentioned in the text or notes of this volume.

A fairly complete list of articles will be found in the relevant sections of J. D. Pearson's *Index Islamicus*, 1906–1955 (Cambridge, 1958) and supplements. Books as well as articles, mostly with brief comments, are listed in *Abstracta Islamica*, published annually as a supplement to *Revue des études islamiques* (Paris). Books and articles up to 1922 are discussed in the work of Pfannmüller mentioned in note 2 to this chapter.

Older works:

Christian Snouck-Hurgronje: 'La légende qorānique d'Abraham et la politique religieuse du Prophète Mohammed' (1880; French translation by G. H. Bousquet, *Revue africaine*, 95 [1951], 273-88).

I. Schapiro: *Die haggadischen Elemente im erzählenden Teile des Korans* (first section only), Leipzig, 1907.

J. Barth: 'Studien zur Kritik und Exegese des Qorāns', *Der Islam*, vi (1915–16), 113-48.

B. Schrieke: 'Die Himmelsreise Muhammeds', *ibid.* 1-30.

Wilhelm Rudolph: *Die Abhängigkeit des Qorāns von Judentum und Christentum*, Stuttgart, 1922.

W. W. Barthold: 'Der Koran und das Meer', *Zeitschrift der deutschen morgenländischen Gesellschaft*, 83 (1929), 37-43.

Karl Ahrens: 'Christliches im Qoran: eine Nachlese', *ibid.* 84 (1930), 15-68, 148-90.

Heinrich Speyer: *Die biblischen Erzählungen im Qoran*, Gräfenhainichen, 1931 (reprinted 1961).

D. Sidersky: *Les origines des légendes musulmanes dans le Coran*, Paris, 1933.

K. Ahrens: *Muhammed als Religionsstifter*, Leipzig, 1935.

Articles by Richard Bell on Qur'ānic subjects (complete list):

'A duplicate in the Koran; the composition of Surah xxiii', *Moslem World*, xviii (1928), 227-33.

'Who were the Ḥanīfs?', *ibid.* xx (1930), 120-4.

'The Men of the Aʿrāf (Surah vii: 44)', *ibid.* xxii (1932), 43-8.

'The Origin of the ʿId al-Adḥā', *ibid.* xxiii (1933), 117-20.

'Muhammad's Call', *ibid.* xxiv (1934), 13-19.

'Muhammad's Visions', *ibid.* xxiv. 145-54.

'Muhammad and previous Messengers', *ibid.* xxiv. 330-40.
'Muhammad and Divorce in the Qur'ān', *ibid.* xxix (1939), 55-62.
'Sūrat al-Ḥashr: a study of its composition', *ibid.* xxxviii (1948), 29-42.
'Muḥammad's Pilgrimage Proclamation', *Journal of the Royal Asiatic Society*, 1937, 233-44.
'The Development of Muhammad's Teaching and Prophetic Consciousness', *School of Oriental Studies Bulletin, Cairo*, June 1935, 1-9.
'The Beginnings of Muhammad's Religious Activity', *Transactions of the Glasgow University Oriental Society*, vii (1934–5), 16-24.
'The Sacrifice of Ishmael', *ibid.* x. 29-31.
'The Style of the Qur'ān', *ibid.* xi (1942–4), 9-15.
'Muhammad's Knowledge of the Old Testament', *Studia Semitica et Orientalia*, ii (W. B. Stevenson Festschrift), Glasgow, 1945, 1-20.

Other recent works:

Michel Allard, etc.: *Analyse conceptuelle du Coran sur cartes perforées*, The Hague, 1963 (2 vols. and cards); explained by Allard in 'Une méthode nouvelle pour l'étude du Coran', *Studia Islamica*, xv (1961), 5-21.
Dirk Bakker: *Man in the Qur'ān*, Amsterdam, 1965.
Harris Birkeland: *The Lord guideth: studies on primitive Islam*, Oslo, 1956.
Régis Blachère: *Le Coran* (Collection 'Que sais-je?'), Paris, 1966.
Robert Brunschvig: 'Simples remarques négatives sur le vocabulaire du Coran', *Studia Islamica*, v (1956), 19-32.
Maurice Causse: 'Théologie de rupture et de la communauté: étude sur la vocation prophétique de Moïse d'après le Coran', *Revue de l'histoire et de la philosophie religieuses*, i (1964), 60-82.
Josef Henninger: *Spuren christlicher Glaubenswahrheiten im Koran*, Schöneck, 1951.
Toshihiko Izutsu: *God and Man in the Koran: semantics of the Koranic Weltanschauung*, Tokyo, 1964.
— *Ethico-Religious Concepts in the Qur'ān*, Montreal, 1966.

Arthur Jeffery: 'The Qur'ān as Scripture', *Muslim World*, xl (1950), 41-55, 106-134, 185-206, 257-75.
Jacques Jomier: 'Le nom divin "al-Raḥmān" dans le Coran', *Mélanges Louis Massignon*, Damascus, 1957, ii. 361-81.
— *The Bible and the Koran* (tr. Arbez), New York, 1964.
Ilse Lichtenstadter: 'Origin and Interpretation of some Koranic Symbols', *Arabic and Islamic Studies in honor of Hamilton A. R. Gibb* (ed. G. Makdisi), Leiden, 1965, 426-36.
John Macdonald: 'Joseph in the Qur'ān and Muslim Commentary: a comparative study', *Muslim World*, xlvi (1956), 113-31, 207-24.
D. Masson: *Le Coran et la révélation judéo-chrétienne*, 2 vols., Paris, 1958.
Julian Obermann: 'Islamic Origins: a study in background and foundation', *The Arab Heritage*, ed. N. A. Faris, Princeton, 1946, 58-120.
Daud Rahbar: *God of Justice: a study in the ethical doctrine of the Qur'ān*, Leiden, 1960.
— 'Reflections on the Tradition of Qur'ānic Exegesis', *Muslim World*, lii (1962), 269-307.
Helmer Ringgren: 'The Conception of Faith in the Qur'ān', *Oriens*, iv (1951), 1-20.
— 'Die Gottesfurcht im Koran', *Orientalia Succana*, iii (1954), 118-34.
Irfan Shahid: 'A Contribution to Koranic Exegesis', *Arabic and Islamic Studies . . . Gibb* (as above), 563-80.
S.H. al-Shamma: *The Ethical System underlying the Qur'ān*, Tübingen, 1959.

2. Problems facing the non-Muslim scholar

(a) *The question of truth.* When the question is asked, 'Is the Qur'ān true?' it has to be countered by another, 'What does that question mean?' Before we can say whether the Qur'ān is true or not, we have to clarify our minds on the whole problem of the relationship of language to experience and more particularly to religious experience or, better, to man's experience of life in its totality. This is a vast subject which can only be adumbrated here.

A starting-point might be a distinction between a cerebral knowledge of religious ideas and an experiential knowledge of these same ideas. This distinction is found in other fields also. A student may be taught the scientific account of the various things that happen to a man's body when he is drunk; but, if he has lived a sheltered life, has never been slightly drunk, and has never seen a drunk man, his knowledge remains cerebral. The point is even more obvious with sexual intercourse. The person who has had no actual experience cannot from reading novels or scientific textbooks form an adequate idea of the 'feel' of the experience. The person without experience may have a perfect cerebral knowledge, but only experience can give experiential knowledge.

The case of religious ideas is even more complex. The ideas may sometimes deal apparently with objective external realities, sometimes with a man's inner states. Children brought up in a community of the adherents of a religion normally acquire a cerebral knowledge of the ideas of the religion long before they have an experiential knowledge. For one thing some of the profounder experiences associated with religion come only to a few and only after the attainment of some degree of maturity. For another thing, since one cannot point to interior states as one can point to external objects like plants, a person may not always recognize in his experience the things of which he has cerebral knowledge. One day it will come with a flash of illumination that 'This (in my present experience) is that which I have known about for years'.

Normally a person can only reach important levels of religious experience through participating in the life of the community in which he has been brought up and basing his activity on its ideas. There are exceptions, but this is the normal case. It is not easy for a person brought up in a Christian environment to appreciate the religious ideas of Islam, far less to make them the basis of a satisfactory life. The same is true for the Muslim with Christian ideas. This means that it is Christian ideas which give the Christian the best chance of attaining a richer and deeper experience, and likewise Muslim ideas the Muslim. Moreover we know that some such experience has actually been attained among both Christians and Muslims. At the same time we have no even approximately objective criterion to decide whose experience of life is richer and deeper.

One of the effects on the scholar of studying a religion other than that in which he was brought up is to produce a more sophisticated attitude in him. He no longer naïvely accepts words at their face value. Phrases like 'the uncreated speech of God' or 'the comfort of the Holy Spirit', he now realizes, do not mean a simple object in the way the phrase 'that tree' means the object at the end of the garden. Rather he has come to understand that he is primarily concerned with realities, which enter into 'man's experience of life as a whole', but at which language can only imperfectly hint. From this sophisticated standpoint the scholar can regard the Christian and the Muslim as being both concerned with the same realities-beyond-language, though each uses his own system of ideas and of language to deal as best he can in his practical living with these realities. The scholar can further see that both these systems are effective for those brought up in the community based on the system; and fortunately he does not require to decide which is the more effective, since in his own practical living he must make use – perhaps in a sophisticated form – of the system of ideas in which he was brought up.

It follows from this that truth is to be regarded as belonging not to separate propositions in a book, but to a whole system of ideas as embodied in the life of a community. Because this is so there is no uncommitted standpoint from which different sets of ideas can be objectively compared. The only possible comparison is one which is linked with a decision to abandon one's own community and attach oneself to some other. Such a decision, however, comes at a relatively naïve level. At the more sophisticated level of the scholar just described, he sees that the systems of ideas followed by Jews, Christians, Muslims, Buddhists and others are all true in so far as they enable human beings to have a more or less satisfactory 'experience of life as a whole'. So far as observation can tell, none of the great systems is markedly inferior or superior to the others. Each is therefore true. In particular the Qur'ān is in this sense true. The fact that the Qur'ānic conception of the unity of God appears to contradict the Christian conception of the unity of God does not imply that either system is false, nor even that either conception is false. Each conception is true in that it is part of a system which is true. In so far as some conception in a system seems to contradict the accepted teaching of science – or, that of history in so far as it is objective – that contradiction raises problems for the adherents of the system, but does not prove that the system as a whole is inferior to others. That is to say, the Qur'ānic assertion that the Jews did not kill Jesus does not prove that the Qur'ānic system as a whole is inferior to the Christian, even on the assumption that the crucifixion is an objective fact.

What then is the non-Muslim scholar doing when he studies the Qur'ānic system of ideas? He is not concerned with any question of ultimate truth, since that, it has been suggested, cannot be attained by man. He assumes the truth, in the relative sense just explained, of the Qur'ānic system of ideas. He is interested, however, in looking at these ideas in their relationships to one another, at their development over the centuries, at their place in the life of the community, and similar matters; and he also tries to express his thoughts and conclusions in 'neutral' language which will neither deny the truth of the ideas in the relative sense nor improperly assert their ultimate truth in some naïve sense.

(b) *The question of sources.* Nineteenth-century European scholars were, as we now think, excessively concerned with the attempt to discover the 'sources' of Qur'ānic statements. Modern work on this subject may be said to have begun in 1833 with the book (in German) of Abraham Geiger entitled *What has Muhammad taken from Judaism?*[5] Numerous other scholars entered the lists, and there was quite a battle between those who thought Judaism was the main source and those who thought it was Christianity. Some of the more recent works will be found in the list above. Since the study of sources has been objected to by Muslims, it seems worth while making some remarks of a general kind.

Firstly, the study of sources does not explain away the ideas whose sources are found, nor does it detract from their truth and validity. Shakespeare's play of *Hamlet* remains a very great play even after we have found the 'source' from which Shakespeare derived the outline of the story. No more does our knowledge of the source tell us anything of importance about the creative processes in Shakespeare's mind. This is admittedly not an exact parallel with the Qur'ān, yet men have often thought that there was some divine inspiration in the work of great poets and that we can properly speak of a 'creative' process.

Secondly, even those who accept the doctrine that the Qur'ān is the uncreated speech of God may properly study 'sources' in the sense of external influences on the thinking of the Arabs in Muḥammad's time. It is repeatedly asserted in the Qur'ān that it is 'an Arabic Qur'ān'; and this implies that the Qur'ān is not merely in the Arabic language but is also expressed in terms of the conceptions familiar to the Arabs. Thus 23.88/90 has frequently been misunderstood by European scholars because it makes statements about God in terms of the distinctively Arab conception of *ijāra* or 'the giving of neighbourly protection'. Again many of the 'narratives' of the Qur'ān are in an allusive style which presupposes that the hearers already have some knowledge of the story.

If these two points are accepted, it will be seen that the study of sources and influences, besides being a proper one, has a moderate degree of interest. It tells us something about the spread of ideas and other cultural features in Arabia before the revelation of the Qur'ān. We can perhaps also learn something of the general laws which cause peoples to take over certain ideas from their neighbours and to reject certain other ideas. Such matters are of interest to students of the social sciences and to like-minded general readers. Such a study of sources and influences, of course, also raises theological problems for the Muslim, or rather gives additional complexity to old problems. The doctrine of the uncreated Qur'ān already raises the problem of the relation of the eternal and the temporal. It may be asserted that the temporal events mentioned in the Qur'ān are eternally known to God, but this still leaves questions unanswered. How can imperfect human language represent the perfection of divine thought? If it is held that language is created by God, this seems to imply that God works through secondary causes; and the relation of these secondary causes to God who is the primary cause of all events, is but another form of the relation between the temporal and the external. Thus the problem has really only taken on another form.

The Qur'ān has been studied and meditated on for about fourteen centuries, and much has been achieved. Yet in this strange new world of the later twentieth century when Muslims are in closer contact with devout and convinced non-Muslims than at any time since the first century of Islam, there is need for still further study of the Qur'ān and study along new lines; and this must be undertaken by both Muslims and non-Muslims.[6]

ABBREVIATIONS

Bell, *Origin* = Richard Bell, *The Origin of Islam in its Christian Environment*, London, 1926 (reprinted 1968).

Bell, *Translation* = do., *The Qur'ān, translated with a critical re-arrangement of the Surahs*, 2 vols., Edinburgh, 1937, 1939.

EI[1], *EI*[2] = *The Encyclopaedia of Islam*, first edition, Leiden, 1913-42; second edition, Leiden and London, 1960-

EI(S) = *A Shorter Encyclopaedia of Islam*, Leiden, 1913.

Jeffery *Foreign Vocabulary* = Arthur Jeffery, *The Foreign Vocabulary of the Qur'ān*, Baroda, 1938; cf. p. 85.

Mecca = W. Montgomery Watt, *Muhammad at Mecca*, Oxford, 1953.

Medina = do., *Muhammad at Medina*, Oxford, 1956.

NS = Nöldeke and Schwally, *Geschichte des Qorāns*, second edition, Leipzig, 1909–38 (reprinted Hildesheim, 1961); cf. pp. 175f.

Origin = *see* Bell, *Origin*.

Translation = *see* Bell, *Translation*.

Watt, *Integration* = W. Montgomery Watt, *Islam and the Integration of Society*, London, 1961.

NOTES

Chapter One

1. Cf. Charles Diehl and Georges Marçais, *Le Monde Oriental de 395 à 1081* (Histoire Générale), Paris, 1936, 123-57.
2. A variant reading with only a difference in pointing gives exactly the opposite sense; but this can hardly be correct, since at no date at which the passage is likely to have been revealed had there been a notable Persian defeat. Cf. NS, i. 49f.
3. Leiden, 1892; a thesis for a German doctorate.
4. E.g. Book, account: 69.19,25; 84.7,10. Reckoning: 69.90,26; 84.8. Balance: 21.47/8; 101.6/5, 8/6. Pledge: 52.21; 74.38/41. Hire: 57.19/18,27; 84.25; 95.6. Loan: 2.245/6; 5.12/15; 57.11,18/17; 64.17; 73.20.
5. *A Study of History*, London, 1934, iii. 7-22, esp. 13f.
6. Cf. G. Rentz, art. "'Arab (Djazīrat al-)', sect. vi (ethnography) in *EI*².
7. Cf. Philip K. Hitti, *History of the Arabs*, seventh ed., London, 1961, 49-66. South Arabian influences on the Islamic religion were emphasized by Hubert Grimme, e.g. in 'Der Logos in Südarabien', *Orientalische Studien Theodor Nöldeke gewidmet*, Leipzig, 1906, i. 453-61; 'Südarabische Lehnwörter im Koran', *Zeitschrift für Assyriologie*, xxvi (1912), 158-68.
8. *Cf. Medina*, 192; D.S. Margoliouth, *The relations between Arabs and Israelites prior to the Rise of Islam*, London, 1924; Werner Caskel, in *Studies in Islamic Cultural History* (ed. G. von Grunebaum), Menasha, 1954, p. 43 speaks of Jews as bearers of Nabatean culture.
9. There is much material about Christianity in Arabia. Cf. *EI*(*S*), art. 'Naṣārā', section A (A.S. Tritton); also Watt, *Medina*, 315.
10. Julius Wellhausen, *Reste arabischen Heidentums*, second ed., Berlin, 1897; Ibn-al-Kalbī's *Book of Idols* is translated by Nabih Amin Faris, Princeton, 1952.
11. *Mecca*, 24f.

12. Cf. 29.61,63,65; 23.84/6-89/91; 39.38/9; 43.8-15/14; 6.136/7; 41.9/8; etc. See also p. 117.
13. Cf. *EI*² art. 'ḥanīf' (Watt); also Annex B, pp. 15f.
14. The following account is based on Watt, *Muhammad at Mecca* and *Muhammad at Medina*. There is a shorter statement in *Muhammad Prophet and Statesman*, Oxford, 1961. Cf. also Tor Andrae, *Mohammed, the Man and his Faith*, tr. Menzel, New York, 1936, 1960 (emphasizing the religious development); and *EI*¹, art. 'Muḥammad' (Frants Buhl).
15. Since the Islamic year consists of twelve lunar months or 354 days, recourse must be had to tables in order to discover corresponding Islamic and Christian dates. Simple tables are given in Sir Wolseley Haig's *Comparative Tables of Muhammadan and Christian Dates*, London, 1932, and G.S.P. Freeman-Grenville's, *The Muslim and Christian Calendars*, London, 1963. The fullest and most satisfactory tables for those who want to know the day of the week and the month are in *Wüstenfeld-Mahler'sche Vergleichungs-Tabellen*, edited by Bertold Spuler, Wiesbaden, 1961. To facilitate comparisons with Byzantine history, dates in this *Introduction* are given in the Christian form.

Chapter Two

1. E.g. 25.5/6, where it accompanies an accusation of fraud; the phrase occurs nine times. From the *Translation* it appears that Richard Bell thought it belonged to the early Medinan period and was sometimes used by Jews; but the passages where it occurs are usually reckoned to be Meccan. Cf. NS, i. 16; Jeffery, *Foreign Vocabulary*, s.v.
2. Cf. Norman Daniel, *Islam and the West, The Making of an Image*, Edinburgh, 1960, chapter 2.
3. *On Heroes, Hero-worship, and the Heroic in History*, various editions, Lecture II, 'The Hero as Prophet: Mahomet: Islam' (8 May 1840).
4. *Mohammed der Prophet*, Stuttgart, 1843; cf. p. 174 above.
5. Cf. p. 174 above.
6. Cf. p. 174 above.
7. *Mohammed and the Rise of Islam*, London, 1905.
8. Cf. NS, i, 1-5 and corresponding section of first edition.
9. In *EI*¹, art. 'Muḥammad', *ad fin.*
10. *Origin*, esp. 71-83.
11. *Mohammed, the Man and his Faith*, esp. 47-52.
12. *Mohammed*, 48f.; he refers to 75.16-19 (movement of the tongue) and 87.6-8.

13. The same phrase is used in 3.44/39 and 11.49/51.
14. Bell, *Origin*, 97f.
15. 22.52/1, which is said to refer to the incident of the 'satanic verses' connected with 53.19,20; cf. p. 88.
16. Cf. Nabia Abbott, *Aishah the Beloved of Mohammed*, Chicago, 1942, 61, with references to the sources; also Andrae, *Mohammed*, 154.
17. Cf. p. 115.
18. 3.21/0; 4.138/7; 9.3,34; 31.7/6; 45.8/7; 84.24. This usage is not discussed by Jeffery, *Foreign Vocabulary*, s.v.
19. P. 25 above; cf. also 12.109; 16.43/5; 21.7f. Wife: 13.38.
20. Cf. Jeffery, *Foreign Vocabulary*, s.v.; also Josef Horovitz, *Koranische Untersuchungen*, Berlin, 1926, 47 (pp. 44-54 of this work deal with 'die Koranische Prophetologie').
21. Cf. lists in 4.163/1 and 6.84-9. Idrīs is called a prophet in 19.56/7; some European scholars favour an identification of Idrīs with a figure in Greek legend (cf. A.J. Wensinck, art. 'Idrīs' in *EI*[1]; Horovitz, 88), while Muslims have usually identified him with the Enoch of the Bible, and this view seems to have been accepted by A.J. Wensinck at a later date (*The Muslim Creed*, Cambridge, 1932, 204); C.C. Torrey suggested that Idrīs was a corruption of Esdras or Ezra (*The Jewish Foundation of Islam*, New York, 1933, 72): cf. also Jeffery, *Foreign Vocabulary*, s.v.
22. Cf. Wensinck, *Muslim Creed*, 203f.; also *EI*[1], arts. '*nabī*' (J. Horovitz), '*rasūl*' (Wensinck); Wensinck, 'Muhammed und die Propheten', *Acta Orientalia*, ii (1924), 168-98.
23. Cf. Jeffery, *Foreign Vocabulary*, s.v.
24. Cf. 42.10/8; 24.48/7; §23 of the Constitution of Medina (*Medina*, 223; Watt, *Islamic Political Thought*, Edinburgh, 1968, 132); also *Medina*, 230.
25. Cf. 4.41/5; 16.89/91. The verse 10.47/8, 'when their messenger comes (to a community), judgement will be given (*quḍiya*) between them fairly', is probably also to be understood eschatologically (contrary to the view expressed in *Medina*, 229; cf. R. Paret, review of *Medina* in *Der Islam*, xxxv/1957).
26. *EI*[2], art. "Arabiyya', A. ii (1), with further references.
27. Cf. p. 4 above.
28. Cf. Frants Buhl, *Das Leben Muhammeds*, Leipzig, 1930, 55 with reference; the extension of writing in Arabia is discussed on pp. 52-6.
29. See NS, ii. 11-14 for full references.
30. Cf. Jeffery, *Foreign Vocabulary*, s.v.

31. Cf. A. Mingana, *Woodbrooke Studies*, Cambridge, 1928, ii. 21.
32. Cf. Jeffery, s.v.
33. For discussions of *ummī* see esp. Horovitz, *Koranische Untersuchungen*, 52f.; R. Paret, art. 'Ummī' in *EI*(*S*).
34. Cf. *Mecca*, 40, 46.
35. E.g. Ibn-Hishām, *Sīra*, ed. F. Wüstenfeld, Göttingen, 1858–60, 747; the English translation by Alfred Guillaume (London, 1955) is entitled *The Life of Muhammad: a translation of (Ibn) Ishāq's Sīrat Rasūl Allāh*, and has Wüstenfeld's paging on the margin.
36. Cf. *Medina*, 5f.
37. Ibn-Hisham, 226f. (*ṣaḥīfa* is rendered 'manuscript', 'sheet' and 'page' in the English translation).
38. Cf. NS, i. 46f.
39. Cf. al-Bayḍāwī, az-Zamakhsharī and other commentators on 6.93; also Ibn-Hishām, 818ff.

Chapter Three

1. The versions of the report are discussed in NS, ii, 11-15; detailed references are given p. 11, note 4.
2. Ibn-Sa'd, *Ṭabaqāt*, Leiden, 1904, etc., iii. 1.202.8f.; cf. NS, ii. 15, n. 2.
3. Friedrich Schwally (in NS, ii. 20) could find the names of only two such persons.
4. See p. 55.
5. Arthur Jeffery, *Materials for the Study of the Text of the Qur'ān*, Leiden, 1937, 212f. (Arabic text, 24f.). The edition of Ibn-Abī-Dāwūd's *Kitāb al-Maṣāḥif* is part of this book.
6. NS, ii. 50-54.
7. Cf. p. 83 above.
8. Cf. Jeffery, *Materials*, 13; and note 5 above.
9. *Op. cit.*, 7; NS, ii. 27-30. It is notable that a prominent position is given in late traditions to the collection by al-Miqdād (b. 'Amr) b. al-Aswad, although nothing is said about him by early writers on the Qur'ānic text (cf. NS, iii, 172f.).
10. NS, ii. 33-8.
11. Ash-Shahrastānī, *Milal*, ed. Cureton, 95; cf. NS, ii. 94.
12. Cf. R. Blachère, *Introduction au Coran*, Paris, 1947, (see also p. 177 for this book).
13. Full name: Abū-Bakr Aḥmad ibn-Mūsā. Cf. Blachère, 127-30; NS, iii. 110-23; Louis Massignon, *La Passion d' . . . al-Hallaj*, Paris, 1922, i. 241-3.
14. Cf. NS, iii. 108.

15. For reff. see A. J. Wensinck, *Handbook of early Muhammadan Tradition*, Leiden, 1927, 130 (*s.v.* Ḳur'ān). The interpretation of *aḥruf* as 'dialects' is to be rejected (NS, i. 51).
16. Or Ibn-Muqsim; also known as Abū-Bakr al-ʿAṭṭār; cf. Yāqūt, *Irshād*, London (Gibb Memorial Series), 1923, etc., vi. 498-501. For the incident cf. NS, iii. 122f.
17. For fuller details cf. NS, iii. 186-9 and Blachère, 118-23. There are variant death-dates for some of these scholars.
18. *Journal des Savants*, 1832, 536.
19. *Historisch-Kritische Einleitung in den Koran*, second edn., Bielefeld, 1878, 52.
20. NS, ii. 82.
21. *Einleitung*, 74.
22. Ibid., 76.
23. *New Researches into the Composition and Exegesis of the Qoran*, London, 1902, 138ff.
24. Ibn-Hishām, 341-3; Watt, *Medina*, 221-5; *Islamic Political Thought*, 130-4.
25. Ibn-Hishām, 747f.
26. Goldziher, *Koranauslegung* (see ch. x, note 1), 24; al-Bayḍāwī ad loc.; etc.
27. Al-Bukhārī, *Shahādāt*, 11; Muslim, *Faḍā'il al-Qur'ān*, 2; cf. NS, i. 47.
28. A fairly full account of these is given in NS, i. 234-61.
29. Cf. Watt, *Integration*, 192; J. Schacht, art. 'Zinā'' in *EI(S)*.
30. NS, i. 242f.; Jeffery, *Materials*, 198.
31. Jeffery, *Materials*, 32.
32. Cf. Watt, *Medina*, 304; also art. 'Ḥanīf' in *EI*².
33. Cf. Watt, *Mecca*, 102.

Chapter Four

1. Edward Sell, *The Faith of Islam*, 3rd edition, London, 1907, contains as appendix A *ʿIlmu't-tajwīd*, where there is a fuller account of the divisions, the symbols to guide the reader, and similar matters.
2. Cf. Jeffery, *Foreign Vocabulary*, s.v.; though originally accepted by Nöldeke, this was rejected in NS, i. 30.
3. Bell, *Origin*, 52; approved by Jeffery, l.c.
4. *Mark* 12.26; *Luke* 20.37.
5. *New Researches*, 141-3.
6. 'Ursprung und Bedeutung der koranischen Siglen', *Der Islam*, xiii (1923), 191-226.

7. In his *Geschichte des Qorāns*, 1860, 215f.
8. Cf. NS, ii. 68-78, esp. 75-7.
9. 'The mystical letters of the Qur'ān', *Studia Islamica*, xvi (1962), 5-11.
10. But cf. *Hebrews*, 6.13.
11. Arabic *lā uqsimu*; it is uncertain whether the *lā* should be regarded as negative or intensive (cf. al-Bayḍāwī on 56.75/4); in his *Translation* Bell prefers the negative, but the intensive seems to give better sense. The uncertainty confirms the suggestion of a formula.
12. Direct address is found in the following verses:
   (*a*) O ye people: 2.21/19, 168/3, 172/67; 4.1,170/68,174; 10.23/4, 57/8; 22.1,5,73/2; 31.33/2; 35.3,5,15/16; 49.13.
   (*b*) O ye who have believed: 2.104/98, 153/48, 178/3, 183/79, 208/4, 254/5, 264/6, 267/9, 278,282; 3.100/95, 102/97, 118/4, 130/25, 156/0,200; 4.19/23, 29/33, 43/6, 59/62, 71/3, 94/6, 135/4, 136/5, 144/3; 5.1,2,6/8, 8/11, 11/14, 35/9, 51/6, 54/9, 57/62, 87/9, 94/5, 95/6, 101, 105/4, 106/5; 8.15,20,24,27,29,45/7; 9.23,28,34-38,119/20, 123/4; 22.77/6; 24.21.27,58/7; 33.9,41,49/8,53,56,69; 47.7/8,33/5; 49.1,2,6,11,12; 57.28; 58.9/10,11/12,12/13; 59.18; 60.1,10,13; 61.2,10,14; 63.9; 64.14; 65.11; 66.6,8. Cf. 29.56.
   (*c*) O thou messenger: 5.41/5, 67/71.
   O thou prophet: 8.64/5, 65/6; 9.73/4; 33.1,28,45/4, 50/49,59; 60.12; 65.1; 66.1,9.
   O thou heavily burdened: 73.1.
   O thou clothed in the *dithār*: 74.1.
   (*d*) O Children of Israel: 2.40/38, 47/4, 49/6, 122/16, 124/18; 20.80/2.
   O People of the Book: 3.65/58, 70/63, 71/64; 4.171/69; 5.15/18,19/22.

Chapter Five

1. *Göttinger gelehrte Anzeigen*, 1909, i; cf. *Wiener Zeitschrift für die Kunde des Morgenlandes*, xxii (1908), 265-86, 'Zur Strophik des Qurāns'; also H. Haham, ibid., xxviii (1914), 370-5.
2. *Die Propheten in ihrer ursprünglichen Form . . .*, Vienna, 1896, i. 20-60, 211f.
3. Cf. Alfred Guillaume, *Prophecy and Divination*, London, 1938, 245-50, etc.
4. The chief asseverative passages are: 36.1-5/4; 37.1-4; 38.1f.; 43.2/1f.; 44.1-6/5; 50.1; 51.1-6; 52.1-8; 53.1-3; 56.75/4-80/79;

68.1-4; 69.38-43; 74.32/5-37/40; 75.1-6; 77.1-7; 79.1-14(?); 81.15-19; 84.16-19; 85.1-7; 86.1-4,11-14; 89.1-5/4; 90.1-4; 91.1-10; 92.1-4; 93.1-3; 95.1-5; 100.1-6; 103.1f. (In some cases there is doubt where the passage ends.)

5. 'When'-passages, introduced by *idhā*: 56.1-9; 69.13-17(?); 74.8-10; 75.7-12,26-30; 77.8-13; 79.34-41; 81.1-14; 82.1-5; 84.1-6; 99.1-6; 110.1-3(?). Do., introduced by *yawma*: 70.8-14; 78.18-16; 80.34-7; 101.4/3f.
6. Cf. F. Bühl, 'Über Vergleichung und Gleichnisse im Qur'ān', *Acta Orientalia*, ii (1924), 1-11.
7. T. Sabbagh, *La métaphore dans le Coran*, Paris, 1953.
8. Such at least would be one of the suggestions of the word to Arab ears; but in its application to the party of 'Abd-Allāh ibn-Ubayy it has doubtless acquired something of the meaning of the Ethiopic *menāfeq*, 'hypocrite'.
9. *Volkssprache und Schriftsprache im alten Arabien*, Strasbourg, 1906.
10. *The Cairo Geniza* (Schweich Lectures for 1941), London, 1947, 78-84; *Goldziher Memorial Volume* (ed. Somogyi), Budapest, 1948, i. 163-82; 'The Arabic Readers of the Qur'ān', *Journal of Near Eastern Studies*, viii (1949), 65-71. His main contention is that the Qur'ān was recited, as modern colloquials are spoken, without *iʿrāb* or case-endings.
11. *Neue Beiträge zur semitischen Sprachwissenschaft*, Strasbourg, 1910, 2-4.
12. Carl Becker, *Der Islam*, i (1910), 391.
13. NS, ii. 59, n. 1.
14. *Histoire de la Littérature arabe*, Paris, 1952, i. 66-82; *Introduction*, 156-69.
15. *Ancient West Arabian*, London, 1951, xii, 1-4; 'The Beginnings of Classical Arabic', *Studia Islamica*, iv (1955), 19-37; *EI*², art. ʿArabiyya, A, ii (1): Eng. ed. i. 565f.
16. Cf. *Arabiya*, Berlin, 1950, 1-5.
17. Quoted in Jeffery, *Foreign Vocabulary*, 10.
18. Baroda, 1938 (Gaekwad's Oriental Series, vol. 79).

Chapter Six

1. Cf. pp. 40-4 above.
2. Cf. pp. 55f. above.
3. Translated by Majid Khadduri under the title *Islamic Jurisprudence: Shāfiʿīs* Risāla, Baltimore, 1961.
4. E.g. *K. an-nāsikh wa-l-mansūkh* by Abū-Jaʿfar an-Naḥḥās (d. 949), printed Cairo, 1938.

5. Chapter 47; in the edition of Cairo, 1935, this is ii. 20-27.
6. It was features of this kind which led Geyer to assume a kind of sonnet-formation; cf. p. 72 above.
7. 3.33/off., 45/off.; 7.160ff.; 10.7-10/11; 13.2ff.; 14.24/9ff.; 16.10ff., 48/50ff., 51/3ff.; 25.45/7ff., 53/5ff., 61/2f.; 27.59/60ff.; 31.15-20; 40.57/9ff., 69/71ff.; 41.9/8ff.; 43.9/8ff. For details see Bell's *Translation.*
8. To be exact, verse 18/16 rhymes in -ī(l), while of later verses 27/6, 30/28, and those mentioned below rhyme in -ā(l).
9. It seems from the *Translation* that Bell thought of one verse as ending at *muḥarraran* in 35/1 and another possibly at the first *unthā* in 36/1, and perhaps a third at *Zakariyyā'* in 37/2. Verse(s) 33-4/30 could be an addition to help the insertion of the passage. Another possibility is to let 33/0 originally end at '*Imrān.*
10. The change of pronoun is concealed by Bell's translation of *anfusa-kum* as 'your own people'. On the other hand, the Constitution of Medina (cf. Watt, *Medina*, 221f.) speaks about ransoms, and the verse probably refers to that.
11. For details see Bell's *Translation*, *ad locc.*
12. 69.3; 74.27; 77.14; 82.17; 83.8,19; 86.2; 90.12; 97.2; 101.3/2,10/7; 104.5. A. Fischer, 'Eine Qorān-Interpolation' (*Nöldeke-Festschrift*, Giessen, 1906, 33-55) thinks also that 101.10/7f. are a later addition.
13. Cf. p. 88 above. For Bell's theory of the original meaning of this verse, cf. his *Origin*, 97f.
14. The more striking cases are: 2.101/95ff., 135/29ff., 144/39ff., 183/79ff., 196/2ff.; 3.48/3ff., 68/1ff., 102/97ff., 110/06ff., 143/37ff., 152/45f., 170/64f., 181/77ff.; 4.23/7ff., 131/0f.; 5.41/5f., 48/52ff., 72/6ff., 90/2f.; 6.87ff.; 7.40/38f., 165/3ff.; 8.72/3f.; 9.86/7ff., (81/2ff.), 111/2f., 117/8f.; 10.104ff.; 11.40/2ff.; 13.19ff.; 15.87ff.; 16.16ff.; 17.45/7; 27.38ff.; 34.51/0ff.; 35.29/6ff.; 36.79ff.; 39.47/8f., 69ff.; 40.30/1ff.; 45.27/6ff.; 50.22/1ff.; 54.43ff.; 57.13f.; 59.5ff.; 63.7f.; 72.25/6ff.; 74.31ff.; 80.33ff. For details see Bell's *Translation.*
15. Richard Bell, on the basis of his written-document hypothesis, thought there had been an interweaving of alternative versions in 3.126/2-129/4 and 36.1-6/5.
16. A more elaborate analysis of this passage will be found in K. Wagtendonk, *Fasting in the Koran*, Leiden, 1968, 47-81.
17. Cf. Bell, 'The Origin of the '*īd al-aḍ'ḥā*', *Moslem World*, xxiii (1933), 117ff.
18. Cf. Bell, 'Muhammad's Pilgrimage Proclamation', *Journal of Royal Asiatic Society*, 1937, 233ff.

19. Other complicated passages are analysed by Bell in the articles 'The Men of the Aʿrāf (vii. 44)', *Moslem World*, xxii (1932), and '*Surat al-Ḥashr* (59)', ibid. xxxviii (1948); see pp. 179f.

Chapter Seven

1. For the history of this work see pp. 175f.
2. J.M. Rodwell's translation of the Qur'ān (1861, etc.) gives the suras in Nöldeke's order with one or two changes in the early suras.
3. See p. 174 above.
4. *Mohammed*, vol. 2, 'Einleitung in den Koran; System der Koranischen Theologie', Münster i. W., 1895, esp. 25ff. There is some discussion of the views of Grimme and others in Frants Buhl, 'Zur Ḳuranexegese', *Acta Orientalia*, iii (1924), 97-108.
5. London, 1902. This followed on earlier works in German: *Jüdische Elemente im Koran*, Berlin, 1878; *Beiträge zur Erklärung des Koran*, Leipzig, 1886.
6. 2 vols. Paris, 1949, 1951, with an introductory volume, 1947 (see p. 177).
7. *Mohammed*, vol. 1, 'Das Leben', Münster i. W., 1892.
8. 'Une nouvelle biographie de Mohammed', *Revue de l'Histoire des Religions*, xxx (1894), 48-70,149-78; reprinted in *Verspreide Geschriften*, Bonn, 1923, i.
9. *Mohammed, the Man and his Faith*, esp. ch. 3.
10. *Origin*, 89f., 102-6.
11. A fuller exposition of these points is given in Watt, *Muhammad Prophet and Statesman*, 22-34; cf. also *Mecca*, 62-72. It is to be noted that the later appeal to the Jews (2.47/4-53/0) speaks of God's goodness and mentions the Last Day briefly; cf. also the appeal to the Bedouin, 16.70/2-73/5.
12. Cf. Julius Wellhausen, *Reste arabischen Heidentums*,[2] Berlin, 1897, 218-22.
13. 39.3/4,43/4f. See also Index, s.v. and chapter 1, note 12.
14. Cf. Edmund Beck, 'Die Gestalt des Abraham am Wendepunkt der Entwicklung Muhammeds', *Muséon*, lxv (1952), 73-94; Beck minimizes the originality of the Qur'ān.

Chapter Eight

1. Cf. A.F.L. Beeston, *Journal of Semitic Studies*, xiii (1968), 253-5.

1a. *Beiträge zur Erklärung des Qorans*, Leipzig, 1886, 37; cf. Horovitz, *Koranische Untersuchungen*, 13f.
2. Ibid., 130.
3. Ibn-Hishām, *Sīra*, ed. Wüstenfeld, 157, 166.
4. Abraham Geiger, *Was hat Mohammed aus dem Judentum aufgenommen?*, Bonn, 1833 (Leipzig, 1902), 58.
5. NS, i. 115; cf. also Nöldeke, *Neue Beiträge*, 26.
6. Aloys Sprenger, *Das Leben und die Lehre des Mohammad*, second edition, Berlin, 1869, 3 vols., i. 462.
7. Horovitz, *Koranische Untersuchungen*, 26f.
8. Cf. *Translation*, vii.
9. The list is (in Nöldeke's order): 96.1-8; 74.1-7; 87.1-9; 73.1-8; 90.1-11; 102; 92; 91.1-10; 80; 99; 82; 81.1-14; 84.1-6, 7-12; 100; 79; 78; 88; 89; 75; 69; 51; 52; 56; 70; 55; 54; 37; 44; 50; 20; 26; 15; 38; 36; 43; 27; 14; 12; 39; 42; 10; 13.
10. This is also the conclusion of K. Wagtendonk in *Fasting in the Koran*, 143.
11. Cf. also: 6.59; 27.75/7; 34.3; etc.
12. Cf. Jeffery, *Foreign Vocabulary*, s.v.
13. Bell later rejected the view expressed in his *Origin*, 118, that the word occurred in late Meccan passages; this was based on the assumption that suras 21 and 25 were Meccan.
14. In the recent discussion of *furqān* by Wagtendonk he appears to take it as the battle of Badr (*Fasting in the Koran*, 67, 87, etc.).

Chapter Nine

1. Cf. EI^2, art. 'Allāh' (Louis Gardet), section 1.
2. Cf. 23.12-14, quoted on p. 91 above. God's shaping of the child in the womb is mentioned occasionally in the Bible; e.g. *Job*, 31.15.
3. Relevant passages are: 6.136/7; 29.61-5; 23.84/6-89/91; 30.33/2; 39.8/11, 38/9; 43.8-15/14.
4. In 37.149-66; 43.16/15-20/19 and 53.27/8f. female deities appear to be regarded as angels either by their worshippers or by other people. For jinn cf. 6.100; 34.40/39f.; 37.158.
5. 53.23.
6. 16.57/9; 53.19-21; and passages quoted in note 3 above.
7. 76.29f.; cf. 81.27-9; 74.56/5; 10.99f.
8. A full account will be found in EI^2, art. '(al-)asmā' al-ḥusnā' (Louis Gardet). There are lists in T.P. Hughes, *A Dictionary*

of Islam, London, 1885, 1935, art. 'God'; and in J. Windrow Sweetman, *Islam and Christian Theology*, London, 1945, i/1.215f.

9. Cf. Wellhausen, *Reste*², 217-19.
10. Cf. NS, i. 121; also 111-14.
11. *Mohammed*, Münster, 1892–5; cf. also p. 112.
12. Cf. *EI*² art. 'Djinn', *ad init.* (D.B. Macdonald, H. Massé); also Wellhausen, *Reste*², 148-59; Paul Arno Eichler, *Die Dschinn, Teufel und Engel im Koran*, Leipzig, 1928.
13. Cf. Guillaume, *Prophecy and Divination*, esp. 243-9.
14. Some are discussed in Thomas O'Shaughnessy, *The Development of the Meaning of Spirit in the Koran*, Rome, 1953. See also Index, s.v.
15. Cf. Jeffery, *Foreign Vocabulary*, s.v.; Horovitz, *Koranische Untersuchungen*, 120f.
16. More fully discussed in Watt, 'The early development of the Muslim attitude to the Bible', *Transactions of the Glasgow University Oriental Society*, xvi (1957), 50-62, esp. 50-53.
17. Cf. Geoffrey Parrinder, *Jesus in the Qur'ān*, London, 1965; Michel Hayek, *Le Christ de l'Islam*, Paris, 1959, esp. ch. 1; Watt, 'The Christianity criticized in the Qur'ān', *Muslim World*, lvii (1967), 197-201; also in *Atti del III Congresso di Studi Arabic Islamici*, Napoli, 1967, 651-6. Cf. also T. O'Shaughnessy, *The Koranic Concept of the Word of God* (Biblica et Orientalia, no. 11), Rome, 1948; R.C. Zaehner, *At Sundry Times* (in America *The Comparison of Religions*), London, 1958, Appendix 'The Qur'an and Christ'.
18. Cf. R. Bell, 'The men on the Aʿrāf', *Moslem World*, xxii (1932), 43ff.
19. For Paradise cf. arts. 'Djanna', section A (L. Gardet), in *EI*², The main article on Hell will be 'Nār', but there is a short article 'Djahannam'.
20. See Index under '*qibla*'.
21. Cf. *EI(S)*, art. '*ẓakāt*' (J. Schacht); Watt, *Mecca*, 165-9; *Medina*, 306.
22. Wagtendonk, *Fasting in the Koran*, 47-9,80, allows that the Muslims observed the fast of the 'Āshūrā', but considers that 2.183/79 does not prescribe it.
23. Wagtendonk, esp. 143. For other discussions of the fast, cf. *EI(S)*, arts. 'Ramaḍān (C.C. Berg), 'Sawm' (J. Schacht); also S.D. Goitein, *Studies in Islamic History and Institutions*, Leiden, 1966, 90-110 ('Ramadan, the Muslim Month of Fasting').
24. For the pilgrimage cf. *EI*², art. 'Hadjdj' (A.J. Wensinck,

etc.); Ahmad Kamal, *The Sacred Journey* (London, 1961), a manual for Muslim pilgrims.

25. For details see Index, s.v. Divorce, Marriage. A fuller discussion will be found in Watt, *Medina*, 272-89. Cf. Sara Kohn, *Die Eheschliessung im Koran*, London, 1934.
26. Cf. Watt, *Medina*, 296-8.
27. Cf. ibid., 293-6.
28. Further details will be found in the Index.

Chapter Ten

1. *Die Richtungen der islamischen Koranauslegung*, Leiden, 1920, 1952. A brief survey of the work of Islamic scholars will be found in NS, ii. 156-87.
2. Cf. Goldziher, *Koranauslegung*, 65-81.
3. *Geschichte des arabischen Schrifttums*, i, Leiden, 1967, 19-49 ('Qur'ānauslegung'). It is noteworthy that he has far more material in this category than Carl Brockelmann in his *Geschichte der arabischen Literatur* (2 vols., second edition), Leiden, 1943, 1949 and (3 supplementary volumes) Leiden, 1937–42. These are usually referred to as *GAL* and *GALS*. The pages corresponding to the section in Sezgin are *GAL*, i. 202-5 and *GALS*, i. 330-6.
4. Cf. Goldziher, 85-98; Sezgin, 323-5,327f.
5. D.S. Margoliouth, *Chrestomathia Baidawiana: the commentary of El-Baidāwī on Sura III translated and explained for the use of students of Arabic*, London, 1894. A.F.L. Beeston, *Baiḍāwī's Commentary on Sūrah 12 of the Qur'ān; text, accompanied by an interpretative rendering and notes*, Oxford, 1963.
6. Cf. J.M.S. Baljon, *Modern Muslim Koran Interpretation*, 1880–1960, Leiden, 1961; also Kenneth Cragg, *Counsels in Contemporary Islam*, Edinburgh, 1965, esp. ch. 11.
7. Cf. J. Jomier, *Le commentaire coranique du Manār*, Paris, 1954.
8. *The Tarjumān al-Qur'ān*, edited and rendered into English by Syed Abdul Latif, vols. 1 and 2, London, 1962, 1967.
9. Cf. Watt, 'Early Discussions on the Qur'ān', *Moslem World*, xl (1950). 27-40, 96-105; some of this requires to be revised in the light of *Integration*, 173f., 240f.
10. Cf. Walter M. Patton, *Aḥmed ibn Ḥanbal and the Miḥna*, Leiden, 1897.
11. Cf. Wensinck, *The Muslim Creed*, Index, s.v. 'Kuran'.

Chapter Eleven

1. Cf. R.W. Southern, *Western Views of Islam in the Middle Ages*, Cambridge, Mass., 1962, esp. 37-40; also Norman Daniel,

Islam and the West: the Making of an Image, Edinburgh, 1960. At the basis of these and other studies is an article by Marie-Thérèse d'Alverny, 'Deux traductions latines du Coran au Moyen Age', *Archives d'histoire doctrinale et littéraire du Moyen Age*, xvi (1948), 69-131. Cf. J. Kritzeck, 'Robert of Ketton's Translation of the Qur'ān', *Islamic Quarterly*, ii (1955), 309-12.

2. Fuller bibliographical details will be found in Gustav Pfannmüller's *Handbuch der Islam-Literatur*, Berlin, 1923, esp. 138-50, 206-29. There is a short account of Qur'ānic scholarship in Europe from about 1800 to 1914 in NS, ii. 193-219. The earlier European translations and those into French are described in Blachère, *Introduction*, vii-xix, while attempts to classify the suras chronologically are described in the same work, 247-63. Cf. also Johann Fück, *Die arabische Studien in Europa vom 12. bis . . . 19. Jahrhundert*, Leipzig, 1944; *Die arabische Studien in Europa bis in den Anfang des 20. Jahrhunderts*, Leipzig, 1955.
3. *The Alcoran of Mahomet*. Translated out of Arabique into French, by the Sieur du Ryer, and newly englished . . ., London, 1649.
4. The edition by E.M. Wherry, entitled *A comprehensive Commentary on the Qur'ān: comprising Sale's Translation and Preliminary Discourse with notes and emendations*, London and Boston, 1882–6, is pleasanter typographically than most other recent editions, but the additional notes are of poor quality and detract from the value of Sale's work.
5. Cf. ch. 8, note 4.
6. A fuller discussion of some of the points raised in this chapter will be found in Watt, *Islamic Revelation and the Modern World*, Edinburgh University Press, 1970.

The left-hand column gives Flügel's numbers; the corresponding numbers in the Egyptian text are obtained by adding or subtracting as shown. At the points of transition this applies only to part of a verse in one of the editions.

[1]	1–6	+1	[3]	180–190	+3	[7]	28–103	+2
[2]	1–19	+1		191–193	+2		103–131	+3
	19–38	+2		194	+1		131–139	+4
	38–61	+3		196–198	+1		140–143	+3
	61–63	+4	[4]	3–5	+1		144–146	+2
	63–73	+5		7–13	−1		147–157	+1
	73–137	+6		14	−2		166–186	+1
	138–172	+5		15	−3		191–205	+1
	173–212	+4		16–29	−4	[8]	37–43	−1
	213–216	+3		30–32	−5		44–64	−2
	217–218	+2		32–45	−4		64–76	−1
	219–220	+1		45–47	−3	[9]	62–130	−1
	236–258	−1		47–48	−2	[10]	11–80	−1
	259–269	−2		49–70	−3	[11]	6	−1
	270–273	−3		70–100	−2		7–9	−2
	273–274	−2		100–106	−1		10–22	−3
	274–277	−1		118–156	+1		22–54	−2
[3]	1–4	+1		156–170	+2		55–77	−3
	4–18	+2		171–172	+1		77–84	−2
	19–27	+1		174–175	+1		84–87	−1
	27–29	+2	[5]	3–4	−1		88–95	−2
	29–30	+3		5–8	−2		96–99	−3
	30–31	+4		9–18	−3		99–120	−2
	31–43	+5		18–19	−2		120–122	−1
	43–44	+6		20–35	−3	[12]	97–103	−1
	44–68	+7		35–52	−4	[13]	6–18	−1
	69–91	+6		53–70	−5		28–30	+1
	92–98	+5		70–82	−4	[14]	10–11	−1
	99–122	+4		82–88	−3		12–13	−2
	122–126	+5		88–93	−2		14–24	−3
	126–141	+6		93–98	−1		25–26	−4
	141–145	+7		101–109	+1		27–37	−5
	146–173	+6	[6]	66–72	+1		37	−4
	174–175	+5		136–163	−1		37–41	−3
	176–179	+4	[7]	1–28	+1		41–42	−2

[14]	42–45	−1
	46–47	−2
	47–51	−1
[16]	22–24	−1
	25–110	−2
	110–128	−1
[17]	10–26	−1
	27–48	−2
	49–53	−3
	53–106	−2
	106–108	−1
[18]	2–21	+1
	23–31	+1
	31–55	+2
	56–83	+1
	83–84	+2
	85–97	+1
[19]	1–3	+1
	8–14	−1
	27–76	−1
	77–78	−2
	79–91	−3
	91–93	−2
	93–94	−1
[20]	1–9	+1
	16–34	−1
	40–41	−1
	42–63	−2
	64–75	−3
	75–79	−2
	80–81	−3
	81–88	−2
	89–90	−3
	90–94	−2
	94–96	−1
	106–115	+1
	115–121	+2
	122–123	+1
[21]	29–67	−1
[22]	19–21	−1
[22]	26–43	−1
	43–77	+1
[23]	28–34	−1
	35–117	−2
	117	−1
[24]	14–18	+1
	44–60	+1
[25]	4–20	−1
	21–60	−2
	60–66	−1
[26]	1–48	+1
	228	−1
[27]	45–66	−1
	67–95	−2
[28]	1–22	+1
[29]	1–51	+1
[30]	1–54	+1
[31]	1–32	+1
[32]	1–9	+1
[33]	41–49	+1
[34]	10–53	+1
[35]	8–20	−1
	20–21	+1
	21–25	+2
	25–34	+3
	35–41	+2
	42–44	+1
[36]	1–30	+1
[37]	29–47	+1
	47–100	+2
	101	+1
[38]	1–43	+1
	76–85	−1
[39]	4	−1
	5–9	−2
	10–14	−3
	14–19	−2
	19–63	−1
[40]	1–2	+1
	19–32	−1
[40]	33–39	−2
	40–56	−3
	56–73	−2
	73–74	−1
[41]	1–26	+1
[42]	1–11	+2
	12–31	+1
	31–42	+2
	43–50	+1
[43]	1–51	+1
[44]	1–36	+1
[45]	1–36	+1
[46]	1–34	+1
[47]	5–16	−1
	17–40	−2
[50]	13–44	+1
[53]	27–58	−1
[55]	1–16	+1
[56]	22–46	+1
	66–91	+1
[57]	13–19	+1
[58]	3–21	−1
[71]	5–22	+1
	26–29	−1
[72]	23–26	−1
[74]	32	−1
	33	−2
	34–41	−3
	41–42	−2
	42–51	−1
	54–55	+1
[78]	41	−1
[80]	15–18	+1
[89]	1–14	+1
	17–25	−1
[98]	2–7	+1
[101]	1–5	+1
	5–6	+2
	6–8	+3
[106]	3	+1

TABLE OF SURAS

Listed in the order of the ʿUthmānic Recension, and indicating for each sura: (1) usual title in Arabic; (2) title in English; (3) the number of verses in the official Egyptian text, followed (after a diagonal) by the number in Flügel's text where the two differ; (4) the length as shown by the number of lines in Redslob's edition of Flügel's text (the *bismillāh* in this edition occupies a full line, which has been counted); (5) the initial letters where they occur (for convenience, *alif* is here indicated by A); and (6) the chronological order according to Muir, Nöldeke, Grimme and the official Egyptian text. The numbers in parentheses indicate the verses which are regarded as belonging to a different time from that of the main part of the sura; only Flügel's numbering is given.

			Verses	Lines	Initials
[1]	*Al-fātiḥa*	The Opening	7	6	
[2]	*Al-baqara*	The Cow	286	715	ALM
[3]	*Āl ʿImrān*	The Family of ʿImrān	200	409	ALM
[4]	*An-nisāʾ*	The Women	176 / 5	445	
[5]	*Al-māʾida*	The Table	120	332	
[6]	*Al-anʿām*	The Cattle	165	358	
[7]	*Al-aʿrāf*	The Heights	206 / 5	398	ALMS
[8]	*Al-anfāl*	The Spoils	75 / 6	149	
[9]	*At-tawba*	Repentance	129 / 30	301	
[10]	*Yūnus*	Jonah	109	215	ALR
[11]	*Hūd*	Hūd	123	221	ALR
[12]	*Yūsuf*	Joseph	111	209	ALR
[13]	*Ar-raʿd*	The Thunder	43	99	ALMR
[14]	*Ibrāhīm*	Abraham	52	99	ALR
[15]	*Al-Ḥijr*	Al-Ḥijr	99	85	ALR
[16]	*An-naḥl*	The Bee	128	217	
[17]	*Al-isrāʾ*	The Night Journey	111	195	
[18]	*Al-kahf*	The Cave	110	184	
[19]	*Maryam*	Mary	98	114	KHYʿṢ
[20]	*Ṭāʾ Hāʾ*	Ṭāʾ Hāʾ	135	159	ṬH
[21]	*Al-anbiyāʾ*	The Prophets	112	145	
[22]	*Al-ḥajj*	The Pilgrimage	78	150	
[23]	*Al-muʾminūn*	The Believers	118	129	
[24]	*An-nūr*	The Light	64	159	
[25]	*Al-furqān*	The Furqān	77	109	
[26]	*Ash-shuʿarāʾ*	The Poets	227 / 8	169	ṬSM
[27]	*An-naml*	The Ant	93 / 5	137	ṬS
[28]	*Al-qaṣaṣ*	The Story	88	168	ṬSM

	Muir	*Nöldeke*	*Grimme*	*Egyptian*
[1]	6	48	79	5
[2]	94	91 (parts later a few vv. Meccan)	93 (192-6 later)	87 (281 later)
[3]	108	97 (parts later)	100	89
[4]	107	100	101	92
[5]	109	114 (parts earlier)	95 (1-14 later)	112
[6]	81	89 (91?)	89	55 (20,23,91,93, 114,152-4,Med.)
[7]	91	87 (156-8,Med.)	88 (156-8,Med.)	39 (163-9,Med.)
[8]	97	95	97	88 (30-37,Mec.)
[9]	114	113	114	113 (129f.,Mec.)
[10]	79	84	87	51 (41, 94-6,Med.)
[11]	78	75	86	52 (15,20,116, Med.)
[12]	77	77	85	53 (1,2,3,7,Med.)
[13]	89	90	84	96
[14]	80	76 (38-42,Med.)	50 (38-42,Med.)	72 (33f.Med.)
[15]	62	57	48	54
[16]	88	73 (43f.,111-125, Med.)	83 (111-25,Med.)	70 (126-8,Med.)
[17]	87	67	82	50 (28,34,35,58, 75-82,Med.)
[18]	69	69	81	69 (27,83-101, Med.)
[19]	68	58	78	44 (59,72,Med.)
[20]	75	55	74	45 (130f.,Med.)
[21]	86	65	77	73
[22]	85	107 (1-24,43-56, 60-65,67-75,Mec.)	49 (25-42,76-8, Med.)	103
[23]	84	64	75	74
[24]	103	105	98	102
[25]	74	66	73	42 (68-70,Med.)
[26]	61	56	71	47 (197,224-8, Med.)
[27]	70	68	70	48
[28]	83	79	69	49 (52-5,Med.,85 on journey)

			Verses	Lines	Initials
[29]	*Al-ʿankabūt*	The Spider	69	129	ALM
[30]	*Ar-Rūm*	The Greeks	60	99	ALM
[31]	*Luqmān*	Luqmān	34	62	ALM
[32]	*As-sajda*	The Prostration	30	46	ALM
[33]	*Al-aḥzāb*	The Confederates	73	158	
[34]	*Sabā'*	Sheba	54	102	
[35]	*Al-malā'ika*	The Angels	45	98	
[36]	*Yā' Sīn*	Yā' Sīn	83	90	YS
[37]	*Aṣ-ṣāffāt*	The Rangers	182	118	
[38]	*Ṣād*	Ṣād	88	90	Ṣ
[39]	*Az-zumar*	The Troops	75	140	
[40]	*Al-mu'min*	The Believer	85	145	ḤM
[41]	*Fuṣṣilat*	Made Distinct	54	94	ḤM
[42]	*Ash-shūrā*	Counsel	53	100	HMʿSQ
[43]	*Az-zukhruf*	Ornaments	89	104	ḤM
[44]	*Ad-dukhān*	Smoke	59	46	ḤM
[45]	*Al-jāthiya*	Hobbling	37 /6	59	ḤM
[46]	*Al-aḥqāf*	The Sand-Dunes	35	75	ḤM
[47]	*Muḥammad*	Muḥammad	40	67	
[48]	*Al-fat'ḥ*	The Victory	29	69	
[49]	*Al-ḥujurāt*	The Chambers	18	42	
[50]	*Qāf*	Qāf	45	46	Q
[51]	*Adh-dhāriyāt*	The Scatterers	60	46	
[52]	*Aṭ-ṭūr*	The Mount	49	40	
[53]	*An-najm*	The Star	62	44	
[54]	*Al-qamar*	The Moon	55	44	
[55]	*Ar-Raḥmān*	The All-Merciful	78	50	
[56]	*Al-wāqiʿa*	The Event	96	54	
[57]	*Al-ḥadīd*	Iron	29	70	
[58]	*Al-mujādila*	The Disputer	22	57	
[59]	*Al-ḥashr*	The Mustering	24	54	
[60]	*Al-mumtaḥana*	The Woman Tested	13	43	
[61]	*Aṣ-ṣaff*	The Ranks	14	28	
[62]	*Al-jumuʿa*	The Congregation	11	22	
[63]	*Al-munāfiqūn*	The Hypocrites	11	23	
[64]	*At-taghābun*	Mutual Fraud	18	31	

	Muir	Nöldeke	Grimme	Egyptian
[29]	90	81 (1-10,Med.,45? 69?)	68 (1-12,45-6,69, Med.)	85 (1-10,Med.)
[30]	60	74	67	84 (16,Med.)
[31]	50	82 (13f.,11-18?)	65	57 (26-8,Med.)
[32]	44	70	64	75 (12-20,Med.)
[33]	110	103	108	90
[34]	49	85	63	58 (6,Med.)
[35]	66	86	62	43
[36]	67	60	61	41 (45,Med.)
[37]	59	50	60	56
[38]	73	59	59	38
[39]	45	80	58	59 (53.5,Med.)
[40]	72	78	57	60 (58f.,-Med.)
[41]	53	71	55	61
[42]	71	83	80	62 (22-4,26,Med.)
[43]	76	61	76	63 (54,Med.)
[44]	58	53	54	64
[45]	57	72	53	65 (13,Med.)
[46]	64	88	51	66 (9,14,34,Med.)
[47]	95	96	96	95 (14,Mec.)
[48]	105	108	112	111
[49]	113	112	110	106
[50]	56	54	47	34 (37,Med.)
[51]	63	39 (24ff., later)	46	67
[52]	55	40 (21,29ff., later)	45	76
[53]	43	28 (23,26-33 later)	44 (21-3,27-33 later)	23
[54]	48	49	43	37 (44-6,Med.)
[55]	40	43 (7,8 later)	42	97
[56]	41	41 (74ff.?)	41	46 (70,71,Med.)
[57]	96	99	102	94
[58]	98	106	106	105
[59]	102	102	99	101
[60]	111	110	105	91
[61]	106	98	104	109
[62]	101	94	94	110
[63]	104	104	109	104
[64]	82	93	103	108

			Verses	*Lines*	*Initials*
[65]	*Aṭ-ṭalāq*	Divorce	12	35	
[66]	*At-taḥrīm*	The Prohibition	12	31	
[67]	*Al-mulk*	The Kingdom	30	40	
[68]	*Al-qalam*	The Pen	52	40	N
[69]	*Al-ḥāqqa*	The Indubitable	52	35	
[70]	*Al-maʿārij*	The Stairways	44	30	
[71]	*Nūḥ*	Noah	28 /9	28	
[72]	*Al-jinn*	The Jinn	28	34	
[73]	*Al-muzzammil*	The Enwrapped One	20	25	
[74]	*Al-muddaththir*	The Shrouded One	56 /5	33	
[75]	*Al-qiyāmā*	The Resurrection	40	22	
[76]	*Al-insān*	Man	31	32	
[77]	*Al-mursalāt*	Those That Are Sent	50	27	
[78]	*An-naba'*	The Announcement	40 /1	24	
[79]	*An-nāziʿāt*	Those Who Draw Out	46	25	
[80]	*ʿAbasa*	He Frowned	42	19	
[81]	*At-takwīr*	The Veiling	29	15	
[82]	*Al-infiṭār*	The Splitting	19	11	
[83]	*Al-muṭaffifīn*	The Stinters	36	25	
[84]	*Al-inshiqāq*	The Rending	25	15	
[85]	*Al-burūj*	The Constellations	22	15	
[86]	*Aṭ-ṭāriq*	The Night-Star	17	9	
[87]	*Al-aʿlā*	The Most High	19	10	
[88]	*Al-ghāshiya*	The Enveloping	26	13	
[89]	*Al-fajr*	The Dawn	30	18	
[90]	*Al-balad*	The Land	20	11	
[91]	*Ash-shams*	The Sun	15	8	
[92]	*Al-layl*	The Night	21	11	
[93]	*Aḍ-ḍuḥā*	The Morning	11	6	
[94]	*Al-inshirāḥ*	The Expanding	8	4	
[95]	*At-tīn*	The Fig	8	6	
[96]	*Al-ʿalaq*	The Blood-Clot	19	10	
[97]	*Al-qadr*	Power (or The Measuring-Out)	5	4	
[98]	*Al-bayyina*	The Evidence	8	12	
[99]	*Az-zalzala*	The Earthquake	8	6	
[100]	*Al-ʿādiyāt*	The Runners	11	6	

	Muir	Nöldeke	Grimme	Egyptian
[65]	99	101	107	99
[66]	112	109	113	107
[67]	42	63	66	77
[68]	52	18 (17ff. later)	38	2 (17-33,48-50, Med.)
[69]	51	38	37	78
[70]	37	42	36	79
[71]	54	51	72	71
[72]	65	62	52	40
[73]	46	23 (20,Med.)	35 (20,Med.)	3 (10,11,20,Med.)
[74]	21	2 (31-4 later)	34 (55 later)	4
[75]	36	36 (16-19?)	33	31
[76]	35	52	32 (30f. later)	98
[77]	34	32	31	33 (48Med.)
[78]	33	33	30 (37f. later)	80
[79]	47	31 (27-46 later)	29	81
[80]	26	17	28	24
[81]	27	27	27 (29 later)	7
[82]	11	26	26	82
[83]	32	37	25	85
[84]	28	29 (25 later)	24 (25 later)	83
[85]	31	22 (8-11 later)	23 (8-11 later)	27
[86]	29	15	22	36
[87]	23	19	21 (7,Med.)	8
[88]	25	34	20	68
[89]	14	35	19	10
[90]	15	11	18	35
[91]	4	16	17	26
[92]	12	10	16	9
[93]	16	13	15	11
[94]	17	12	14	12
[95]	8	20	13	28
[96]	19	1 (9f. later)	12	1
[97]	24	14	56	25
[98]	100	92	90?	100
[99]	3	25	10	93
[100]	2	30	9	14

			Verses	Lines	Initials
[101]	*Al-qāri'a*	The Striking	11/8	6	
[102]	*At-takāthur*	Rivalry	8	5	
[103]	*Al-'aṣr*	The Afternoon	3	3	
[104]	*Al-humaẓa*	The Backbiter	9	5	
[105]	*Al-fīl*	The Elephant	5	4	
[106]	*Quraysh*	Quraysh	4	3	
[107]	*Al-mā'ūn*	Charity	7	4	
[108]	*Al-kwathar*	Abundance	3	2	
[109]	*Al-kāfirūn*	The Unbelievers	6	4	
[110]	*An-naṣr*	Help	3	3	
[111]	*Tabbat*	Perish	5	3	
[112]	*Al-ikhlāṣ*	The Purifying	4	2	
[113]	*Al-falaq*	The Daybreak	5	3	
[114]	*An-nās*	The People	6	3	

All arrangements place sura 2 as the first of the Medinan suras.

Muir	has therefore	93	Meccan and	21	Medinan
Nöldeke	”	90	”	24	”
Grimme	”	92	”	22	”
Egyptian	”	86	”	28	”

With regard to the Medinan suras, there is a fair amount of unanimity as to their order, though all the Western scholars recognize that they contain passages of different date. The doubtful suras are 98 and 22.

The Westerns divide the Meccan suras into groups, within which they do not profess that their order is strictly chronological. Muir places 18 suras before the Call, thus like Nöldeke agreeing with Tradition in regarding 96 as the sura marking the Call. His other groups are 19-22, 23-41, 42-63, 64-91, 92, 93 (113, 114 undatable).

Nöldeke's groups are 1-48, 49-69, 70-90. Grimme's are 1-30 (113, 114 doubtfully along with these) 41-50, 51-89 (98, 112, 109 doubtfully with this group).

	Muir	*Nöldeke*	*Grimme*	*Egyptian*
[101]	7	24	8	30
[102]	9	8	7	16
[103]	1	21 (3 later)	6 (3 later)	13
[104]	10	6	5	32
[105]	13	9	4	19
[106]	5	4	3	29
[107]	39	7	2	17
[108]	18	5	11	15
[109]	38	45	92?	18
[110]	30	111	111	114
[111]	22	3	1	6
[112]	20	44	91?	22
[113]	92	46	39?	20
[114]	47	47	40	21

INDEX TO THE QUR'ĀN

Containing all instances of proper names and a selection of other topics; 'Muḥammad' is abbreviated to 'M'.

Aaron (Ar. Hārūn): brother and helper of Moses, 7.142/38; 10.75/6, (87); 20.29/30-32/3,71/3,90/2-92/4 (calf); 21.48/9; 23.45/7; 25.35/7 (*wazīr*); 26.13/12,48/7; 28.34f.; 37.114,120 a prophet, 4.163/1; 6.84; 19.53/4 Mary called his sister, 19.28/9 also, 2.248/9; 7.122/19

Abel, *see* Adam (two sons of)

ablutions (Ar. *wuḍū'*): as preparation for prayer, 5.6/8f.

Abraham (Ar. Ibrāhīm): abandons idolatry, 6.74-83; 21.51/2-72; 26.69-102; 29.16/15-25/4; 37.83/1-101/99; 43.26/5-28/7; 60.4 leaves father, 9.114/5; 19.41/2-49/50 promise of son and warning about Sodom, 11.69/72-76/8; 15.51/8; 29.31/0 f.; 51.24-34 sacrifice of son, 37.102/0-113 his religion as *ḥanīf* and *muslim*, 2.130/24-135/29; 3.95/89; 4.125/4; 6.161/2; 16.120/1-123/4; 22.78/7 (your father) at Mecca with Ishmael, 2.125/19-129/3; 3.97/1; 14.35/8; 22.26/7-31/2 not a Jew or Christian, 2.140/34; 3.65/58-68/1 God took him as friend, 4.125/4 also, 2.124/18 (imām), 136/0, 258/60 (? Nimrod); 3.33/0,84/78; 4.54/7,163/1; 9.70/1; 12.6,38; 19.58/9; 22.43; 33.7; 38.45; 42.13/11; 53.37/8; 57.26; 87.19 ('scrolls')

abrogation (Ar. *naskh*): cancellations, deletions or substitutions by God, 2.106/0; 13.39; 16.101/3 God removes verses intruded by Satan, 22.52/1f. *see also* pp. 86-9 here

Abū-Bakr: mentioned as 'second of two' (*sc.* M.'s companion on Hijra), 9.40 possibly referred to, 24.22

Abū-Lahab 111.1

'Ād: tribe to which Hūd sent, disobeyed, 7.65/3-72/0; 11.50/2-60/3; 26.123-40; 46.21/0-26/5; 54.18-20; 69.4-8 also, 7.74/2; 9.70/1; 14.9; 22.42/3; 29.38/7; 38.12/11; 40.30/2; 41.13/12,15/14f.; 50.13; 51.41f.; 53.52/1; 89.6/5

booty (Ar. *anfāl;mā ghanimtum*): belongs to God and M., 8.1 a 'fifth' to be given to God, 8.41/2 destination of 'fifth', etc., 59.6-10 booty (from Khaybar?) promised, 48.15,19-21
burial: taught to Adam's son by raven, 5.31/4
Byzantines (Ar. *Rūm*), *see* Greeks

Cain, *see* Adam, two sons of
calendar, *see* months
calf: worshipped by Israelites, 2.51/48,92/86;4.153/2;7.148/6; 20.87/90-98
caliph, *see khalīfa*
camels (Ar. *ibl*, etc): wonder of their creation, 88.17 passing through eye of needle, 7.40/38 may be eaten, 6.144/5
cattle (Ar. *an'ām*): include sheep, goats, camels, oxen, 6.143/4f.; cf. 39.6/8 ('eight in pairs') are beasts of burden and for food, 6.142/3 pagan taboos rejected, 5.103/2;6.138/9 God's provision for men and cattle 79.33;80.32
Cave, Men of (Ar. *Ahl al-kahf*): their story (identified with Seven Sleepers of Ephesus), 18.10/9-26/5
children: suckling, 2.233;31.14/13;46.15/14 rules for inheritance, 4.11/12 wealth and ch. a temptation, 8.28;64.14f. pagans dislike daughters, 16.58/60f.;43.17/16 children not to be killed out of fear of want, 17.31/3;cf. 16.59/61;81.8f. attitudes to parents, 31.14/13f.;6.137/8,140/1.
Christ, *see* Messiah, Jesus
Christians (Ar. Naṣārā): worshippers of God, 2.62/59;4.46/50f.; 5.69/73 friends of Muslims, 5.82/5-85/8 are kind and monastic, 57.27 their errors, 2.111/05-113/07,120/14,135/29, 140/34;3.67/0;4.171/69;5.14/17-18/21,51/6 (not to be taken as friends), 72/6-75/9;9.30-2;23.50/2-56/8;98.4/3 challenged to mutual cursing, 3.61/54 among religions between which God distinguishes, 22.17 their churches, etc., 22.40/1 *see also* Jesus, Messiah, Book (People of the)
clothing (Ar. *libās*, *zīna*): given by God for concealment, 7.26/5f. to be worn in mosques, 7.31/29f.
commerce: seaborne by ships, 16.14;17.66/8 measures to be just, 17.35/7 permissible during pilgrimage, 2.198/4
concubines: marriage with those whom your right hands possess, 4.3,24/8f.;23.6;70.30
Confession of Faith, *see* Shahāda
contributions (Ar. *mā yunfiqū*, etc.): required for God's cause, 2.195/1,215/1,254/5,261/3-265/7,267/9,270/3-274/5; 3.92/86,180/75;4.37/41f.;34.39/8 from nominal Muslims

contributions (*contd.*) from nominal Muslims rejected, 9.53f. 'voluntary' contributions or alms (*ṣadaqāt*), 2.196/2 (in place of pilgrimage), 263/5f.,271/3,276/7; 4.114; 9.58-60 (how to be divided), 79/80,103/4f. (as purification); 58.12/13f. (before interview with M.) gifts to women (*ṣaduqāt*), 4.4/3

corruption of scriptures (Ar. *taḥrīf*, etc.): Jews 'alter words from their sets', 4.46/8f.; 5.13/16,41/5 Jews 'alter the word of God', 2.75/0,(79/3) Jews substitute another word, 2.58/5; 7.161 Jews twist tongues in the book, 3.78/2 concealing of scriptures, 2.42/39,76/1,140/34,146/1, 159/4,174/69; 3.71/64; 5.15/18

covenant (Ar. *'ahd*, *mīthāq*): with Adam, 20.115/4 with posterity of Adam, 7.172/1 with prophets, 3.81/75; 33.7 violation of covenants with M., 8.55/7-58/60 with Israelites at Sinai, 2.83/77,93/87; 3.187/4(?); 5.12/15f. with Christians, 5.14/17 with M. and people of Medina, 2.84/78

coveting (*tamannā*): forbidden, 4.32/6

creation (Ar. *khalq*, etc.): God says 'Be' to a thing, 2.117/1; 3.47/2 (Mary's child), 59/2 (Jesus); 6.73/2; 16.40/2; 19.35/6 (Jesus); 36.82; 40.68/70 creation of heavens and earth, 7.54/2; 41.9/8-12/11; 65.12 creation is for a purpose, 21.16f.; (30.8/7) *see also* Adam, man

crucifixion of Jesus denied, 4.157/6

daughters: ascribed to God, 16.59; 53.21 *see* children

David (Ar. Dāwūd): killed Goliath, 2.251/2 a prophet, given psalms, 4.163/1; 17.55/7 given wisdom and skill, and mountains and birds join him in praising God, 21.78/80; 27.15f.; 34.10; 38.17/16-20/19 story of ewe and his repentance, 38.21/0-26/5 cursed disbelieving Israelites, 5.79/82 also 6.84; 34.13/12; 38.30/29

Day of Judgement (Ar. *yawm ad-dīn*, etc.): comes suddenly, 6.31; 7.187/6; 12.107; 22.55/4; 43.66; 47.18/20 portents of the Day, 20.105-108/7; 22.1f.; 36.53; 39.68; 50.20/19; 54.1; 56.1-7; 69.13-16; 73.14,17f.; 74.8; 75.7-10; 77.8-13; 78.18-20; 79.6; 80.33; 81.1-14; 82.1-5; 84.1-6 descriptions, 7.6/5-9/8; 11.103/5-105/7; 21.47/8; 28.62-7,74f.; 34.31/0-33/2; 37.20-32; 41.19/18-23/2; 43.67-73; 45.27/6-35/4; 50.21/0-29/8; 69.13-37; 75.12-15; 77.28-50; 78.38-40; 79.6-14; 80.33-42; 84.7-15; 89.21/2-30 date known only to God, 7.187/6f.; 79.92-4 God is supreme Judge, 1.4/3; 22.56/5; 40.20/1 each man stands alone, 31.33/2; 82.19 *see also* balances, intercession

Enoch, sometimes identified with Idrīs (*q.v.*)
Eve (referred to without being named), 2.35/3f.;7.19/18-23/2; 20.117/5-121/19;39.6/8
expiation: an expiation or 'covering' (*kaffāra*), 5.89/91 (for broken oath), 95/6 (for hunting in state of sanctity) remitting strict retaliation is expiation (for unspecified offence), 5.45/9 redemption or compensation (*fidya*), 2.184/0 (for omitting fast), 196/2 (for omitting shaving head at pilgrimage); 57.15/14 (none for Hypocrites) after unintentional homicide, 4.92/4 *see also* fasting
Ezra ('Uzayr): regarded by Jews as son of God, 9.30

faith (Ar. *īmān*): content of faith or belief, 2.3/2f., 285;4.136/5; 7.158 *see* believers
fall of man, *see* Adam
fasting (Ar. *ṣawm*): prescribed for Muslims in Ramaḍān, 2.183/79-185/1,187/3 vowed by Mary, 19.26/7 as expiation, 4.92/4 (for unintentional homicide);5.89/91 (for broken oath), 95/6 (for hunting in state of sanctity);58.4/5 (for using pagan formula of divorce)
fathers (Ar. *abā'*): pagans follow fathers' errors, 2.170/65; 5.104/3;7.28/7,173/2;11.109/11;21.53/4;26.74;31.21/0; 34.43/2;37.69/7f.;43.23/2 pagans want fathers made alive, 45.25/4 pagans, even fathers, to be treated as enemies, 9.23f.;58.22 *see also* parents
fate (or time, Ar. *dahr*): pagan belief in fate, 45.24/3
Fātiḥa: name of sura 1
fifth (Ar. *khums*), *see* booty
fire (Ar. *nār*): compared with resurrection, 36.80 made by friction, 56.70-2 *see also* Hell
food regulations: most foods lawful, 2.168/3-172/67;3.93/87 (except what Jacob forbade himself);5.1,4/6 (including game caught by dogs), 5/7 (also food of People of the Book), 87/9f.;6.118f.,142/3;16.114/5 forbidden is carrion, blood, pork, slaughtered without God's name, 2.173/68;5.3/4 (with additions);6.121,145/6;16.115/6 special rules for Jews (3.93/87);4.160/58;6.146/7;16.118/9 other lawful foods, 5.96/7 (fish) food offences venial, 5.93/4;6.115/6 pagan taboos not to be observed, 6.119,143/4f.;10.59/60;16.116/7 *see also* wine
forgiveness: of Muslim offenders, 24.22;42.37/5 of unbelievers(?), 45.14/13 better than retaliation, 42.38/6-43/1
fornication, *see* unchastity

Friday (Ar. *yawn al-jumu'a*): worship specially commended, 62.9f.
Furqān (salvation), 2.53/0,185/1;3.3/2;8.29,41/2;21.48/9; 25.title, 1 *see* pp.145-7 here

Gabriel (Ar. Jibril): mentioned by name, 2.97/1 (has brought revelation to M.), 98/2 (unbelievers hostile);66.4 (supports M.) said to be referred to, 53.4-16 (in visions);81.19-21 (noble messenger) also identified with the Spirit (*q.v.*), esp. 2.87/1,253/4;5.110/09;16.102/4;19.17;26.193;78.38
gambling: 'consuming property in vanity' (? gambling) forbidden, 2.188/4;4.29/33 gambling for camel with arrows (*maysir*) forbidden, 2.219/6;5.90/2f.;cf. 5.3/4
garden(s) (Ar. *janna, jannāt*), i.e. Paradise (*q.v.*): parables about terrestrial gardens, 18.32/1-44/2;68.17-33
Gehenna (Ar. Jahannam): a name of Hell (*q.v.*)
Genie(s), *see* Jinn
God (Ar. Allāh): his bounty and goodness, 2.268/71f.; 10.58/9-60/1;14.32/7-34/7;22.63/2-66/5;35.3;55.1-28; 80.24-32 his omniscience 6.59;10.61/2;11.5-5/7; 13.8/9-10/11;22.70/69;27.65/6;58.7/8 his power, 22.5-7; 28.68;29.19/18f.;35.43;37.6-11;42.49/8f.;56.57-73;79.27-33; 88.17-20; the only deity, 16.51/3;23.116/7-117; 27.59/60-64/5;37.4f.;38.65f.;39.2-3/4,64-6;112.1-4 the beautiful names, 17.110 has no offspring, 10.68/9; 19.88/91-95;37.149-57;43.16/15,81f. predetermines man's fate, 45.26/5;57.22;cf. 3.145/39 *see also* creation
gods, false, *see* idols
Gog and Magog (Ar. Yājūj, Mājūj): barbarous tribes (or evil spirits) confined behind a wall by Dhū-l-Qarnayn, 18.93/2-97/6 their release (shortly before the Day of Judgement), 21.96
Goliath (Ar. Jālūt): terrified Saul's army but killed by David, 2.249/50-251/2
Gospel (Injīl): the book revealed to Jesus, 3.3/2,48/3,65/58; 5.46/50f.,66/70,68/72,110/09;9.111/2;48.29;57.27 M. mentioned in it as *ummī*, 7.157/6;cf. 61.6
Greeks (Ar. Rūm), 30.title, 2/1f.
Grove (or Thicket) (Ar. *ayka*): the men of the Grove disobeyed, 15.78f.;26.176-89 (Shu'ayb sent);38.13/12;50.13
guidance (Ar. *hudā*), often mentioned, e.g.: true guidance from God, 2.120/14;etc. the Qur'ān as guidance, 2.2/1;etc.

Ḥafṣa: one of M.'s wives, referred to (without name), 66.4
ḥajj, *see* pilgrimage
Hāmān: an associate of Pharaoh, 28.6/5,8/7,38; 40.24/5,36/8
ḥanīf, pure monotheist, *see* pp. 15f. here
Hārūn, *see* Aaron
Hārūt: angel in Babylon, 2.102/96
Ḥawāriyyūn, *see* Apostles of Jesus
Heaven, *see* Paradise
heavens: seven heavens created, 41.12/11; 65.12
Hell (Ar. *an-nār*), etc.: descriptions, 38.55-8; 70.15-18; 73.12f.; 74.27-30; 104.5-9 punishment in it eternal, 2.81/75; 20.74/6; 43.74-8 has seven gates, 15.44 guarded by angels, 40.49/52; 74.30f. to be filled with many jinn and men, 7.179/8; 11.119/20; 32.13; 38.85; cf. 50.30/29 ('Art thou full?')
Helpers, *see* Anṣār
Ḥijr (Al-): a place whose people disobeyed, 15.80-4
Holy Spirit (Ar. *rūḥ al-qudus*), *see* Spirit
honey: produced from bees, 16.69/71
horses (Ar. *khayl*): used as cavalry by Muslims, 8.60/2; 59.6 by cavalry of Iblīs, 17.64/6 also, 3.14/12; 16.8
houris (Ar. *ḥūr*, dark-eyed ones): consorts in Paradise, 44.54; 52.20; 55.72; 56.22 cf. also 2.25/3; 4.57/60 ('pure spouses')
Hūd: the prophet sent to ʿĀd, 7.65/3-72/0; 11.title, 50/2-60/3,89/91; 26.123-40
Ḥunayn: a battle, 9.25
hunting: forbidden in state of sanctity, 5.1,2/3,(94/5) use of dogs, 5.4/6
Ḥuṭama (Al-), ('Crusher'): name of Hell, 104.4f.
Hypocrites (Ar. *munāfiqūn*): disaffected nominal Muslims in Medina, 4.61/4,88/90,138/7-145/4; 8.49/51; 9.64/5-68/9,73/4; 29.11/10; 33.1,12,24,48/7,60,73; 48.6; 57.13; 63,title,1-8; 66.9 among Bedouin, 9.101/2 'those in whose hearts is disease' (*fī qulūbi-him maraḍ*), (2.10/9); 5.52/7; 8.49/51; 9.125/6; 22.53/2; (24.50/49); 33.12,(32),60; 47.20/2,29/31; 74.31/3

Iblīs, the Devil: an angel (?) who refused to worship Adam, 2.34/2; 7.11/10-18/17; 15.28-44; 17.61/3-65/7; 20.116/5; 38.71-84/5 'one of the jinn', 18.50/48 also, 26.95 (his hosts); 34.20/19f. *see also* Satan
Ibrāhīm, *see* Abraham
idols, false gods: various deities named, 53.19f.; 71.23/2-23 their powerlessness, 7.191-198/7; 16.20-2; 25.3f.; 35.40/38 unable to

idols, false gods (*contd.*) unable to intercede, 6.94; 10.18/19; 30.13/12; 39.3/4,38/9 turn against worshippers at Judgement, 10.28/9f.; 19.82/5; etc. regarded as females, 16.57/9 (*see also* daughters) are angels or jinn, 34.40/39f.; cf. 6.100 are mere names, 53.23 *see also* Ṭāghūt
idolatry: unforgivable sin is *shirk*, 'associating' (others with God), 4.48/51,116 idolaters (*mushrikūn*) to be excluded from Mecca, 9.28 idolaters not to be prayed for, 9.113/4f. idolaters like a spider, 29.41/0 apparent belief in a 'high god' and lesser deities, 6.136/7; 23.84/6-89/91; 29.61,63,65; 43.8-15/14
Idrīs: a prophet (sometimes identified with Enoch), 19.56/7f.; 21.85
'Ifrīt: type of jinnī, 27.39
'Illiyyūn, 83.18-21
Ilyās, Ilyāsīn, *see* Elias
imām: leader or model, 2.124/18 (of Abraham); 11.18/20 (of the book of Moses); 17.71/3; 25.74; 46.12/11 (of the book of Moses) model-book (?), 15.79; 36.12/11 leaders, 9.12; 21.73; 28.5/4,41; 32.24
'Imrān: father of Mary, 3.33/0-35/1; 66.12
infidels (Ar. *kāfirūn*), *see* unbelievers
injīl (Evangel), *see* Gospel
inheritance: basic principle, 4.7/8f.,32/6f. detailed rules, 4.11/12-14/18,19/23 (wives?), 176/5 making of wills, 2.180/76-182/77; 5.106/5-108/7 *see also* orphans
intercession (Ar. *shafā'a*): none (for sinners) on Last Day, 2.48/5,123/17,254/5; 26.100; 40.19; 74.48/9 only by God's permission, 2.255/6; 6.51,70/69; 10.3; 19.87/90; 20.109/8; 21.28/9; 32.4/3; 34.23/2; 39.43/4f. that of deities unavailing, 10.18/19; 30.13/12; 36.33/2; 43.86; 53.26 (of angels)
Iram: a place, 89.7/6
'Īsā, *see* Jesus
Isaac (Ar. *Is'ḥaq*): given to Abraham, a prophet, 6.84; 11.71/4; 14.39/41; 19.49/50; 21.72; 29.27/6; 37.112f. also, 2.133/27,136/0,140/34; 3.84/78; 4.163/1; 12.6,38; 38.45 unnamed son of Abraham as sacrifice, 37.102/0-111
Ishmael (Ar. *Ismā'īl*): a prophet, 2.133/27,136/0,140/34; 3.84/78; 4.163/1; 6.86; 14.39/41; 19.54/5f.; 21.85; 38.48 with Abraham at Mecca, 2.125/19-127/1 unnamed son of Abraham as sacrifice, 37.102/0-111
Islam (Ar. *islām*): as name of the religion, 3.19/17,85/79; 5.3/5; 6.125; 39.22/3; 61.7 as 'submission' (to God), 9.74/5; 49.17
isrā' (night journey): 17.1 (and title)

Israel (Ar. Isrā'īl): 3.93/87; 19.58/9 *see also* Jacob
Israelites, Children of Israel (Ar. Banū Isrā'īl): occurrence of name (usually connected with Moses or Jesus), 2.40/38, 47/4,83/77,122/16,211/07,246/7; 3.49/3,93/87; 5.12/15,32/5, 70/4,72/6,79/82,110; 7.105/3,134/1,137/3f.; 10.90,93; 17.2,4,101/3,104/6; 20.47/9,80/2,94/5; 26.17/16,22/1,59,197; 27.76/8; 32.23; 40.53/6; 43.59; 44.30/29; 45.16/15; 46.10/9; 61.6,14 perversity of, 2.54/1-66/2,83/77-87/1; 4.153/2-162/0; 5.20/3-26/9,70/4f.; 23.49/51-56/8 (and Christians) *see also* Jews

Jacob (Ar. Ya'qūb): given to Abraham, 6.84; 11.71/4; 19.49/50; 21.72; 29.27/6 a Muslim, 2.132/26-140/34 a prophet (in lists), 3.84/78; 4.163/1; 19.6; 38.45 father of Joseph, 12.6,38,68
Jahannam ('Gehenna'): a name of Hell (*q.v.*)
Jālūt, *see* Goliath
Jesus (Ar. 'Īsā): a prophet, 2.87/1,253/4; 3.48/3-51/44; 5.46/50,110/09; 43.63-6; 57.27; 61.6 messenger of God, 4.171/69 in lists of prophets, 2.136/0; 3.84/78; 4.162/1; 6.85; 33.7; 42.13/11 his annunciation and birth, 3.45/0-47/2; 19.16-33/4(not named) supported by his apostles, 3.52/45f.; 5.111; 61.14 is God's word, a spirit from him, 4.171/69 to be raised to God, 3.55/48; (4.158/6) a created being, 3.59/2 not killed by Jews, 4.157/6-159/7 not son of God or a god, 4.171/69; 9.30; 19.34/5-36/7; 43.58/7 (not named) cursed unbelievers, 5.78/82 sending down of table, 5.112-15 announces Aḥmad, 61.6 *see also* Mary (son of), Messiah
Jethro: sometimes identified with Shu'ayb (*q.v.*)
Jews: occurrence of name (Yahūd, Hūd, *alladhīna hādū*), 2.62/59,111/05,113/07,120/14,135/29,140/34; 3.67/0; 4.46/8,160/58; 5.18/21,41/5,44/8,51/6,64/9,69/73,82/5; 6.146/7; 9.30; 16.118/9; 22.17; 62.6 appeals to Jews of Medina, 2.40/38-44/31,47/4-53/0,122/16-129/3; 3.64/57; 5.15/18 criticisms of Jews, 2.75/0-82/76,88/2-96/0,111/05-117/1 (also Christians); 3.72/65-85/79; 4.44/7-70/2,150/49-153/2; 5.64/9f.,78/82-81/4; 62.6-8 creed of Abraham superior, 2.130/24-141/35; 3.65/58-71/64; 5.44/8-50/5 Jewish(?) believers in M., 3.199/8 expulsion of Jewish clan, 59.2-5 *see also* Israelites
Jibrīl, *see* Gabriel
Jibt: demons(?), 4.51/4
jihād ('effort', 'holy war'), *see* warfare

Jinn (or genies; singular *jinnī*): created of fire, 15.27; 55.15/14 made to serve God, 51.56 Hell will be filled with jinn and men, 6.128; 11.119/20; 32.13; 41.25/4 jinn, like men, lead people astray, 41.29 jinn subject to Solomon, 27.17,39-42 'ifrīt, a type of jinnī, 27.39 listen to Qur'ān from Muḥammad and some are converted, 72.1-19; 46.29/8-32/1 messengers sent to them, 6.130 pagans make them partners to God, 6.100 Iblīs was one, 18.50/48 *see also*, 55.31

iẓya: tribute to be paid by non-muslims, 9.29 (later more especially 'poll-tax')

Job (Ar. Ayyūb): his sufferings, 21.83f.; 38.41/0-44 a prophet (in lists), 4.162/1; 6.84

John (the Baptist), (Ar. Yaḥyā): his miraculous birth, 3.38/3-41/36; 19.2/1-15; 21.89f. also, 6.85.

Jonah (Ar. Yūnus): his story, 37.139-48; 68.48f. ('him of the fish', *ṣāḥib al-hūt*) his success, 10.98 a prophet (in lists), 4.163/1; 6.86 *see also* Dhū-n-Nūn.

Joseph (Ar. Yūsuf): his story, 12 also, 6.84; 40.34/6

Judaism, *see* Jews

Jūdī (Al-): a mountain, 11.44/6

Ka'ba: sanctuary of Mecca, 5.95/6,97/8 'the House' founded by Abraham, 2.125/19-127/1; 22.26/7 'this house', 106.3 *see also* Mosque, Holy

Kāfūr ('camphor'): said to be fountain in Paradise, 76.5

khalīfa: deputy, vicegerent, 2.30/28 (Adam); 38.26/5 (David); 6.165 (in pl. of some Muslims)

Khaybar (a Jewish oasis): reference to the expedition, 48.15

Khidr (Al-): 'one of our servants' usually identified as, 18.65/4-82/1

Korah (Ar. Qārūn): Moses sent to him along with Pharaoh, 29.39/8; 40.23/4-25/6 swallowed by the earth, 28.76-82

Koran, *see* Qur'ān

Koreish, *see* Quraysh

Lāt, *see* Allāt

'light verse' (Ar. *āyat an-nūr*), 24.35

Lot (Ar. Lūṭ): sent as prophet, 7.80/78-84/2; 21.74f. the people to whom he was sent punished, 11.77/9-83/4; 15.57-74; 26.160-73; 27.54/5-58/9; 29. 26/5,28/7-35/4; 37.133-8; 54.33-40 also, 6.86; 11.70/3,74/7,89/91; 21.71; 22.43; 38.13/12; 50.13; 66.10 (his wife)

Luqmān (an Arabian sage): is given wisdom by God and admonishes his son, 31.12/11-19/18

Madyan, *see* Midian
Magians (Ar. Majūs), 22.17
magic (Ar. *siḥr*): taught by Hārūt at Babel, 2.102/96 Moses accused of magic, 7.109/6f.; 10.76/7f.; 26.34/3f., 49/8; 27.13 Pharaoh's magicians, 7.112/09-122/19; 10.79/80-81; 26.36/5-51 Jesus accused of magic, 61.6 (?) Muḥammad accused of magic, 37.15; etc.
Mājūj (Magog), *see* Gog
Majūs, *see* Magians
Mālik: said to be name of angel, 43.77
man (Ar. *insān*): his creation (as embryo, etc.), 22.5; 23.12-14; 40.67/9; 75.37/9; 76.2; 86.5-7; 96.1f. creation of mankind, 6.98; 7.189-193/2; 15.26, 28f.; 39.6/8 God's covenant with mankind, 7.172/1f. men are subject to death, 21.34/5f. men are created weak, 4.28/32 creatures subjected to man, 14.32/7-34/7; etc. called to God at night, 6.60; 39.42/3 *see also* Adam
Manāt: name of idol, 53.20
marriage (Ar. *nikāḥ*): no intermarriage with idolaters, 2.221/0 marriage with Jewish and Christian women, 5.5/7 marital intercourse, 2.223 marriage of widows, 2.234f. four wives permitted, 4.3 rules of incest, 4.22/6f.; 33.4 (fictive relationships) various rules, 4.4/3 (dowry), 24/8-28/32, 127/6-129/30; 24.26, 32f.; 60.11 slaves (as concubines), 4.25/9; 23.5-7; 70.29-31 general, 30.21/0 M.'s special privileges 33.50/49-52 M.'s wives, 33.6 ('mothers' of believers), 28-34, 53-5, 59; 66.3-5 temporary marriage (*mut'a*), 4.24/8 (rejected interpretation) *see also* divorce, women
Mārūt: angel in Babylon, 2.102/96
Marwa: hill near Mecca, 2.158/3
Mary (Ar. Maryam): birth and upbringing, 3.35/1-44/39 annunciation and birth of Jesus, 3.45/0-47/2; 19.16-33/4 her chastity and faith, 66.12 slandered by Jews, 4.156/5
Mary, son of: 'son of Mary' (alone), 23.50/2; 43.58/7 'Jesus son of Mary', 2.87/1, 253/4; 3.45/0; 4.157/6, 171/69; 5.46/50, 78/82, 110/09, 112, 114; 19.34/5; 33.7; 57.27; 61.6, 14 'the Messiah, son of Mary', 5.17/19, 72/6, 75/9; 9.31
Mary the Copt: referred to as 'one of his (M.'s) wives', 66.3
Masīḥ, *see* Messiah
maysir, *see* gambling

Mecca (Ar. Makka): named, 48.24 'mother of towns' (*umm al-qurā*), (or perhaps Medina), 6.92; 42.7/5 *see also* Bakka, Ka'ba, Mosque (Holy)

Medina (Ar. *al-madīna*, 'the city'): as a proper name (probably), 9.101/2,120/1; 33.60; 63.8 *see also* Yathrib, Anṣār, Mecca

Merciful, the (Ar. ar-Raḥmān): apparently as a proper name of God, 19.18,26/7,45/6, etc.; 55.1; etc. (in all about 50 times)

Messenger of God (Ar. *rasūl Allāh*): designation of M., 7.158/7, etc. *see also* Muḥammad

Messengers of God (Ar. *rusul, mursalūn*): M. similar to previous messengers, 4.163/1-165/3; cf. 40.78 no distinctions to be made between messengers, 2.136/0; 4.150/49-152/1 messengers differ in rank, 2.253/4 are human beings, 7.35/3; 16.43/5; cf. 22.75/4 (or angels) use speech of own people, 14.4 always meet opposition, 15.10f.; 23.44/6; 46.35/4; 51.52 aspects of the message, 6.48; 16.36/8; 18.56/4 stories revealed to confirm M., 11.120/1 always attacked by Satan, 22.52/1; cf. 27.11 may produce 'signs' (miracles), 40.78

Messiah (Ar. *al-masīḥ*, i.e. Jesus): annunciation, 3.45/0 not killed by Jews, 4.157/6 only a messenger, etc., not divine, 4.171/69f.; 5.17/19,72/6,75/9; 9.30f. *see also* Jesus, Mary (son of)

Michael (Ar. Mīkāl): an angel, 2.98/2

Midian (Ar. Madyan): the people to whom Shu'ayb was sent, 7.85/3-93/1; 11.84/5-95/8; 29.36/5 Moses among them, 20.40/2; 28.22/1-28 also, 9.70/1; 22.44/3; 28.45

money: a talent, a large sum (*qinṭār*), 3.14/12,75/68; 4.20/4 a dīnār (small gold coin, denarius), 3.75/68 a dirham (silver coin, drachma), 12.20

monks (Ar. *ruhbān*): found among Christians, so friendly to Muslims, 5.82/5 taken for lords (gods) by Christians, 9.31 many consume people's wealth, 9.34 monasticism (*rahbāniyya*) invented by Christians, not prescribed by God, 57.27

month (Ar. *shahr*): of twelve four are sacred, 9.36 no intercalary month, 9.37 the sacred month, 2.194/0,217/4 (fighting); 5.2,97/8 (appointed by God); 9.5 *see* Ramaḍān

moon (Ar. *qamar*): appointed for reckoning time, 6.96; 10.5 Abraham rejects worship, 6.77 in Joseph's dream, 12.4 subject to God's command for man's sake, 7.54/2; 13.2; 14.32/7; 16.12; 29.61; 31.29/8; 35.13/14; 39.5/7 gives light, 10.5; 25.61/2; 71.16/15 the crescent, 36.39 rites at new moons (*ahilla*), 2.189/5 not to be worshipped, 41.37 split (on Last Day), 54.1; cf. 75.8,9 in oaths, 74.32/5; 84.18; 91.2 also, 21.33/4; 22.18; 36.40; 55.5/4

pilgrimage, lesser (Ar. *'umra*): mentioned with greater, 2.158/3,196/2   probably referred to, 9.17f.
plagues of Egypt: 7.133/0–135/1; 17.101/3f.   *see also* Pharaoh
pledge (Ar. *bay'a*): of the women, 60.12   under the tree, 48.18   *see* covenant
poet(s) (Ar. *shā'ir*): M. is not a poet, as pagans say, 21.5; 36.69; 37.36/5; 52.29f.; 69.40–2   poets, inspired by demons, fall in love in every wadi, 26.221–6
polygamy, *see* marriage
polytheism, *see* idolatry, idols
prayer
(1) formal worship (Ar. *ṣalāt*): enjoined on prophets, 20.11/14 (Moses); 73.20 (M. and Muslims)   times of prayers, 2.238/9; 11.114/6; 17.78/80; 20.130; 30.17/16; 32.16 (night); 50.39/8f.; 73.2–4 (night), 20 (abrogated); 4.103/4 (general)   to be made facing Mecca, 2.144/39   shortening of prayers on expeditions or in danger, 2.239/40; 4.101/2–103/4   bowing (*rukū'*) as part of worship, 2.125/19; 22.26/7,77/6; 48.29; etc.   prostration (*sujūd*) as part of worship, 2.125/19; 4.102/3; 25.64/5; 48.29; 50.40/39; 76.26; 96.19(?); etc.   marks of prostration on believers, 48.29   Friday prayer, cessation of work, 62.9f.   no funeral prayer for pagans, 9.84/5   various rules, 4.43/6; 6.52; 17.110; 107.4–7 (*see also* ablutions)   opponents prevent worship, 96.9f.
(2) informal supplication (Ar. *du'ā'*, *istighfār*): God is hearer of prayer, 3.38/3; 14.39/41; 19.4; etc.   prayer only to God, 13.14/15   false gods do not answer, 13.14/15; 35.14/15   no supplication for pagan kinsmen, 9.113/4f.; cf. 71.28/9 (Noah)   supplication for hypocrites unavailing, 9.80/1; 63.5,6   *see also* intercession
Preserved Tablet (Ar. *lawḥ maḥfūẓ*): Qur'ān written on it, 85.21f.
priests (Ar *qissīsīn*): found among Christians, so friendly to Muslims, 5.82/5
prophets (Ar. *nabī*): God raised up prophets, 2.213/09; 5.20/3; 43.6/5f.; 45.16/15   covenant with prophets to acknowledge others, 3.81/75   Jews kill and oppose prophets, 2.61/58,91/85; 3.21/0,112/08,181/77; 4.155/4   lists of prophets, 4.163/1; 6.83–9; 19.58/9; 29.27/6; 33.6; 57.26   M. the 'seal of the prophets', 33.40   each has an enemy, 6.112; 25.31/3   *see also* Messengers
Psalms (Ar. *ẓabūr*): a book given to David, 4.163/1; 17.55/7; cf. 21.105   representing Ar. *ẓubur* (perhaps 'scriptures'), 3.184/1; 16.44/6; 23.53/5; 26.196; 35.25/3; 54.43,52

Purgatory: possible references, 3.24/3 (limited period in Hell); 7.46/4-49/7 (men of the *a'rāf*); 9.113/4 (asking pardon for idolaters); 23.99/101f. (request for second chance, mention of *barzakh*)

Qārūn, *see* Korah
qibla (direction of prayer): change from Jerusalem as *qibla*, 2.142/36, 143/38 Muslims to face Sacred Mosque, 2.144/39-150/45 houses in Egypt a *qibla* for Moses, 10.87
Qur'ān: 'a qur'ān', 10.15/16, 61/2; 13.31/0; 15.1; 17.106/7; 36.69; 41.44 ('foreign'); 56.77/6; 72.1; 85.21 an Arabic Qur'ān, 12.2; 20.113/2; 39.28/9; 41.3/2; 42.7/5; 43.3/2 the Qur'ān (Koran), 2.185/1; 4.82/4; 5.101; 7.204/3; 9.111/2; 15.87, 91; 16.98/100; 17.45/7, 46/9, 60/2, (78/80), 82/4; 20.2/1; 25.32/4; 27.1, 6, 91/3; 36.1; 38.1; 46.29/8; 47.24/6; 50.1, 45; 54.17, 22, 32, 40; 55.2/1; 73.4, 20; 76.23; 84.21 this Qur'ān, 6.19; 10.37/8; 12.3; 17.9, 41/3, 88/90f.; 18.54/2; 25.30/2; 27.76/8; 30.58; 34.31/0; 39.27/8; 41.26/5; 43.31/0; 59.21. 'the reciting (of it)', 75.17f.
Quraysh: tribe inhabiting Mecca, 106.1

Raḥmān, *see* Merciful
rain: as God's mercy, 7.57/5f.
Ramaḍān: month of fasting, 2.185/1
Raqīm (Ar-): mentioned with Men of the Cave, 18.9/8
Rass (Ar-): the people of it unbelievers, 25.38/40; 50.12
rasūl, *see* Messenger of God
refrains: found in Suras 26, 37 (81/79, etc.), 54, 55, 77 *see also* p. 72 here
religion (Ar. *dīn*): to fight till religion is God's, 2.193/89 no compulsion in religion, 2.256/7 religion before God is Islam, 3.19/17 God only object of religion, 7.29/8; 98.5/4 religious instruction on campaign, 9.122/3 Muslims as brothers in religion, 9.11; 33.5 religion of Muslims that of Abraham, (2.132/26); 22.78/7; 42.13/11 (also that of Noah, Moses, Jesus) pagans have their religion, Muḥammad his, 109.6 *see* Abraham
repentance (Ar. *tawba*): nature of repentance, 4.16/20-18/22 repentance as conversion, 9.5 from corrupt religion, 19.60/1 the importance of repentance, 25.70f.; 39.54/5; 42.47/6; 85.10; etc.

responsibility: each accountable for his good and evil deeds, 17.15/16; 35.18/19; 41.46; 74.38/41; 99.6-8; etc. 2.48/5; 16.93/5 none responsible for another, 10.41/2 degrees of reward, 6.132 none burdened beyond capacity, 2.286 responsibility for attitude to revelation, 10.108
resurrection (Ar. *baʿth*, etc.): historical examples, 2.243/4,259/61 unbelief in resurrection, 13.5; 19.66/7; 27.67/9f.; 32.10/9; 34.7; 36.78; 37.16f.; 44.35/4f.; 45.24/3f.; 75.3f.; 79.10f. period between death and resurrection, 2.259/61; 20.103f.; 23.112/4-115/7; 30.55/4 prefigured by rain and springtime, 7.57/5; 22.5; 30.19/18,50/49; 35.9/10; 50.9-11 parallel to creation, 29.19/18; 36.79; 46.33/2; 50.15/14; 56/62; 75.36-40 (creation of man); 80.22 fire a symbol of resurrection, 36.80 ransacking of graves, 82.4; 84.4; 100.9 'day of resurrection' (*yawm al-qiyāma*), *passim*
retaliation (Ar. *qiṣāṣ*): rules prescribed, 2.178/3f.,194/0; 42.40/38f. in Mosaic law, 5.45/9 not to exceed injury, 16.126/7 also 22.39/40,60/59
rites (Ar. *mansak*, pl. *manāsik*): at Mecca, 2.128/2 (Abraham), 200/196 (pilgrimage) a rite for each community, 22.34/5,67/6
Romans: inhabitants of eastern Roman empire, *see* Greeks
rūḥ (ar-), *rūh al-qudus*, *see* Spirit, Gabriel
Rūm, *see* Greeks

Sabā, *see* Sheba
Sabaeans (Ar. Sābi'ūn): a people of believers (along with Jews and Christians), 2.62/59; 5.69/73; 22.17 (also with Magians)
Sabbath (Ar. *sabt*): Jewish day of rest, 4.154/3; 16.124/5 punishments for those who break it, 2.65/1; 4.47/50; 7.163
sacrifice: sacrifice (*naḥr*) commanded along with prayer, 108.2 sacrifice (*dhabḥ*) of cows by Moses, 2.67/3-71/66 sacrificial animals as an offering (*hady*) at the Kaʿba, 2.196/2; 5.2,95/6,97/8 the name of God to be pronounced over such animals, 22.34/5,36/7 (*budn*, camels) the value of sacrifice is in piety, 22.37/8 the offering (*qurbān*) of the sons of Adam, 5.27/30 an offering (*qurbān*) consumed by fire as a sign, 3.183/79 Abraham's sacrifice (*dhabḥ*) of his son, 37.102/1,107
Ṣafā: hill near Mecca, 2.158/3
sakīna (assurance, or the Hebrew Shechina): 2.248/9; 9.26,40; 48.4,18,26
ṣalāt, *see* prayer (1)

sleep (Ar. *nawm, manām*): God has appointed sleep as rest, 25.47/9; 78.9 human souls return to God in sleep, 39.42/3 God does not sleep, 2.255/6
social behaviour: gait in walking, 17.37/9; 25.63/4 salutation of 'Peace', 4.86/8; 6.54; 25.63/4; cf. 24.61 domestic privacy to be observed, 24.27f., 58/7f. modesty in men and women, 24.30f., 60/59; 33.55 (M.'s wives) eating in other houses, 24.61/0 respect for M.'s houses, 33.53; 49.4f. voices not raised when M. present, 49.2f. avoidance of private conclaves, 58.7/8-10/11
Solomon (Ar. Sulaymān): the demons in S.'s reign, 2.102/96 wind and demons or jinn subjected to S., 21.78-82; 34.12/11-14/13; 38.36/5-40/39 repents and is forgiven, 38.30/29-40/39 controls birds, 27.15-21 meets Queen of Sheba, 27.22-45 also, 4.163/1; 6.84
soothsayer (Ar. *kāhin*): M. is not one, 52.29; 69.42
spider (Ar. *'ankabūt*): parable of spider, 29.41/0
Spirit, the (*ar-rūḥ*): is sent down (from God), 16.2 (to warners, with angels); 40.15 (to warners); 19.17 (to Mary); 26.193 (Faithful Spirit, with revelation); 97.4 (with angels on Night of Power) inspires M., 42.52 is of God's 'affair', 17.85/7; cf. 40.15; 42.52; 94.4(?) along with angels, 70.4 (mounting to God), 78.38 (in ranks); also 40.15; 97.4 Jesus a spirit from God, 4.171/69 God's spirit breathed into man, 15.29; 32.9/8; 38.72; 21.91 (into Mary); 66.12 (into Mary?) the Holy Spirit (*rūḥ al qudus*) aided Jesus, 2.87/1, 253/4; 5.110/09 the Holy Spirit revealed Qur'ān, 16.102/4 a spirit from God supports believers, 58.22 *see also* Gabriel
spoils, *see* booty
star(s) (Ar. *najm*): stars created by God to guide men by land and sea, 6.97; 7.54/2; 16.12, 16 do obeisance to God, 22.18 Abraham turned from worshipping a star, 6.76; 37.88/6 stars blotted out on Last Day, 77.8; 81.2 shooting stars as stones thrown at demons, *see* demons constellations (*burūj*), 85.1 *see also* Sirius
ṣuḥuf (sheets?): *see* book (2); also p. 33 here
Sulaymān, *see* Solomon
sun (Ar. *shams*): created by God to serve men, 7.54/2; 14.33/7; 16.12; 29.61; 31.29/8 not to be worshipped, 41.37 worshipped by Queen of Sheba, 27.24 Abraham turned from worshipping, 6.78 sun and its brightness in oath, 91.1 on Last Day, 75.9; 81.1

unbelievers (*contd.*)
their punishment, 3.10/8;7.41/39;14.29/34;22.19/20-22,72/1; 25.11/12-14/15;27.5;33.64/5;36.63f.;40.71/3;64.5f. (of former unbelievers);67.6-9
unchastity (Ar. *zinā*): forbidden, 4.16/20;17.32/4;25.68 punished by scourging, 24.2 restrictions on marriage, 24.3,26 four witnesses needed against women, 4.15/19;24.4f. accusations by husband, 24.6-9 accusation against 'Ā'isha 24.11-25
usury (Ar. *ribā*, gain): forbidden to Muslims, 2.275/6-281; 3.130/25;30.39/8 forbidden to Jews, 4.161/59;5.62/7(?)
'Uzayr, *see* Ezra
'Uzzā (Al-): an idol ('the strong one'), 53.19

visions: of Muḥammad, 17.1 ('night-journey'), 60/2;53.1-18; 81.19-24 of Joseph, 12.4f. of Pharaoh, 12.43-9 of Abraham, 37.102/0-7

Wadd: an idol, 71.23/2
warfare: meritorious to 'expend effort' (*jihād*) 'in the way of God', 2.218/5;3.142/36;4.95/7;5.35/9,54/9;8.72/3,74/5f.; 9.19f.,24;49.15;etc. command to 'expend effort' (*jihād*), 9.41,73/4;22.78/7;66.9 command to fight, 2.190/86,244/5; 4.71/3,95/7;8.39/40;9.13f., 29,36,123/4;22.39/40;47.4,35/7; 61.10f. fighting in the sacred months, 2.217/4;9.36 reluctance to fight, 2.246/7;4.77/9f.;9.38,42-8,86/7f.;47.20/2 merits of death 'in the way of God', 2.154/49;3.157/1, 169/3,195/4;47.4/5-6/7 superiority of believers, 8.65/6f. *see also* Badr, booty, Uḥud, etc.
wine (Ar. *khamr*): forbidden, 2.219/6 (but also uses);5.90/2 wine supplied in Paradise, 47.15/16 from grapes an intoxicating drink (*sakar*) 16.67/9
women: rules for fair treatment, 4.127/6-130/29 good men and women rewarded, 33.35 rules for widows, 2.234f. provision for widows, 2.240/1 suckling of children, 2.233 avoidance of defamation, 24.4-9,23f. modest behaviour, veiling, 24.31 precautions to avoid insult(?), 33.59 reception of believing women, 60.10-12 women inferior to men, 2.228;4.34/8

Yaghūth: an idol, 71.23
Yaḥyā, *see* John
Yājūj, *see* Gog
Ya'qūb, *see* Jacob

INDEX

The Arabic article al-, *with its variants,* an-, ash-, *etc.,* *is neglected in the alphabetical arrangement*